Confronting Suburban School Resegregation in California

CONTEMPORARY ETHNOGRAPHY

Kirin Narayan and Alma Gottlieb, Series Editors

A complete list of books in the series
is available from the publisher.

CONFRONTING SUBURBAN SCHOOL RESEGREGATION IN CALIFORNIA

Clayton A. Hurd

PENN

UNIVERSITY OF PENNSYLVANIA PRESS

PHILADELPHIA

Published by
University of Pennsylvania Press
Philadelphia, Pennsylvania 19104-4112
www.upenn.edu/pennpress

Printed in the United States of America
on acid-free paper

10 9 8 7 6 5 4 3 2 1

Library of Congress Cataloging-in-Publication Data
ISBN 978-0-8122-4634-6

CONTENTS

PART III. ATTEMPTS TO MAKE HIGH-QUALITY, SHARED SCHOOLING WORK

TIMELINE OF EVENTS

Date	Chapter	Events
1967	2	Residential communities of Farmingville and Allenstown are consolidated into the Pleasanton Valley United School District (PVUSD)
1971	2	PVUSD cited by federal government for its racially segregated schools, falls under desegregation mandate
1976	2	PVUSD submits "good faith" desegregation plan to the state
1987	3	School overcrowding in Farmingville requires busing of two hundred Farmingville students to Allenstown High
1991	3	PVUSD begins busing 250 Farmingville students per year to Allenstown High
1994	3	Brown Berets chapter forms in Farmingville
	3	MEChA Club founded at Allenstown High
	3	Mexican immigrant students are elected president and vice president of Associated Student Body (ASB) at Allenstown High
	3	Student walkouts opposing California Proposition 187 occur at Allenstown High
1995	3	Allenstown High ASB president impeached
	4	PVUSD call for parent meetings to address social unrest at Allenstown High
	4	PVUSD-sponsored parent meetings break down and dissolve

Date	Chapter	Events
(1995)	4,5,7	Allenstown citizen group goes public with intention to leave the PVUSD and establish their own school district (Allenstown secession campaign officially begins)
1996	5	California State Board of Education rejects Allenstown District Reorganization proposal
1999		Author begins field-based research at Allenstown High
2000	6	Student conflicts emerge at AHS surrounding commemorations of Mexican holidays
2002	6	Over 1,100 Allenstown High students absent for Cinco de Mayo (May 5)
2003	7	Allenstown school secession plan publicly reemerges in PVUSD-commissioned District Reorganization Feasibility Study
	7	Together for a United PVUSD (TFAU-PVUSD) coalition is formed
2004	7	TFAU-PVUSD coalition shuts down school district-sponsored community forum in advance of the planned decision on the District Reorganization Plan
	7	PVUSD decides to "indefinitely" shelve District Reorganization/Allenstown Secession Plan
2005	7	TFAU-PVUSD coalition endorses three candidates for the PVUSD school board; all are elected

Introduction

Time magazine has called the continuing racial segregation of U.S. public schools one of the most underreported news stories of our time (Fitzpatrick 2009). While it is historically viewed as an African American/White issue, Latinos[1] are now in fact more segregated than African Americans in southern and western regions of the country. In the Western states,[2] the number of Latinos in intensely segregated minority schools—that is, schools with a 90–100 percent racial minority population—increased from 19 percent in 1980 to over 40 percent in 2005 (Orfield and Lee 2007). California is now the national leader for the isolation of Latino youth, with approximately 90 percent attending majority minority schools and nearly half (47 percent) attending intensely segregated minority schools (Orfield and Lee 2006).

A distinguishing feature of this increasing White/Latino segregation is that it is no longer limited to metropolitan areas. Rapid increases in the ethnoracial and socioeconomic diversity of U.S. suburbs has led to thousands of communities experiencing significant shifts in their public school enrollments, many for the first time (Frankenberg and Orfield 2012; Frankenberg and Lee 2002). As Latino immigrant and nonimmigrant populations move beyond "suburban ring" satellite areas of metropolitan centers to further removed, more affluent, and traditionally White suburban areas as well as small to mid-sized towns across the United States (Orfield and Luce 2012), they often find themselves in communities that have relatively little experience in bringing youth and adults together across lines of racial, ethnic, cultural, and socioeconomic difference (Frankenberg and Orfield 2012), and that lack adequate services to facilitate the adaptation of immigrant students (Waters and Jiménez 2005).

Unfortunately, in a number of U.S. suburbs facing increased immigration and ethnic and racial diversification, public school resegregation has become an *active* process led by concerned citizens and elected school board collaborators whose proclaimed interests are to reorganize school districts in ways that best meet the alleged "needs" of all children. School district reorganization campaigns in which resegregation has become a significant factor have proliferated across the country—most notably in California, but also in Arizona, Illinois, Kansas, Maine, Massachusetts, Missouri, Nevada, New Jersey, New Mexico, New York, North Carolina, Oregon, Pennsylvania, South Carolina, Texas, Utah, Wisconsin, and Washington (Murray 2009). In California alone since the 1990s, public school district reorganization campaigns in which White/Latino racial resegregation has become a politicized issue include those in Alta Dena (Pasadena), Aptos (Santa Cruz County), Fremont (San Francisco Bay Area), Grand Terrace (near Riverside), Lakewood (Long Beach), Lomita (Los Angeles County), Marina (Monterey County), Pleasanton Valley (Ventura), Rio Linda (North Sacramento), San Rafael (Marin County), and Santa Clarita Valley (Los Angeles County), to name a few. The proliferation of these campaigns has gone hand in hand with a string of U.S. Supreme Court decisions that suggest a growing legal and political interest in abandoning the goal of integrating children and moving (back) toward the idea of the "neighborhood school" and arrangements favoring "parental choice."[3] While this tendency of federal courts to support residential level control of schooling can be potentially liberating for both majority and minority populations in some areas of the country, it has provided, in others, tacit support for the efforts of affluent White populations to *resegregate* on the basis of class-based interests.

Many of these suburban school resegregation movements—including the one that will be highlighted in this study—take the form of grassroots district reorganization campaigns led predominantly by White, middle-class residential communities whose residents justify their actions as *anything other than* racially, culturally, or socioeconomically motivated. These citizen movements, and the policy decisions their activism inspires, are typically couched in language such as promoting quality education, meeting the linguistic and academic needs of diverse students, holding all students accountable to basic educational standards, bridging the achievement gap, exercising local control, or assuring the integrity and benefits derived from "neighborhood schools." Despite the avowed good intentions and clear democratic appeals, the outcomes of these efforts are often the increased isolation of Latino students in high-poverty schools with fewer resources, less-experienced teachers, and fewer social networks that cross lines of racial, class, and ethnic differences (Orfield and Lee 2005, 2006, 2007).[4]

Central Questions and Arguments of the Book

The purpose of this book is to examine the political and educational processes that are contributing to active White/Latino school resegregation in suburban areas of the United States. Rather than focusing primarily on shifts in legal discourse and educational policy at the state and federal levels, the book investigates school resegregation processes through a grounded ethnographic study of a suburban school district on California's central coast where a predominantly White residential community has undertaken an active, decade-long campaign to "secede" from what has become an increasingly Latino school district. Based on five years of extensive school and community-based ethnographic research, the analysis pays close attention to the local, regional, and national politics that have shaped the direction of debates, decisions, and patterns of action and response regarding school resegregation, as well as to the justifications to "reorganize" the school district in ways that accomplish resegregation. The book's analytical focus on "cultural politics" is meant to situate local interactions within and around schools in relation to larger macro-level discourses regarding race and class entitlement, as well as current conceptions of what constitutes "quality education" and equality of educational opportunity.

A growing body of academic literature is focusing on public school resegregation processes in the United States, including the expansive research associated with the Civil Rights Project/Proyecto Derechos Civiles at UCLA.[5] This work has focused primarily on quantitative analyses of shifting societal attitudes, aggregate demographic data, and changing court orders, decisions, deliberations, and legal proceedings. While these approaches are valuable in assessing what kinds of resegregation are happening, and to some extent how they are happening, but they provide less insight into *why* resegregation is occurring and *how it is being justified*, particularly given the paradoxical reality that U.S. citizens appear to value integrated schooling as much now as (if not more than) ever.[6] This book intends to help fill the existing gap in qualitative research by providing a micro/macro account of White/Latino suburban school resegregation processes that moves beyond quantitative data analysis to delve more deeply into the explanations, justifications, and community-level processes through which increasing school segregation is being accomplished, in what appears in the case at hand to be a very active fashion.

The theoretical and ethnographic analysis in the book is informed by three related interests. The first is a desire to analyze and understand the core issues at the root of campaigns to reorganize suburban school districts in ways that accomplish Latino/White resegregation. Why are these efforts being pursued despite the existence of state laws that prohibit reorganization on such terms, and how is such activity being justified? To what extent are racism and/or classism a significant factor? A second area of interest relates to the different visions of entitlement to "quality education" that characterize battles between students, school officials, and citizen groups who occupy various sides of the school district secession debate. What differential visions of "quality education" exist, and how do they inform the perspectives of policymakers, community activists, parents, and school officials, as well as the academic and social engagement of students in racially diverse school settings? Third, this study seeks to examine some of the diverse ways Mexican-descent[7] populations—from migrant residents to later generation Mexican American youth and their families—are experiencing and responding to the school district secession campaign and efforts to exclude them from low-poverty, middle-class schools and the potential benefits derived from them. Of particular interest are forms and expressions of resistance that are being mobilized against school resegregation campaigns. From what angles have these potent citizen initiatives been resisted, particularly from those within the working-class Latino community, and to what effect? Correspondingly, what alternative visions for developing successful, integrated, and equitable suburban schools are being imagined and articulated, and to what extent might such visions inform broader, equity-based school reform efforts aimed at establishing high-quality, integrated education as a fundamental right for all U.S. citizens? A deeper conceptual engagement with this set of questions is undertaken in the first chapter of this book.

Beyond these foundational concerns, this study seeks to address a practical set of questions regarding the challenges and prospects for developing successful models of high-quality, integrated education, particularly in bimodal (White/Mexican-descent), socioeconomically diverse school settings. For example, what obstacles do administrators, teachers, and students in such settings face in their efforts to facilitate educational transformation toward equity and broad inclusiveness, particularly in areas historically opposed to changes in schooling status quo? How and why do teachers and school administrators who are committed to improving learning environments and facilitating access to resources for Latino children and their families—even in well-resourced schools—face such difficult challenges achieving these goals? For what complex reasons do some people oppose types of educational reform and policies that are specifically designed to transform schooling conditions to include and better serve working-class Mexican-descent students?

To pursue these diverse concerns, the book offers a kind of contrapuntal narrative. In one line of inquiry, it examines a school district reorganization process, initiated by concerned citizen groups rather than local teachers or school officials, to establish separate schooling systems between two residential communities in central California that have long shared a common school district. One community, which I call Allenstown,[8] is a predominantly White, middle- to upper-class professional suburb; the other, Farmingville, is a largely Mexican-descent working-class town. In a related line of analysis, the study looks closely at the struggles of a well-resourced desegregated high school in the district's White residential community to establish an inclusive, integrated schooling environment capable of promoting the broad-based success and academic achievement of an increasingly diverse student body.

In this sense, the case study provides a unique opportunity to simultaneously investigate a political process pushing for ethnically separate "local schools" and the efforts of a well-resourced high school to create the conditions for the positive operation of a racially diverse and inclusive school. This dual ethnographic focus is intended to provide a lens from which to see how the recent campaign to split the school district along racial, ethnic, and class lines—an effort touted by its proponents as a *response/reaction* to an institutional failure to create effective integrated schools locally—is better understood as an *outcome* of the continued mobilization of normative discourses, restrictive citizenship narratives, and forces of privilege-in-action that have served to undermine a range of courageous and well-intentioned efforts to establish conditions of equal status and shared control that are the essential prerequisites for effective and equitable integrated education in racially and socioeconomically diverse settings (Allport 1954; Fine et al. 1997; Pettigrew and Tropp 2006; Slavin 1985, 1995; Tropp and Prenovost 2008).

Here, an important distinction must be made between a willingness to establish *desegregated* schools—that is, those that allow for the coexistence of students from different racial and ethnic groups in the same institutional space—and the commitment to effectively sustain *integrated* schooling conditions, which requires intentional, well-informed, and often courageous efforts to establish intellectual and social engagement, as well as relationships of equal status, across lines of racial, ethnic, and socioeconomic difference and in settings inside and outside the formal classroom. A major aim of this ethnography is to investigate the political and educational processes that have contributed to this failure of *integration* in a desegregated school setting, and to identify the dimensions of shared responsibility for the conditions of educational inequality that continue to exist between middle-class Whites and working-class Latinos.

Chapters 3 through 7 offer a set of extended case studies, covering a ten-year period from the mid-1990s to the mid-2000s, that focus on a series of highly politicized encounters between youth and adults in Allenstown and Farmingville as they attempt to negotiate a shared vision for equitable, high-quality schooling that reflects and validates their varied (and sometimes divergent) wants, needs, and senses of entitlement. By way of the vested and emotional narratives of local students, parents, teachers, school administrators, and community activists, the case studies critically analyze the school and community-level practices and policies that have sustained ongoing structures of segregation in ways that have resisted change and made conditions of segregation seem so sensible to those currently privileged. At the same time, each case study includes attention to the concerted efforts of local working-class Latino youth and their families to challenge schooling arrangements and practices that have long favored the affluent and that have excluded them from the benefits of equal access to, and participation in, well-resourced, low-poverty schools.

By design, this study is not concerned with the formal analysis of curricular content, pedagogical methods, or student assessment in ways that suggest specific technical remedies for classroom-based educational reform. Instead, the ethnographic approach highlights *normative* educational processes and forces of privilege-in-action that limit efforts to promote equity-based educational change. The study suggests that, until we address these normative issues that challenge equity-based school reform, and imagine paths and strategies for altering them, our technical reform endeavors will continue to fall flat (Oakes et al. 2005; Rogers and Oakes 2005).

Racialization and Mexican American Experiences of (De-)segregation

A substantial body of scholarly research has addressed the historical, socioeconomic, political, and legal factors and conditions that have undermined the institutionalization of racial integration since *Brown v. Board of Education* and justified what appears to be a return to more "separate but equal" public schooling conditions in the United States. A more detailed outline of these explanatory frameworks is offered in Chapter 1. Fewer studies, however, have focused specifically on the Mexican American experience of (de-) segregation despite a significance history of Latino struggle that includes hard-fought legal victories predating the Supreme Court's decision in *Brown*.[9] While African Americans and Latinos have faced common obstacles in their respective struggles for equal schooling, there are important distinctions that should prohibit any attempt to collapse the Latino experience into the dominant White/Black binary that constitutes much of the historical analysis of school (de)segregation. Shifting racial categorizations applied to Mexican Americans from the mid-nineteenth century to the early 1970s generated a unique set of political statuses and inspired a distinct array of educational policy decisions that have differentially impacted how Latino communities have experienced, responded to, and resisted the intersectional forms of subordination they have faced—forms that can be at once legal, political, economic, cultural, linguistic, and [hetero]sexual (Donato and Hanson 2012; Valencia 2008; Yasso and Solórzano 2007).[10]

For these reasons, scholars of Latina/o education, notably those writing from a Critical Race Theory perspective (Latina/o CRT), have emphasized moving beyond the Black/White binary in the study of Mexican American experiences of (de)segregation to focus more specifically on processes of *racialization*—that is, on the sociohistorical processes through which particular racial categories have been maintained and shaped through social struggles over time.[11] A racialization perspective encourages attention not only to the (often shifting) forces of exclusion and discrimination that have been directed at particular communities of color, but also to minority populations' own histories of responding to such treatment, including the manners in which they come to organize themselves around racial discourse (Omi and Winant 1994; Solórzano and Delgado-Bernal 2001; Villenas and Deyhle 1999; Yasso and Solórzano 2007). Highlighting processes of racialization draws attention to the ways "race" can serve as a source of meaning for minority populations in their own struggle against intersectional forms of cultural, political, and socioeconomic oppression, and how racial solidarity and identities may serve as bases for social and political action, informing broader social mobilizations and community capacity-building activities to assert political rights and promote social and racial justice (Gilroy 1987; Gregory 1998).

The CRT framework has drawn increased scholarly attention to the agency and lived experience of Latino populations in both historical and contemporary contexts, inspiring a host of critical qualitative/ethnographic studies examining processes of community empowerment and collective struggle, including important explorations of how Latina/o communities have successfully used experiential knowledge, drawn from community-based relationships, as a source of strength in their struggles against intersectional forms of oppression, building on such "cultural wealth"[12] to politically organize, assert rights in society, and excel academically in the educational realm (Dyrness 2008; González, Moll, and Amanti 2005; Villenas and Deyhle 1999; Warren et al. 2011; Yasso 2005; Yasso and Solórzano 2007).

In investigating the politics of school integration and resegregation, attention to processes of racialization prove useful for a variety of reasons. First, a racialization perspective warns against any tendency to represent the conflicts that arise in battles over integration, or any other form of equity-based school reform, as struggles between distinct races of people, or bearers of specific "cultures" or national heritages (e.g., as struggles between White/Mexican "races" or "cultures"). Instead, conflicts must be examined as negotiations over the meanings and relative value ascribed to racial and cultural categories, in specific historical terms and institutional contexts, with attention to the processes and practices of inclusion and exclusion through which categorical boundaries are maintained, and for what reasons and at whose benefit or disadvantage. Second, with respect to the current study, a racialization perspective calls for attention to the historically specific manner in which Mexican Americans in the U.S. Southwest have themselves participated in the racialization process, not simply as victims of class and racial oppression but as contributors to the making and unmaking of racial and class categories in ways that have been consequential to the relative distribution of political, economic, and educational opportunities and resources in the region. Moreover, attention to processes of racialization permits space to consider how racism can operate in a more complex fashion among minority populations, taking such forms as self-aggrandizement at the expense of more vulnerable representatives of racially subordinate groups (Omi and Winant 1994: 73).[13] This perspective helps explain why actions and attitudes in racially politicized educational encounters do not always fall neatly along racial or cultural lines.

It is at this level of boundary construction and maintenance that I concentrate much of my ethnographic attention in the following study. In doing so, I attend not only to individual and group-ascribed actions and attitudes but also to the ways *institutional routines* and interactions *between* social groups, as they occur within and around schools, have shaped schooling structures, policies, and modes of community-building. This strategy requires ethnographic attention to multiple levels of the schooling process, including (1) district-level politics and policies, (2) the activism of community-based groups around schooling related issues, (3) the attitudes and practices of staff at the school level, (4) the social organization of students within the school, and (5) students' particular responses to school structures and programs.

The Ethnographic Field Site

The following study takes place in the Pleasanton Valley of California, a rich agricultural basin situated between the mountain foothills and the jagged cliffs of the state's central coast. The focus of analysis is on the Pleasanton Valley Unified School District (PVUSD), consolidated in 1967, which currently serves two physically separate, residential communities characterized by sharp contrasts in culture, "race," and socioeconomic status. At the center of Pleasanton Valley is Farmingville, a largely Mexican and Mexican American working-class town of about 50,000 residents (with a median household income of $46,500 and per capita income $16,200)[14] whose livelihoods have long been tied to the Valley's rich and productive commercial farmland. Ten miles north on the state highway is Allenstown, a predominantly White, middle- to upper-class professional town of just under 20,000 residents (with a median household income of $80,000 and per capita income $41,500) that has been populated largely since the 1950s and serves as a bedroom community for a nearby corporate center and wealthy coastal tourist town.

Historically speaking, Farmingville's regional reputation as a "Mexican town" is quite recent. It was not until the 1942 passage of California's Public Law 78, popularly known as the Bracero Program, that thousands of Mexican nationals (mostly single men) were brought to the Valley to work on temporary, low-wage work contracts with agricultural companies. The termination of the Bracero Program in 1965, along with the relatively generous amnesty terms associated with the federal Immigration Act of 1965, supported a large and relatively unregulated in-migration from Mexico. Between 1960 and 1995, Farmingville's population grew over 130 percent, with Latinos—the vast majority of them Mexican immigrants—representing 97 percent of the new arrivals. As a percentage of the town's population, Latinos increased from less than 15 percent in 1960 to nearly 75 percent by 2000. Over the same time period, the enrollment of Latino students in PVUSD schools grew from under 8 percent to over 70 percent.

The sociocultural transformations that reshaped Farmingville in the post-World War II period were not equally manifest in Allenstown, due in large degree to Allenstown's higher real estate values, its relative distance from the center of agricultural production and employment, and its history of active political resistance to low-income residential development that might have attracted working-class Mexican-descent populations. As an unincorporated area without a city council or planning commission, Allenstown politics have long been dominated by homeowner associations (HOAs) representing the coastal subdivisions, and leaders have traditionally included those heavily invested in local real estate and interested in preserving desirable rural characteristics that would keep land values high. This long-established de facto private residential government has continued to yield a political leadership in Allenstown that is conservative and isolationist, despite what would appear to be growing political heterogeneity among its residents.

Since the PVUSD was consolidated in the late 1960s, community leaders in Allenstown have successfully repelled a series of state and federal mandates, continuing through the mid-1990s, that have sought to integrate working-class, Mexican-descent children from Farmingville with the predominantly White, middle-class children from the Allenstown area. In spite of this active resistance, some level of school desegregation has been achieved. This resulted not from capitulation to legal mandates, but as a consequence of dire overcrowding at Farmingville's only comprehensive high school in the late 1980s. This lack of classroom space in Farmingville, combined with the district's inability to secure public bond support for the construction of a new high school, compelled the district to begin a busing arrangement that would send an increasing number of Mexican-descent students from Farmingville to Allenstown High School. By the mid-1990s, Allenstown High held the status as the district's only truly racially mixed school, with Mexican-descent youth from Farmingville constituting nearly half the school's 2,000 students. Chapters 2, 3, and 6 of this book provide a deeper look at the highly politicized experience of integration at Allenstown High from the late 1980s to the mid-2000s.

In its current form, the PVUSD is a predominantly bi-modal school system (72 percent Mexican American/25 percent White),[15] with nearly 18,000 students enrolled, making it one of the largest K-12 districts in northern California. Nearly 50 percent of the district's students are identified as having limited English proficiency, and approximately 30 percent are the children of migrant farm worker families.

Research Engagements and Methods

My research experience in the PVUSD began in the late 1990s as a graduate student researcher in a larger, longitudinal study of peer relationships among Mexican-descent and European American students at Allenstown High School.[16] Aptly named the "Peers Project," the research was designed to investigate the ways in which peer groups and networks at the high school mediated Mexican American and Euro-American students' academic orientations, engagement, and relative participation in schooling activities. In three years as a lead researcher at the high school site, I worked with a team of ethnographic researchers that included, over time, ten undergraduate students, four Master's-level graduate students, and two postdoctoral fellows. Nearly all the researchers were bilingual, including myself, and a smaller number were first- or second-generation Mexican immigrants themselves.

The collaborative, cohort-based nature of the Peers Project allowed me the unique opportunity to participate in ongoing critical discussions with a diverse group of colleagues regarding our separate (but often overlapping) field experiences at the school, including constant dialogue about our evolving relationships with students, teachers, and parents. This sense of collegiality and deep collaboration was instrumental in helping me compile the diverse, poignant, and profoundly revealing stories of students, teachers, parents, and community activists that appear in this book. The Peers Project yielded a massive archive of ethnographic material that included hundreds of transcribed, semistructured individual and focus group interviews with both White and Mexican-descent students (including a representative sampling of first-, second-, and third-generation Mexican-descent students), teachers and support staff, and parents (the latter interviewed in visits to students' homes). Beyond my own field notes and individual/focus group interviews, I had access to all my colleagues' ethnographic materials as well. These included thousands of pages of field notes chronicling each researcher's interactions, conversations, and observations with students and focal peer groups across the campus.

I maintained an everyday presence at Allenstown High for the entirety of three academic years, working closely with the office of the Migrant Education Program (MEP), the Advancement via Individual Determination (AVID) program, and the English-as-a-Second-Language (ESL) classrooms. I first served as a class assistant and student mentor in the ESL classrooms, after which I began shadowing a smaller group of ESL students who elected to enroll in the AVID classes. Since students in both the AVID and ESL programs tended to utilize the social and academic support services offered by the Office of Migrant Education at Allenstown High, I began to involve myself daily in tutoring sessions and social gatherings taking place there. Outside these formal institutional contexts, I interacted daily with smaller groups of students in the social spaces where they gathered between classes, before and after school, and during lunch periods.

To the extent that I was able to establish deeper, trusting relationships with some of the Mexican-descent students with whom I interacted, it was over time and through opportunities I had to serve as a longer-term conversation partner, mentor, and homework helper—and sometimes just a sympathetic sounding board, particularly for those students from Farmingville who experienced a sense of marginalization or mistreatment in the larger school or community context of Allenstown. I was fortunate to be able to make multiyear commitments to my relationships with students, their families, and school staff. Some of these relationships became very strong, such as those with MEP staff and AVID students whose narratives are highlighted most notably in Chapter 6. Other relationships were more episodic in nature, like those I developed with a much wider range of White and Mexican-descent student peer groups and teachers across the campus, whose narratives appear as interview excerpts throughout the book.

Beyond my ongoing, school-based participation observation, I interacted with Mexican-descent students and their families through visits to homes and workplaces, attendance at sporting and cultural events, and by serving as a chaperone on student trips to movie theaters, college visits, youth leadership conferences, and local recreational centers. I also spent a year living in a migrant farmworker housing complex adjacent to the agricultural fields in Farmingville, and several weeks during two consecutive winters traveling as a guest with migrant students and their families to their small hometown *ranchos* in Michoacán, Mexico. These towns constitute the other end of a significant transnational network that connects families in Pleasanton Valley to the central Mexican province, a network that has been sustained by decades of migration, travel, and resource sharing across national borders. This cross-border experience helped me to deepen some of my relationships of trust with parents and students and also increased my visibility and recognition among Latino leaders in the community of Farmingville, many of whom also traveled to visit extended family in the Mexican province.

Segregation and Nonbelonging at Allenstown High

Early in my research experience at Allenstown High, it became clear to me that the decade-and-a-half of racial togetherness at the school had not led, as one might hope, to the progressive academic and social integration of students. Instead, it had produced what was essentially two high schools—one "White" and one "Mexican"—mirroring the two separate communities in the region. This segregation was apparent in both the formal and informal spatial separation of students on campus and their differential participation in co- and extracurricular activities. School tracking practices and student classifications further reinforced segregation. Where segregation was perhaps most clearly and powerfully exhibited was in the aggregate patterns of academic performance, where White students outperformed Mexican-descent students by nearly every method of academic assessment.

The high degree of social and academic marginalization Mexican-descent students experienced at Allenstown High, despite how well resourced the school was financially, was troubling and seemed to defy any simple explanation. My curiosity was raised in the second year of my research when a social studies teacher mentioned, in passing, that just a few years earlier, two first-generation Mexican immigrant students—running on a platform to "end racism" and improve the status of Latino students at Allenstown High—were elected president and vice president of the school's Associated Student Body (ASB). He explained how the student leaders, supported by a handful of Euro-American student allies and the mentorship of a Latino social studies teacher of Cuban descent, undertook a bold campaign to promote racial integration on the campus through strategies that included a series of social mixing and intercultural awareness activities, the design of a multicultural mural for the school gymnasium, and a controversial demand to institute an elective course on Chicano studies (this full campaign is explored in detail in Chapter 3).

The teacher's passing reference left me to wonder: How could such Latino student empowerment have happened, given the current and seemingly systematic nature of their marginalization on the campus? And why, after only a few years, did the high school students seem to know so little about it? Why had it not come up in my conversations with long-time teachers and administrators with whom I had been communicating for nearly two years about questions of equity and diversity at the school? Was it a form of institutional amnesia? If so, what was being forgotten, and why? I wondered how something as significant as broad-based Latino student empowerment could end up, just a few years later, so difficult to talk about, so seemingly forgotten, and so clearly absent at the school. As I inquired more extensively into what had happened during that time, I was led to realize that it was the Latino student leaders' demands for institutional change at Allenstown High that triggered the decade-long attempt by a group of parents and business leaders to "secede" from the increasingly Latino school district.

Moving the Analytical Lens from School to Community

As I continued my school-based research with the Peers Project through the early 2000s, I began to inquire more deeply into the history of the high school, the school district, and the community politics of schooling in the region. It was through this juxtaposition of site-based ethnographic data collection and historical-archival research that I began to see how the practices and politics of (re-) segregation that I saw clearly at play in the high school were a microcosm of the larger, regional struggles that had taken place in the school district over the place of culture, language, and class/racial entitlement in the schooling process. It occurred to me that if I wanted to develop a more profound understanding of the set of perplexing forces of inequality and alienation that seemed to act on Mexican-descent students in their everyday experiences in the high school, I would need to look beyond the school site and investigate the historically situated nature and "roots" of the marginalization I was witnessing. So it was, then, that in 2002 I elected to leave my research position in the Peers Project to pursue independent research that would lead me to the subject material of this book and the analytical focus on the cultural politics of school resegregation.

Over the next three years (2002–2005) of research, I leveraged my connections with Mexican-descent students, parents, and teachers from Allenstown High to visit and build relationships with civic leaders in Farmingville, including city council members, grassroots community activists, and members of the parent, youth, and citizen organizations (these interactions are described in Chapters 4, 5, and 7). Over time, I was included in ad hoc resident meetings, e-mail exchanges, and telephone calls about political developments in the community, particularly those surrounding the issue of the proposed school district split. The data I collected during this time included over 350 hours of transcribed field notes from ongoing participant-observation in community-level events and activities, including public meetings (e.g., school board meetings, district-sponsored community fora, and civic organization membership meetings) and semiprivate, ad hoc gatherings with Latino activists. In addition, I completed and transcribed semistructured individual and group interviews (about an hour each) with a purposive sample of Mexican-descent parent and parent group representatives (15), Farmingville city council, PVUSD school board, and county board of education members (9), current and former district teachers and administrators (15), Allenstown parents who supported the district reorganization plan (6), current Allenstown High and community college students (15), and former students at Allenstown High (6). I limited the interview sample to those with some level of involvement (and often a strong investment) in the activities surrounding the school district secession campaign. Additional data sources included personal notes, memos, and email communications shared by research subjects, as well as information from local and regional media sources including newsletters and newspapers, U.S. Census reports, local library collections, and school district records and archival documents. All data collected for this book were imported into a single NVivo qualitative software database and analyzed for relevant and emergent themes.

Positionality and Politics in the Field

As a White, male, middle-class individual whose field research included significant interactions with working-class (and often socially and legally vulnerable) Mexican immigrant youth and their families, I have to acknowledge my own positionality in the very complex web of racialized class inequalities that made it possible for me to conduct research in the ways, and through the means, that I did.[17] During my three years at the school, I held the status of a young adult, English/Spanish bilingual "nonteacher" who enjoyed the privilege of moving relatively freely across campus. This meant that I occupied a somewhat unconventional role that allowed me to develop some unique friendship and mentor relationships with students as well as some astonishingly candid relationships with teachers. This did not mean that I was provided with anything like "insider" status among students. In fact, my ability to gain trust in the areas through which I moved, both on and off campus, was far from automatic. Many of the students with whom I interacted—both Latino and Anglo—were initially, and sometimes permanently, ambivalent or distrustful of my activities on campus. Moving through socioeconomically segregated and racialized spaces in the school, I found my positionality made me a trusted ally in some contexts and a distrusted outsider in others. This was not always in a manner one might expect, however. For example, working closely with Mexican immigrant students in a school environment characterized by acute racial/ethnic and class polarization meant that I had somewhat limited access to the more enfranchised Anglo students, particularly those who (or whose parents) may have felt anger or ambivalence about the "bussed-in" presence of Mexican-descent students. Also, because I worked primarily with recent immigrants and those in the AVID and MEP programs that tended to be more overtly school-oriented and/or college-minded, I was regarded with more distrust by some of the later generation and less enfranchised Mexican-descent students.

Unavoidably, my background as a graduate student of cultural anthropology in a university known to be politically progressive (and "Leftist" in the minds of many more conservative Allenstown residents) limited my ability to directly interview some White parents, including a pair of the more highly visible leaders of the school district secession movement. I felt an ethical and professional obligation to be as truthful as I could about my research interests, and in doing so, I was aware that I was by default "taking sides" in some people's minds, even as I echoed my desire to understand the issues from multiple perspectives. However, I also enjoyed some privileged access to teachers at Allenstown High as well as community leaders in both Allenstown and Farmingville. That my mother was employed as a special education resource teacher at Allenstown High allowed me some legitimacy as a "well-intentioned" researcher among teachers and administrators. My father also served as a visible leader of a local community college with a strong reputation among residents, business leaders, and educators in both Allenstown and Farmingville. These familial connections provided me with some "room to move" in the bureaucratic institutions at the high school, school district, city, and county levels. For example, in some cases I was provided with privileged access to people in positions of power who might have otherwise ignored or sought to deny my solicitations for their time and requests for information.

My relationships with Latino leaders in Farmingville, including city council members, community activists, and members of the Migrant Parent Advisory Committee (MPAC), developed more slowly over time. I did not even schedule formal interviews with community leaders until the third year of my research. By that time, many of them had some knowledge of my work with students at the school, my interactions with parents, and my participation in community events and gatherings, including visits to Mexico. I found that initial interviews with Farmingville community leaders, rather than serving as an ends in themselves, often allowed me access to greater networking opportunities. Over time, I was included in email messages and telephone calls about ad hoc resident meetings on political developments in the community, particularly around the issue of school district secession.

It is important to note that I was not viewed benevolently by all residents in the larger Pleasanton Valley context. For example, soon after completing my initial research, I requested a 15-minute time slot in a regularly scheduled PVUSD school board meeting to provide a brief overview of my general findings. As a matter of public record, I left a full copy of the larger working paper in the district office. While it appeared as if my brief presentation was generally well received, I received a phone call from a school board member a few weeks later informing me that my manuscript had disappeared from the district office. As it turned out, a school board trustee who was a strong supporter of the Allenstown secession movement had taken the document into her possession. Following a demand from a fellow trustee to return the document, she did so, but not without first crafting her own three-page response, which she added as a preface to my report and copied and circulated to all board members, articulating her assessment of the "merits" of the findings. She attacked a number of specific statements in the document and claimed that "the underlying analysis appears to be focused on generalizations made about an entire community (Allenstown) based on interviews with a limited number of people, and with the author minimizing or twisting the meaning of comments that did not specifically agree with his belief system." In defense of her claims, she intimated:

> I have lived much of the story of Allenstown High . . . and in the story I lived, there were a few bad apples mixed in with a bunch of good people with good intentions who had differing opinions. The good and bad came from both Allenstown and Farmingville, and from several races, [with] a few ready to undermine processes every step of the way, and to portray the "other side" as the enemy. There were mistakes made, and lessons learned. Again, most people involved, from all opinions, were good, decent people with differing opinions.

With regard to the decentness of the people involved, I would be hard pressed to disagree. But I believe that it is also the case that people's opinions are laden with a number of personal and shared interests and desires (including, in the context of this study, desires for self, cultural, and community/residential preservation as well as the generational reproduction of wealth and opportunity) that inform people's attitudes and actions, and contribute to histories of privilege-in-action that have served to reproduce political and educational conditions in ways that have benefited and privileged some residents in Pleasanton Valley while marginalizing and disempowering others. It is these historicocultural and interactional processes—rather than a moral judgment of the "decentness" of the people—on which my analysis rests.[18]

At the same time, I must acknowledge that I agree with anthropologists Aihwa Ong, Marvin Harris, and Nancy Scheper-Hughes (1995), who claim that anthropology cannot be divorced from ethics, and that our models of inquiry should speak to "how we have used or failed to use anthropology as a critical tool at crucial historical moments (Scheper-Hughes 1995: 419). In this book, it should be clear that my own moral and ethical frameworks have, to some degree, shaped the content, structure, and development of my analysis. It cannot, in fact, be otherwise. Ultimately, however, I hope this book will serve as an example for a kind of politically engaged anthropology that accepts, as Marvin Harris has noted, that "what we choose to study or not study in the name of anthropology is a politico-moral decision" (423).

In the narrative of events and social relations that I construct, I do not wish to create a single, linear account out of what were (and surely remain) a multiplicity of interests, concerns, and motivations among a diverse Pleasanton Valley citizenry. Nor would I argue that earlier history in the area inevitably produced the more contemporary conditions and particular events I describe, including the highly politicized racial and class conflicts that occurred at Allenstown High and that have long surrounded the Allenstown secession campaign. History is not, in fact, so structural, orderly, and goal-oriented. Although I try to represent more than one side of the issues I choose to highlight, I do not pretend to present an "objective" or exhaustive accounting. There are a number of limitations, among them that I tended to focus my analysis more on the stories of those residents who were centrally involved and who maintained strong investments in the events I highlight, and within that group, I focused more (although not exclusively) on the narratives/voices of Mexican-descent residents. By highlighting perspectives that have tended to be marginalized or actively silenced, I expected the analysis would challenge, to some extent, prevailing institutional explanations and authoritative accounts of the historical experiences in the region and within the school district. Ultimately, my narrative rendering follows how I imagine my informants would ideally like to narrate their own personal experiences, that is, by providing an interpretive frame for others that does justice to complexity of the events that occurred.

Outline of the Chapters

To orient the reader to the timing of the various happenings described in the book, I offer a chronology of significant events, along with the corresponding chapters in which they are discussed (see Timeline of Events, p. vii).

In Chapter 1, I provide an overarching discussion of the theoretical frameworks that I deploy to explain the political, material, and normative forces that have contributed to the deprioritization of racial integration as a means of promoting equity-based public school reform in the United States. Here, I focus special attention on the cultural norms of race, merit, and citizenship that have driven and, to a great extent limited, the scope of equity-based educational reform in U.S. schools. The chapter ends with a discussion about the relative promise of grassroots social activism, led primarily by working-class Latino populations, to help generate the political will to protect and sustain shared schooling environments and to establish high-quality integration as a fundamental right in the United States.

Chapter 2 begins with an ethnographic introduction to students' social worlds at Allenstown High, with specific attention to the highly essentialized understandings of racial and cultural difference that characterize students' narratives and help generate students' experiences of sociospatial segregation on the campus. I explore how students' particular understandings of social difference limit their social interactions in ways that impact the relative levels of academic and social engagement experienced by Mexican-descent and White students at the school. In order to make sense of the extreme levels of student segregation, I offer a wider analysis of the economic, political, social, and cultural realities that have shaped the political exercise of community in the larger Pleasanton Valley region, arguing that this history helps explain the racially oppositional politics of identity that has come to shape not only student interactions at the high school but also broader patterns of parent and citizen involvement in the schooling process. The chapter ends with a historical overview of the highly politicized battles over school desegregation that marked schooling politics in Pleasanton Valley from the 1970s to the early 1990s, with particular attention to how conditions of racial polarization in school and community have long served to hinder efforts to establish educational equity and opportunity between White and Mexican-descent populations in the region. This historical analysis of desegregation politics provides what I believe to be essential background for the more recent effort of a citizen group in Allenstown to "secede" from the increasingly Latino school district.

Chapters 3 and 4 chronicle a series of events that led up to the Allenstown school district secession campaign. Because the events in these chapters took place in the mid-1990s—several years before I began ethnographic fieldwork in the area—I take great care to reconstruct the events, relying heavily on narratives from individual and group interviews with parents, educators, community activists, and former students as well as archival sources that include local and student media press accounts, internal school memos and personal notes shared by former school staff and teachers, and school- and district-level meeting notes and transcripts. Chapter 3 focuses on the remarkable set of events that followed the election of two first-generation Mexican immigrant students to top leadership positions in student government at Allenstown High School. Here, I document and analyze the manner in which student leaders and their supporters challenged the status quo of local schooling practices that had historically failed to prioritize the integration of students and to assure equal access and participation for Mexican-descent students at the high school. Despite a series of thoughtful and sincere attempts by students and their adult mentors to create conditions for unity and mutual respect at the school, the efforts ultimately failed to generate any significant transformations in schooling structures and practices. A more detailed analysis demonstrates how students' efforts were undermined by adults at many different levels of the schooling process. Because of the contentious nature of events that transpired during this time, and the painful impact they had on some of those who experienced them, it is important to note that two of the central participants who acted as my informants—Diego Omán and Luis Sandoval—requested that I not quote them directly or reveal the level of information they provided during the course of our interactions. For this reason, I provide a second-hand account of their experiences in this chapter.

Chapter 4 shifts the focus of analysis from the high school to the larger community, chronicling a series of district-sponsored parent fora that were convened to resolve conflicts surrounding the political empowerment of Latino students at Allenstown High. Despite courageous efforts by a group of Mexican migrant parents from Farmingville to have their voices heard, the parent meetings ultimately dissolved before significant action could be taken. As the meetings began to break down, a group of White parents from Allenstown met separately to discuss a plan to separate from the larger PVUSD and create their own Allenstown School District, a plan they made public several weeks later. In proposing their plan for district reorganization—which became widely known as the "Allenstown secession campaign"—the parent group denied that race was an issue, arguing instead that their interests were to create smaller schools, less bureaucracy, and higher-quality education. I analyze the competing notions of entitlement that shaped the convictions of those supporting and opposing the Allenstown secession movement, as well as the role of local discourses of place and community in arguments for and against secession. From either side of this debate, questions about "deservedness"—who deserves what and why, based on entitlements proper to one's racial, class, and residential status—are central to understanding how particular claims about the nature of educational "problems" are constructed, and how these claims acquire wider acceptance by framing debates about how school reform should best be pursued.

Chapter 5 pursues a more in-depth analysis of Allenstown's school secession movement. I consider whether the significance of race was overdetermined in the conflict, and I explore the ways its supporters use discourses proposing its "overdetermined" nature to dismiss the racial dimensions of their own rhetoric and political action. While I warn against collapsing the movement into a simple narrative of White racism, I highlight the ways in which the Allenstown secession effort has resonated with strategies historically employed by local Whites to defend their neighborhoods against racial and class Others.

Chapter 6 shifts to more contemporary conditions at Allenstown High School, where I draw from three years of site-based, participant-observation research to analyze the well-intended, institutional effort at Allenstown High to create a more welcoming and inclusive environment for Mexican-descent students on the campus. I then narrow my focus to one particular effort in this regard: the promotion of "cultural celebrations," including those commemorating Mexican holidays. I argue that the conflicts that have accompanied these events reveal the complex challenges teachers and students face in even the most modest attempts to promote multicultural educational practices that value and validate the cultural and linguistic heritage of Mexican-descent students.

Chapter 7 shifts attention back to the school district secession battle, highlighting the mid-2000s appearance of a broad-based, Latino-led coalition of engaged citizens, community leaders, and civic groups that set out to delegitimize the well-established district secession movement and provide an alternative vision for high-quality, shared schooling in the district. The chapter looks closely at the process and outcomes of civic capacity building among Mexican-descent youth and adult citizens, demonstrating how and why they were drawn powerfully into local politics for school improvement despite conditions of concentrated poverty that can often serve to stifle such mobilization. The analysis focuses specifically on two Latino-led collectivities that served as central organizing contexts for opposition to school resegregation, addressing how each group provided a unique social, cultural, and political space from which formerly marginalized youth and adults could engage in critical conversations about the role and purpose of public schooling, speak out against unjust educational conditions, and articulate counter-narratives stressing the importance of racial justice and a fundamental entitlement to shared, high-quality education. I also explore some of the specific strategies developed by local Latino activists to consolidate cross-class coalitions sympathetic to the cause of equal educational opportunity. The article ends with a discussion of the challenges inherent in translating grassroots activism into broader educational reform efforts aimed at establishing high-quality integrated education as a fundamental right.

The concluding chapter uses a recent controversy over the naming of a newly constructed high school after civil rights leader Cesar Chavez to bring together several of the central arguments developed in the book. The book concludes with a more personal discussion of the importance of integrated schooling in a twenty first-century context, putting in perspective both the inherent challenges to such efforts, and the strategies that would be necessary to sustain public school environments in ways that might more equally serve all students across class, racial, ethnic, and cultural difference.

The story I tell about Pleasanton Valley, its school district, and Allenstown High in particular, cannot be generalized as the "normal" experience of all bimodal (predominantly White/Latino) school systems in the United States, nor is it necessarily a proper representation of the challenges other multiracial schools and school systems may face. However, what became clear to me in the course of my fieldwork is that increasing White/Latino public school segregation, while national in scope, is locally produced. This realization is significant in that it obligates school personnel at both the district and school site levels—as well as officials at the level of regional government—to acknowledge and come to an informed understanding of their own role in perpetuating and reproducing inequity in education and blocking equal access to important academic and social resources for Mexican-descent students. What has been a crux of the problem in

Pleasanton Valley are agencies, administrators, and teachers who are, at worst, unwilling to challenge status quo schooling practices that generate racial segregation and unequal access to educational resources and, at best, lacking the ability, resources, and knowledge to maintain the kind of resolve necessary to transform them.

PART I

Contextualizing Educational Inequality

CHAPTER 1

White/Latino School Resegregation, the Deprioritization of School Integration, and Prospects for a Future of Shared, High-Quality Education

Latino School Segregation as a Twenty-First-Century Problem

Why, from an equal educational opportunity perspective, should there be any significant concern about the school segregation of Latino youth? What does racial balance have to do with effective, equity-based schooling practice? To understand how Latino school segregation constitutes such a potent challenge to equal educational opportunity in the United States, it is imperative to view the situation beyond a simple "racial balance" issue. In reality, Latino school segregation is systematically linked to other forms of isolation including segregation by socioeconomic status, residential location, and increasingly by language. What has been much less politicized in the integration debate is the *class* component of segregated schools, that is, the socioeconomic injustice that segregated schools tend to perpetuate, based on the concentrated poverty that is so strongly associated with race in the United States. Unfortunately, Latino segregation almost always involves double or triple segregation, including conditions of concentrated poverty and linguistic separation.

Research statistics from the Civil Rights Project/Proyecto Derechas Civiles at UCLA provide dimension to the problem. Nationally, Latinos are three times more likely than Whites to be in high-poverty schools and twelve times as likely to be in schools where almost everyone is poor

(Orfield and Lee 2006). In the western United States, Latinos make up 55 percent of students attending high-poverty schools (defined as schools with 50–100 percent poor students) and 76 percent of those in extreme-poverty schools (defined as 90–100 percent poor students). This is in stark contrast to White students, who represent 26 percent of those in high-poverty schools and only 7 percent of those in extreme-poverty schools. Put another way, 82 percent of White students and only 7 percent of Latinos attend low-poverty schools (20).

In these terms, the problem of Latino school segregation is not a simple psychological burden of racial isolation but a larger syndrome of inequalities related to the double and triple segregation Latino students face in racially isolated schools.[1] Latino youth segregated in high-poverty schools—what Orfield and Lee have called "institutions of concentrated disadvantage"—face a host of challenges that impede their access to high-quality K-12 education as well as to college. Students in such schools often face linguistic isolation, with large numbers of native Spanish speakers and few fluent speakers of academic English, which severely limits their opportunities to practice and acquire English, an element considered essential for success in high school, higher education, and beyond (Gándara and Hopkins 2009; Gifford and Valdes 2006). Other significant disadvantages include less contact with teachers credentialed in the subjects they are teaching, a more limited curriculum often taught at less challenging levels, less availability of advanced placement courses that prepare (and sometimes qualify) students for college admission, generally lower levels of parental education, less access to pro-academic peer groups, violence in the form of crime and gangs, dropout problems, lower college-going rates, and lack of proper nutrition and other untreated health problems (Balfanz and Legters 2004; Clotfelter, Ladd, and Vigdor 2005).

In other words, Latino students in racially segregated, high-poverty schools face isolation not only from the White community, but from middle-class schools and the potential benefits derived from them. Low-poverty schools tend to offer stronger academic competition, the ability to attract and hold more qualified instructors teaching in their subject areas, the availability of more accelerated and academically demanding courses, more active involvement of parents, stronger relationships with colleges, better campus facilities and equipment, greater access to pro-academic peer groups, greater access to social networks and experiences that can lead to increased educational and job opportunities, and higher graduation and college-going rates (Betts, Rueben, and Danenberg 2000; Haycock 1998; Orfield 2001).

Beyond the obstacles that confront working-class Latino youth and their families in segregated schooling contexts are the extreme challenges faced by the urban and suburban school systems that serve them. Besides often severe inequalities in school finance due to differential property tax bases, such schools are burdened by added instructional costs related to language training and some forms of special education, constant retraining and supervision of new teachers due to high turnover, frequent student movement and midyear transfers that lead to instability in school enrollments (which also affects consistency of state and federal funding), higher needs for remedial education, increased need for counseling/social work support for students experiencing crises related to living in conditions of poverty, and health emergencies that may arise given many working families' limited access to preventive care (Orfield and Lee 2005). Taking into account these additional costs, it is clear that even liberal educational reforms aimed at equalizing school funding are likely to fall short, as equal dollars simply cannot produce equal opportunities. From an equity-based schooling perspective, the challenge posed by school segregation is not one of simple racial imbalance, but of the clear disadvantages and burdens faced by students isolated in high-poverty schools versus students who enjoy the relative advantages of low-poverty schools.

A critical question is why, given the tangible and damaging consequences of school segregation to Latino youth, so little attention is given to the current crisis. This is particularly perplexing in the United States, where public opinion has become steadily more supportive of desegregated schools. Since the early 1980s, a vast majority of Americans have tended to endorse desegregation in principle, claiming a philosophical preference for racially integrated schools.[2] This popular preference is guided by the wisdom that children must learn how to understand and work with others across differences in order to develop the skills for success in cross-cultural and multiracial work and living environments. In fact, recent longitudinal studies on the experiences of youth who have attended integrated primary and secondary schools point to significant long-term social and career benefits to all students, including improved chances of a desegregated future life, higher educational and occupational aspirations, and an increased likelihood of living and working in interracial settings (Wells 1995; Wells et al. 2009; Yun and Kurlaender 2004; Eaton 2001).

Furthermore, a long-held justification among parents for resistance to integrated schooling—that shared educational environments of this kind cannot be made conducive to high-quality learning for all students—has been challenged by an increasingly rich body of scholarly research identifying a broad range of evidence-based practices that promote effective, shared learning in socioeconomically and racially mixed school settings. This includes development of a variety of curricular models for engaging students in academic learning across politicized social difference (Burris and Welner 2007; Landsman and Lewis 2006; Nieto 2010; Oakes 2005; Pollock 2008) and strategies for socially organizing students within the school and classroom to promote more equal status and engagement in curricular and co-curricular activities (Fine, Weis, and Powel 1997; González, Moll, and Amanti 2005; Hawley 2007; Phelan, Davidson, and Yu 1993; Slavin 1995). Within this literature is a growing body of research that specifically addresses the opportunities and challenges that arise in schooling contexts that bring together working-class Latino populations with middle-class Whites (Cammarota 2007; Conchas 2001; Espinoza-Herold 2003; Gándara 2002; González and Moll 2002; Grady 2002; Mehan et al. 1996; Reyes and Laliberty 1992; Slavin et al. 1996).

If an increasing number of U.S. citizens believe in the potential virtues of integrated schooling—and there are tested, evidence-based models to facilitate learning in such settings—why is school integration in such retreat, and how is it being justified? It would seem important to get at the root of this paradox.

Retreat from Integration and Advancement of School Resegregation in the United States

To date, a broad range of scholarly research has sought to explain the sociohistorical, economic, political, and legal factors that have marred the institutionalization of racial integration as an equity-based school reform strategy in the United States since *Brown v. Board of Education*. For the purposes of my analysis, I wish to identify and discuss two dominant lines of this inquiry.[3] One approach, which I will call the *White resistance/deserved segregation* framework, relies heavily on macrohistorical analyses of shifting material conditions, race- and class-related interests, and federal court decisions in the twentieth century that have shaped public policy, citizenship narratives, and legal-discursive regimes in manners that have undermined or weakened mandates for school integration and justified a return to more "separate but equal" public schooling conditions. The second, which I will call the *normative whiteness/subtractive assimilation* framework, pays closer attention to the impact of local-level forces, intergroup relations, and racialization processes and the ways in which they combine to generate the social and institutional conditions that limit school integration efforts on the ground. My discussion here is meant not only to identify how each framework contributes significantly to our understanding of continuing processes of school segregation but also to consider how, by integrating insights from each approach, it may be possible to imagine what a democratic countertendency capable of challenging school resegregation processes might look like. In the final section of this chapter, I draw on the work of Jeannie Oakes and her colleagues to consider how a broad rearticulation of values of fairness and inclusion in the schooling process—spread widely through mobilizations and social movement activism led primarily by working-class communities of color—may have the potential to disarm resegregation campaigns by promoting the idea of shared, high-quality public schooling as a fundamental right of all citizens in the United States. While seemingly far-fetched, such a rearticulation of values and norms was accomplished, on a smaller scale, in a series of Latino-led citizen mobilizations against a ten-year campaign to resegregate local schools in the Pleasanton Valley region of central California, and it is worth considering how such a feat was accomplished and what might be learned from it (the extended case study is offered in Chapter 7).

Suburban Development, White Entitlement and Shifting Discourses of Citizenship in the United States

The *White resistance/deserved segregation* explanatory approach to the retreat from public school desegregation is perhaps best exemplified in the work of educational scholar Gary Orfield and sociologist George Lipsitz. Each, in separate lines of research, has looked deeply into the political and material histories of race and class in twentieth-century United States that have fueled a process of "refusal, resistance, and renegotiation" (in Lipsitz's 1998 terms) on the part of residents in predominantly White, middle-class residential communities to avoid a host of federal and state desegregation mandates meant to secure equal access to educational resources and to offer minority students opportunities they have historically been denied (see also Orfield and Eaton 1996). Rather than portraying such political strategies of resistance as predicated on openly racist beliefs, Lipsitz identifies what he calls a "possessive investment in whiteness" whereby "white supremacy is usually less a matter of direct, referential, and snarling contempt than a system for protecting the privileges of whites" (1998: viii) by denying communities of color opportunities for such things as asset accumulation, upward mobility, and—in this case—high-quality integrated education.

To account for the construction of White entitlement in these terms, Lipsitz and others (see, for example, Omi and Winant 1994; Brodkin 1998) have pointed to a key set of twentieth-century politico-historical developments in the United States that have fundamentally reshaped the country's race/class demographics, political identities, and notions of citizenship in the post-civil rights era. Chief among these developments was the creation and expansion of U.S. residential suburbs from the early twentieth century to the late 1960s as "expressedly racist and exclusionary housing markets" (Lipsitz and Oliver 2010) whose occupation was facilitated, in large part, by federal government-sponsored home loan and mortgage assistantship programs that actively and systematically promoted racial segregation (see also Massey and Denton 1998; Mahoney 1997; Jackson 1985). By condoning racial covenants on the purchase of suburban properties, refusing to lend money to people of color, and colluding with private citizens and local real estate agents in an array of associated discriminatory practices that included racial zoning, redlining, steering, and block busting, the U.S. federal government assured that 98 percent of Federal Housing Act loans disbursed between 1934 and 1968 were provided exclusively to Whites (Lipsitz and Oliver 2010; Roithmayr 2007). Further safeguarding suburban areas as reserved largely for White, middle-class settlement was the prioritized allocation of federal funds for highway construction to the suburbs and the associated financing of urban renewal programs that tended to displace urban minority residents into further racially and socioeconomically segregated living arrangements within metropolitan areas (see Massey and Denton 1997). As Martha Mahoney has remarked, racial segregation and the "Whiteness" of suburbs in the United States are not incidentally paired; "government-sponsored segregation helped inscribe in American culture the equation of 'good neighborhoods' with White ones" (1997: 274–75).

U.S. residential suburban areas continued to swell through the mid- to late twentieth century, enhanced significantly in the mid-1960s by processes of "White flight" from metropolitan areas that were increasingly subject to, or threatened by, federal and state school desegregation mandates. Here it is important to note that while the Supreme Court decision in *Brown v. Board of Education* was handed down in 1954, its broad enforcement remained limited for nearly a decade, and its requirements were generally not assumed to extend beyond the U.S. South. The passage of the Civil Rights Act of 1964 changed things considerably, as it provided for denial of federal educational funds to school districts continuing to discriminate on the basis of race. It also established the federal Department of Health, Education, and Welfare (HEW) in the Office of Civil Rights, an agency that took the lead in enforcing desegregation by initiating litigation against districts not responding to federal mandates. A string of Supreme Court decisions followed the Civil Rights Act (continuing through the early 1970s) that called for increasingly strict measures for school desegregation, including mandates to extend school integration requirements beyond the U.S. South to western and eastern states, and to expand the right of desegregated schooling to other "protected" minority groups, including Mexican Americans.[4]

This intensification of federal enforcement for desegregation, along with the extension of minority group entitlements to integrated education, had the effect of generating fervent backlash among segments of the White population in various areas of the country, particularly those who felt dislocated by the economic, political, and cultural shifts they believed to be a product of civil rights strategies.[5] The result was massive protests, impassioned political lobbying, and a proliferation of state ballot measures meant to curb or dismantle desegregation efforts, often in open contradiction to federal court decisions in ongoing litigation (Orfield 1997). The ensuing racial-reactive atmosphere fostered the growth of a neoconservative political movement that, incorporating a populist mistrust of "big government" and a distain for the social welfare state, took among its central aims to delegitimize the very civil rights legal framework that had allowed for the conferral of group-based political rights to "protected" racial minorities in the first place. Here, the political intention was to reduce discourses of racial equality and justice from their then-current rootedness in "group rights" principles (a legal recognition hard-earned in the civil rights movement) to largely *individual* terms—that is, that any individual could be subject to discrimination based on being a victim of the unjust practice of racial preferencing. In other words, the civil rights framework calling for collective equality based on a desirable "equality of result" was to be delegitimized and replaced with one meant to provide a less-specific *equality of opportunity for individuals*, which could only be achieved through neutral, color-blind policies and strict opposition to any kind of "race thinking" in public policy decision-making.

This reframing of *civil-rights-as-individual-rights* could find its justification in U.S. liberal democratic principles that have long held group identity and status to be obstacles to the possibility of individual freedom, favored national unity over equality, and viewed the successful American as a self-motivated agent who values a concept of self free from group affiliation and from the past (Schmidt 2000). By intentionally rooting citizenship entitlements in individual rights, those whose wished to roll back the gains of the civil rights movement could present themselves as opponents of both racial discrimination and any antidiscrimination measure based on "group rights" principles—namely, desegregation and affirmative action policies (Omi and Winant 1994: 130).

This powerful populist development, reflected in and amplified by the election of U.S. president Richard Nixon in 1969, led to broad attacks on civil rights strategies, with Nixon himself taking an open and active stance against busing as a means of desegregation, and promising "to restrain HEW's efforts in the South and to produce a more conservative Justice Department and Supreme Court" (Orfield 1978: 6). Nixon's appointment of four political conservatives to crucial federal justice positions helped fuel a division in the U.S. Supreme Court regarding its role in directing the desegregation process (Chemerinsky 2003). The Court's 1974 opinion (5-4) in *Milliken v. Bradley* reinforced the importance of the "local control" of schools "as essential to both the maintenance of community concern and the support for public schools and to the quality of the educational process," while its 1977 decision in *Dayton Board of Education v. Brinkman (Dayton I)* affirmed "local autonomy" with the status of a "vital national tradition . . . long been thought essential both to the maintenance of community concern and the support of public schools and the quality of the educational process" (Bell 1995: 23). By the late 1980s and continuing through the 1990s, the Supreme Court's rulings on school desegregation more clearly reflected a growing political interest in abandoning the goal of integrating children and moving (back) toward the idea of the "neighborhood school" and arrangements favoring "parental choice."[6] Backing away from hard-fought efforts to push racial integration, federal courts increasingly endorsed "separate but equal" schooling situations, authorizing the diversion of federal desegregation funds from financing integration to enhancing the quality of curriculum at all schools.[7]

These shifts in school desegregation decision making, and the transformed notions of citizenship they reflected, must also be understood in relation to the extensive suburbanization underway in the late twentieth century, as unprecedented White flight harkened a distinctive transformation in regional politics, particularly in California, where significant political power shifted toward the suburbs. As Ewan McKenzie (1996) has noted, the rise of suburban homeowners associations and other private common interest developments (CIDs) led to the growth of de facto private (residential) government and an increasingly privatized notion of citizenship rights among suburban-dwelling homeowners (see also Kruze 2005; Cashin 2001). Widespread fees levied by residential associations for private services fueled a growing sense of resentment among suburban homeowners for having to "pay more than their share" in allegedly "duplicate" public services, and helped generate a belief that, should they be expected to pay more, it ought to come with the assurance that such spending serve their own interests and not be earmarked for "redistributional" purposes.[8] The political legitimacy and justification for such claims of entitlement could be rooted in a longer tradition of U.S. individual rights-based liberalism that assumes the right of citizens, as property owners and taxpayers, to rule their own matters on as local a scale as possible (Lehning 1998).

Under the rubric of "local community control" and through claims of local autonomy, residents of suburban communities were increasingly able to justify utilizing their assets to benefit their own communities and fight for upwardly redistributive policies (and against downwardly redistributive policies) for the expenditure of state and federal funds with little or no reference to the race and class composition of the communities benefiting from these policies (Barlowe 2003).[9] This "common sense" suturing of property rights and political rights gained significant traction during the late twentieth century expansion of U.S. suburbanization, as the right to "local control" of public resources and institutions—including public schools—came to be increasingly understood as an entitlement akin to homeownership, merited by virtue of one's privileged (suburban) residential location and relative socioeconomic status. As McKenzie has argued, the rise of private residential government has helped create a society of suburban homeowners who tend to equate citizen rights with property rights and who seem to share one strong political cause: a near obsessive concern with maintaining or upgrading property values. McKenzie spoke, somewhat prophetically, of a time in which suburban homeowners "may develop an attenuated sense of loyalty and commitment to the public communities in which their CIDs are located, even to the point of virtual or actual secession" (1996: 186). Richard Reich (1991) has called this phenomenon the "secession of the successful," and Charles Murray warns that it may be the beginning of a new "caste society" in which privatization of local government will lead to a powerful public constituency campaigning to bypass the social institutions they don't like (quoted in Reich 1991:187).[10]

Suburban School District "Secessionism" and the Politics of Deserved Segregation

The school district reorganization campaign that is the focus of this study, emerging as it did in the mid-1990s, became immediately known by its opponents as the "Allenstown school district secession campaign." In my own analysis of the decade-long initiative, I have elected to retain the politicized language of secession because I believe that this campaign—and other citizen-led, suburban school district "reorganization" efforts like it—can be related to other, largely middle-class movements to "secede from responsibility" in a political opportunity structure made possible by the reigning influence of economic neoliberalism, the increase of suburban privatization, and the combined role they have played in reshaping U.S. political and economic life (Boudreau and Keil 2001). Suburban school secession movements, I argue, should be viewed in relation to similar kinds of phenomena emerging not just in the United States, but on a global scale, including territorial secession efforts (like those in Los Angeles in the 1990s) and the increased construction of gated communities and walled cities about which there is an interesting and growing body of ethnographic literature (Caldeira 2000; Lowe 2003; Rivera-Bonilla 1999). What suburban school secession campaigns share with these territorial and community-fortification counterparts is their status as mostly class-based and strongly racialized movements of social separation couched in political terms, that is, articulated in a language of civil rights and liberalism (Boudreau and Keil 2001: 1702). In other words, they tend to use a common set of arguments to justify their actions, including an expressed desire for local control, an expectation of greater return on tax dollars locally, a fear of bureaucracy and big government, and a sense that they, as privileged members of the suburban middle class, are not getting a fair share of what they deserve. Moreover, citizen groups see themselves as fair players, claiming that they—as well as the regions from which they seek separation—will be better off in a "divorce" (1718–19). The populist appeal of citizen-led school district secession campaigns, much like that of their territorial counterparts, is predicated on their ability to frame their arguments in a rhetoric of efficiency and boosterism in ways that effectively capture the imagination of middle-class residents (1723). In the case of school district secessionism, this is done primarily through the promise of an elite, high-quality education as well as liberation from corrupt, unruly school district bureaucracies that fail to prioritize their specific needs and desires.

More difficult to ascertain, from a democratic point of view, is how proponents of school district secessionism find it possible to cast and imagine themselves as fair players despite often compelling empirical evidence that suggests high levels of negative fiscal and educational impact on communities from which they seek separation—communities that, in many cases, are made up of working-class immigrants and people of color. One manner of accounting for such political behavior, as Andrew Barlowe (2003) has argued, is to see it as reflective of contemporary forms of neoliberal, corporate capitalist development and their influence on current social, political, cultural, and economic relationships in the United States. Barlowe's analysis looks at how a set of neoliberal economic developments in the United States since the 1970s—which have resulted in an acceleration of an income disparity between the rich and the poor; the expansion of nonunionized, part-time, and temporary jobs that provide lower wages and little security; the increased privatization of basic resources like education, health care. and retirement; and the production of a recurring series of economic recessions, including the most recent financial industry bailout—have served to undermine the security of the nation's middle class (see also Comaroff, Comaroff, and Weller 2001; Harvey 2007, 1991).[11] Downward pressures on much of the middle class have provided a context in which the "haves" have taken on an increasingly defensive posture, viewing claims of the "have-nots" on social resources with outright hostility and fear. Moreover, it has allowed a fertile ground for intensification of racism, as middle-class people feel the need to mobilize any and all privileges available to them, including racial privileges, even if they might not recognize them as such, in order to buffer themselves against the fear of downward mobility (Barlowe 2003: 22). In other words, a "fear of falling" has generated a defensive mentality among middle-class citizens, compelling them to exercise social entitlements in ways that increasingly exploit race, class, and national privileges.

While seeking empirical evidence to validate or refute claims about the influence of recent neoliberal economic developments on social, political, and economic behavior is not a central focus of this study, I believe these broader shifts deserve mention for the role they play in providing a political opportunity structure that has facilitated the growth of suburban school secessionism and lent credibility to suburban citizens' assertions of rights to a separate education rooted in residentially based "local control," even when the expected outcomes may be unequal access to public resources across lines of both class and race.

Strengths and Limitations of Material-Historical Accounts of the "Failure" of School Integration

The explanatory framework outlined above, with its careful attention to the macro-level demographic, political, and judicial shifts that have limited school integration efforts and normalized privatization over time, proves a useful lens for interpreting the attitudes of entitlement and privilege that some affluent White suburbanites may feel toward their own segregation—an entitlement they have historically achieved in housing but struggle to sustain in schooling, particularly in light of significant growth of ethnoracial diversity in U.S. suburban areas (Frankenberg and Debray 2011; M. Orfield and Luce 2012). Such felt-entitlements can be considered key components of what Stephen Gregory (following W. E. B. Du Bois) has called "wages of whiteness," a [middle] class struggle through which Whites "evaluate and experience class identity and mobility" as well as engage in a form of antistate and antiminority politics of deserved segregation (1998: 80). In this case, local resistance to integration is rarely voiced in terms of racial or class interests but rather as a (White, middle-class) fear of losing "local control" over the schooling process.

In the present study of the Pleasanton Valley of California, the *White resistance/deserved segregation* framework proves valuable in accounting for the discourses and behaviors that have come to surround school resegregation efforts. As the extended case studies in the following chapters will attest, parent and civic leaders from the White residential community who have spent nearly a decade pushing for more locally operated (and racially separate) schooling arrangements have framed their struggles primarily as ones meant to sustain the quality of schools, to protect community resources (particularly financial ones), and to maintain local ways of managing their affairs and finances. In this manner, they have achieved significant success in persuading the school board to accept their positions. However, these same residents have also repeatedly mobilized to resist state policies mandating legal rights to Latino children and their families under desegregation laws as well as the forms of social activism, often led by local Mexican-descent citizens, that have attempted to secure those rights (see Chapters 2 and 3). This has included strong opposition to school programs, structures, and practices designed to accommodate Latinos' native language skills, and to incorporate cultural elements in ways that might make the schools more equally accessible to Latino students and their families (see Chapters 5 and 6). At the same time, local school district board members and senior school site administrators—positions held overwhelmingly by White residents—have continually dismissed allegations that racial, class, and cultural concerns impact how they manage issues of equity and diversity in the district, yet they have nevertheless repeatedly failed to provide leadership in efforts to integrate students and to assure the provision of state-mandated services and resources designed to ensure equal opportunity and services to Latino youth (see Chapter 2). Ultimately, the entitlement that White suburbanites in Pleasanton Valley have felt to their own "quality schools" has meant excluding minority students. In this sense, struggles for segregated schooling conditions in Pleasanton Valley have truly been, in Gregory's words, a "struggle over what it meant to be white and middle class in postwar, racially segregated American society" (1998: 81).

Yet, even as the *White resistance/deserved segregation* framework offers essential insights into the macrohistorical conditions that have fueled a retreat from school integration and advanced the growth of suburban school resegregation in the United States, it remains limited as an explanatory model for a number of reasons. One reason is that it fails, in broad terms, to adequately account for the importance of (often hard-fought) "on-the-ground" efforts to develop and institute integration plans at the district and school levels, and how the trajectory of such activities can play a significant role in determining citizens', parents', and educators' attitudes about the viability and desirability of shared schooling. In other words, macro-level accounts tend not to include qualitative and comparative attention to the relative challenges of instituting integration on a school-by-school basis as it relates to curricular and pedagogical development and efforts to facilitate relational cultures and strong partnerships between educators, parents, and school administrators to assure commitment and accountability to educational models that can successfully engage student across racial, class, and linguistic difference (see, for example, strategies highlighted in Warren 2005 and Warren, Mapp, and the Community Organizing School Reform Project 2011).

Another limitation of the dominant *White resistance/deserved segregation* explanatory framework is that, by privileging processes of White racism and entitlement claims, it tends to obscure the various ways in which historically oppressed racial minority populations have responded to such treatment, denying them any agency outside of victim. Due to this largely unidirectional historical lens, a deep consideration of what school desegregation initiatives have historically expected of racial minority populations has too often been overlooked. As well, little analytical space is given to an exploration of the ways in which racial minority populations may be internally differentiated by various forms of racial, class, and gender-based discrimination, and the consequences of such differentiation on political agency and engagement at local, regional, and national levels (Gilroy 1987; Gregory 1998). Put another way, the explanatory approach, taken alone, fails in broad terms to adequately account for what school desegregation efforts *have required of minority groups*, and how such expectations have generated conflicts and spawned political subjectivities that have shaped the very terrain on which integration politics, and equity-based school reform debates more broadly, have taken place at local, regional, and national levels.

Normative Whiteness and the Limits of the Integrationist Project Set Forth in *Brown*

While the *White resistance/deserved segregation* framework emphasizes the resistance of privileged White citizens to the vision, expectations, and implications of the mandates set forth in *Brown v. Board of Education*, the fact is that significant voices of critique have also come from within the very minority communities that the *Brown* ruling was intended to vindicate. These voices of resistance go back to the period before and during the original *Brown* proceedings when, for example, Black Nationalist leaders spoke strongly against the court's vision for school integration based on what they regarded as the incomplete understanding of racism and race relations on which the decision was based, and the limited view of racial domination and racial justice that it appeared to reflect (Peller 1996). Because the *Brown* agenda was framed primarily as a struggle against pathological or psychological manifestations of racist attitudes or behaviors, the court assumed that overcoming prejudice and arriving at racial justice could best be achieved through the social practice of equal treatment. Such a practice would require the establishment of a color-blind position, or a sort of race neutrality within public schools, in which all students would have access to an objectively defined, racially integrated form of "quality education" based on neutral standards of professionalism and universal testing paradigms that could serve as effective and appropriate measures of schooling equality and individual ability (Peller 1996: 131).

What Black Nationalist leaders like Malcolm X and Stokely Carmichael found problematic about this particular framing of the integrationist project was the manner in which it diverted attention away from how race and class backgrounds and experiences have structured socioeconomic, political, and educational opportunities over time, eluding consideration of how racism has operated within a historical context related to centuries of unequal distribution of social, economic, and political opportunities and through normative practices that have served to produce systematic White privilege. Viewing racism as primarily a "problem of psychology" evaded not only issues of class exploitation and struggle but also trivialized and mystified the deeper sources of racial inequality that have never been located solely, or even primarily, in individual actions or prejudices but in a racialized social order sustained through enduring systems of hierarchically organized racial inequality that include de facto occupational, residential, and school segregation (Omi and Winant 1994: 133; see also Lipsitz 1998).[12]

The Black Nationalist critique of the *Brown* agenda was not a rejection of integration per se, but a rejection of the particular assimilationist terms under which that integration was expected to take place. *Brown* promoted a form of integration that was assimilative in nature, based on the dominant paradigm of citizenship and belonging in the United States, which asks all citizens regardless of race, class, or cultural background and experience to assimilate to "American culture" by conforming to normative cultural and linguistic practices, and to concede the use of nonstandard or native linguistic and cultural practices in the public realm. Against the *Brown* court's idea that the absence of race consciousness in schools would allow fair, impersonal criteria to inform merit-based decision making and assure "quality education," the Black Nationalist perspective "characterized the norms that constituted the neutral, impersonal, a-racial, and professional character of school integration as particular cultural assumptions of a specific economic class of Whites" (Peller 1996: 140). In doing so, they sought to deny the very possibility and feasibility of an "ideal," objective, neutral, and skills-oriented "quality education"; instead, they meant to demystify it as the arbitrary establishment of middle-class, Anglo-American cultural practices and cultural capital as the preferred and rewarded norms of behavior, learning, and interaction within schools (see also Heath 1996; Kelley 1997).[13] What was considered dangerous about an approach to desegregated schooling that dismissed as irrelevant—or, at worst, inferior—the cultural and linguistic resources, skills, and experiences of the non-White, non-middle class, was the manner in which it could serve to promote the supposition that cultural deficits explain low achievement, an assumption that was used to justify lowered expectations for working-class racial and ethnic minority students and to encourage disparagement of racial minority group status in ways that have promoted student disengagement from normative educational models (see Foley 1997; McDermott 1997; Valenzuela 1999). The fears articulated by Black Nationalist leaders were that assimilative integration, in practice, would serve as a "subterfuge for White supremacy" (Peller 1996: 139) in which "successfully" desegregated environments would become settings for resegregation due to tracking practices, ability grouping, and expectation of Anglo conformity for equal access, participation, and respect in important schooling activities.

Dangers of White Normativity in Racially and Socioeconomically Diverse Schooling Contexts

Unfortunately, these early concerns about the dangers of assimilative integration have, to a large degree, been realized in public schools in the United States up to the present day. An expansive body of ethnographic literature has been exploring the negative forms and consequences of White normativity in U.S. public schools, including attention to how discourse and practices of "color-blindness" can lead to subtle forms of discrimination and privilege that aid in the production of unequal schooling experiences and outcomes (Kailin 1999; Lewis 2003); how Whiteness can come to function as a status associated with giftedness and privileged entitlement, disproportionally channeling educational resources to White students (Fine 1991; Staiger 2004); and how everyday racialization processes in educational settings can impact student identifications and social affiliations in ways consequential to school success (Bettie 2003; Chesler, Peet, and Sevig 2003; Davidson 1996; Hurd 2008; Olsen 1997; Perry 2002).

This notion of white normativity draws from a more general concept within the social sciences of *normative cultural practice*, a term that describes a set of dominant expectations, values, principles, and modes of representation that tend to guide interactions within public institutional settings in the United States. Normative whiteness, as Pamela Perry has argued, draws from a set of ideological understandings that, although broadly shared within the population, tend to be linked to particular ways of understanding history, citizenship, notions of self and other, and the very concept of culture itself (2001: 61). The notion of normative whiteness, to paraphrase Margaret Andersen, is less about bodies and skin color than about discursive and material practices that privilege and sustain the dominance of White imperial and middle-class Eurocentric worldviews (2003: 29).

In the United States, two popular discourses underlie practices of White normativity and help account for the damaging forms they may take in racially and socioeconomically diverse schooling contexts, particularly—I will argue—in school settings shared by White and Latino students. The first is that of assimilationist integration which, while typically allowing for some level of public expression of culture and language by ethnic citizens, tends to limit toleration to safe, "folk" genres such as festivals, cultural celebrations, ethnic restaurants, and some forms of media (Baquedano-López 2000; Hill 1999). Strong public expression of cultural and linguistic diversity beyond those contexts—for example, in institutional settings like public schools, workplaces, and voting booths—is often taken to be threatening to national unity and encouraging of ethnic separatism. A second pillar of normative whiteness, which finds justification in the same liberal democratic principles that support the assimilationist perspective, is the racial ideology of color blindness. From a color-blind perspective, the role of multicultural public schooling is to transcend racial consciousness through race neutrality and the social principle of equal treatment, thereby reaffirming the meritocratic idea in U.S. society that economic and social mobility are possible for all those who will work hard and conform to norms and habits of those already in power.

Problems arise in racially and ethnically diverse public schools when these foundational discourses of normative whiteness find themselves at odds with a range of common strategies and practices used by self-proclaimed "multicultural" schools to pursue their inclusive educational missions. These include, for example, racial and cultural pride activities and events, cultural commemorations, ethnic and cultural clubs, and various "ethnic studies" curricular offerings. The result is a certain schizophrenia inherent in many multiracial, socioeconomically diverse schools today, which says that the promotion of multiculturalism is good, but only if it takes noncritical forms that do not interrupt the assimilative function and "neutral" (color-blind) stance of schools. This has justified attacks on anything but the most muted and power-neutral forms of multicultural education, particularly with regard to educational programs designed specifically to address questions of power and status along lines of race, class, and culture. Moreover, wide-ranging reforms like the 2001 No Child Left Behind Act, with their focus on basic skills development, have had the consequence of reinforcing more monocultural, class-located norms for schooling, as well as condoning a long-standing refusal to acknowledge difference or diversity as a resource. In this manner, even resourceful practices of biculturalism and bilingualism (including code-switching varieties) can be viewed as political challenges or "anti-assmilationist apparatus(es) that challenge the norming process" (Guiterrez, Baquedano-López, and Álvarez 2000: 223). Ultimately, systematic attempts to engage sensitive issues surrounding socioeconomic, racial, or cultural differences in White/Latino shared schooling contexts tend to be vilified as ethnically interested, subversive forms of "victim politics" that promote racial polarization, focus on historical injustices rather than contemporary color-blind conditions, appeal to White guilt, or are motivated by the resentment of Whites (Ovando and McLaren 2000: xix). Moreover, school-based programs that extend beyond the "heroes and holidays" approach to cultural and racial diversity risk being dismissed as "extracurricular" and a distraction from the more "academically rigorous" technical skills training believed to constitute quality education (see Chapter 6 for a case study).

Student Responses to Practices of Normative Whiteness in Schools

Institutional practices of normative whiteness do not, of course, go unchallenged in schools. A long line of student-centered ethnographic research in U.S. public schools has examined the ways in which working-class racial minority youth (including African American, Mexican American, Puerto Rican, and Native American) have employed diverse forms of cultural practice to produce a sense of belonging and solidarity against the White middle-class norms required in the school context (see, for example, Davidson 1996; Foley 1996; Gitlin et al. 2003; Philips 1983). In many cases, such practices take the form of willed resistance against the acquisition of school-valued knowledge, but this is not necessarily the case. Angela Valenzuela (1999), in her study of Mexican American students in a South Texas high school, demonstrates that what would *appear to be* students' posture of resistance or "not caring" about school, is actually experienced by them as a sense of ambivalence—a feeling of being caught between a desire to succeed in school, and a level of resignation to the dominant attitudes that marginalize their cultural and linguistic heritage, which they experience as a key element of their group social status (for related analyses, see Davidson 1996; Gibson and Bejínez 2002; Gibson, Gándara, and Koyama 2004; Gitlin et al. 2003; Zentella 1997). In each of these cases, what may appear to be student resistance or academic disengagement may have less to do with an ability or motivation to succeed academically in school than with a desire, as a member of a stigmatized social group, to find a space of equal status among others and to "construct a positive self within and economic and political context which relegates its members to static and disparaged ethnic, racial and class identities" (Zentella 1997: 13).

Collectively, these studies focus on the ways in which unexamined norms of Whiteness and commitments to color-blindness may serve not only to reproduce the school success of middle-class White students in racially mixed school settings but also to actively promote the marginalization of working-class Latino students and discourage their involvement in school contexts that are known to facilitate students' social integration and academic success, including high-impact co- and extracurricular activities (Davidson 1996; Gibson and Bejínez 2002; Stanton-Salazar, Vásquez, and Mehan 2000). It is in this sense that White normativity can pose a significant and often unacknowledged limit on the effectiveness of educational programs in White/Latino desegregated schooling environments, particularly when student success depends on deep engagement, equal participation, and collaborative learning across what may be significant lines of politicized racial, ethnic, socioeconomic, or gender differences (Fine, Weis, and Powell 1997).

By identifying challenges posed by institutional practices of normative whiteness in racially and socioeconomically diverse school settings, I do not mean to suggest that effective integration is impossible. Instead, I mean to emphasize that the co-location of students in a desegregated setting may do more harm than good if there is not also a strong understanding of, and willingness to address, a broader set of sociocultural and contextual factors—powerfully at play within schools—that mediate student learning, motivation, engagement, and academic success. Ultimately, student learning is a social and political process influenced not only by the school's formal curriculum and the experiences that students bring *into* school with them but also by students' interactions *within* the school, both with peers and with the staff who organize opportunities for student learning and participation based often on their own (classed, raced, and gendered) assumptions, orientations, and belief systems that often go unacknowledged (Bartolomé and Trueba 2000). In a reframing that challenges popular educational reform logic, Ray McDermott suggests that "instead of asking what individuals learn in school, we should be asking what learning is made possible by social arrangements [*within* schools] . . . and see differential patterns of academic success along racial lines as an institutionalized, social event rather than a one-by-one failure in psychological development" (1997: 120). McDermott's admonishment suggests a reimaging of the pursuit for "quality education" from one that seeks to promote a near-exclusive focus on improving classroom instruction to one that seeks to address how schools, as whole institutions, may structure success and failure for particular groups of students (see also Stanton-Salazar, Vásquez, and Mehan 2000).

Hope for a Future of Effective, High-Quality Integrated Education in U.S. Public Schools?

Given the combined reality of rapidly resegregating schools, the deprioritization of integration as an equity-based education reform measure, an escalating desire among affluent residential communities to establish schooling arrangements on their own terms, and the ubiquity of normative practices within desegregated schools that can limit students' engagement across difference, there would appear to be little room for envisioning how to sustain equitable, high-quality educational environments that could be shared across socioeconomic and racial difference. Yet addressing this challenge would seem all the more timely and critical in light of the rapidly increasing rates of racial and socioeconomic diversity in U.S. suburban areas (M. Orfield and Luce 2012) and the educational injustices that we can expect will be perpetuated if the differential production of low- and high-poverty, racially isolated schools is allowed to continue at pace. Is it feasible, or even possible, to imagine a way to generate the political will to protect and sustain integrated public school contexts and the shared, high-quality, and equitable learning environments they have the potential to provide? If so, from where might such an impetus be likely to come?

In recent writings on equity-based school reform, educational scholar Jeannie Oakes and her colleagues have explored the extent to which grassroots political organizing and activism, led primarily by low-income populations of color, might play a catalytic role in equity-based educational reform in the United States (Oakes et al. 2008; Oakes and Lipton 2002; Rogers and Oakes 2005). Their scholarly project reflects a deeper interest in the possibilities of social movement activism to "win" better schools for working-class Latino and African American communities that have long been the most disadvantaged in terms of access to educational resources, opportunities, and school achievement. Their particular interest in social activism "led primarily by working class communities of color operating largely outside of the educational system" reflects a specific understanding of the primary obstacles to equal educational opportunity in U.S. public schools. This view is that the historical failure to establish high-quality, equitable education in U.S. public schools—despite decades of substantial investment in well-intentioned interventions—is largely the consequence of a long-misguided emphasis in educational reform policy on generating consensus-based, *technical* solutions to what are primarily *normative* and *political* impediments to educational equity (see also Nygreen 2006). In other words, what has long impeded the effectiveness of conventional school reform policy is investment in the faulty assumption that educational problems—including those related to differential achievement—are primarily the consequence of a lack of sufficient knowledge about how to design and implement high-impact teaching practices for diverse learners in ways that support standards-based competencies. As a result, the preferred path of reform has been to focus on programmatic innovations to improve teaching practice and create evidence-based "replicable" programs that, when competently applied, support high-quality learning for all students across (or often in spite of) lines of social difference. Yet decades of educational policy reform in this vein have done remarkably little to disrupt the all-too-familiar patterns of school success and failure across lines of politicized race, class, ethnicity, and gender difference in U.S. schools.

This intractability, Oakes and her colleagues suggest, is better understood as the consequence of normative forces that have long fueled aggressive political opposition to a broad range of equalization efforts designed to improve resources, opportunities, and outcomes on behalf of low-income students of color. These normative forces take the guise of a set of dominant "logics" that define the nation's thinking about public education (Oakes et al. 2008) and include assumptions about *resource scarcity* (that the financial resources to support high-quality education are in limited supply); *meritocratic privilege* (that such limited educational resources ought to be competed for and provided in a privileged manner to those students who are most deserving based on their ability level and preparation, often cast erroneously as their "potential"); and a belief in the existence of *unalterable deficits* (that low-income students of color face cultural, situational, and individual deficits that schools cannot be expected to alter).

Taken together, these popular logics portray public schooling as a zero-sum game in which opportunities for sought-after high-quality education are in small supply and should be competed for by students, families, and residential communities. When middle-class populations affirm these normative logics, calls for funding to remediate educational inequalities become viewed as an illegitimate redistribution of resources that allegedly "takes away" from the more deserving middle class, provoking fierce resistance to a perceived attack on their "earned" right to transfer educational and socioeconomic opportunities intergenerationally to their children.

A prime example of these normative logics powerfully at play is in the hard-fought (but still largely unfulfilled) effort to institute high-quality integrated education in U.S. public schools. Despite more than fifty years of technical development of effective, evidence-based models for high-quality integrated education, attempts to institutionalize the vision of *Brown v. Board of Education* have brought "retrogressive action and inertia by elites, anger among nonelite Whites who see themselves as losers in such reform, and disillusionment among excluded groups themselves about the possibility of racial equality and the desirability of racial integration" (Oakes et al. 2008: 2185). The *Brown* court, by viewing the solution to segregated schools in largely technical terms, failed to fully appreciate the broader socioeconomic conditions, power relations and cultural norms of race, merit, and deficit that have sustained structures of segregation and inequality within public schools and made segregated conditions seem so sensible to those who are privileged by them.

Social Movement Activism as a Potential Subterfuge for Resegregating Schools

This *Brown* miscalculation, as Derrick Bell (2004: 170) has noted, offers important lessons to advocates of racial justice and equal educational opportunity, suggesting they "rely less on judicial decisions and more on tactics, actions and even attitudes that challenge the continuing assumptions of white dominance." In Bell's terms, effective equity-based school reform requires a direct challenge to the dominant cultural norms that have framed debates over "quality education" and the need for advocacy strategies that aim to transform schools away from normative models that have long favored the more affluent, monolingual White middle-class and justified White dominance in educational contexts.

In this sense, social movement activism—particularly when rooted in assertions to high-quality education as a social priority and fundamental right to which all citizens should have an equal entitlement—may have an important role to play (Oakes 1995: 9). Such activism has the potential to succeed where technical, consensus-based reform has not, by addressing in a direct manner the political and normative obstacles to equity-based school reform through efforts to expose, disrupt, and challenge the prevailing logics of public schooling that make segregated schooling conditions appear so normal and unquestionable. As well, social movement activism, and grassroots organizing in particular, can make available political spaces from which to frame, articulate, and establish alternative visions, or critical counternarratives (Villenas and Deyhle 1999; Yasso and Solórzano 2001), capable of shifting the popular meaning of high-quality education from one in which citizens and residential communities are expected to compete for scarce resources toward the idea that high-quality education is essential to human dignity and the civic/economic health of a community without reference to the socioeconomic, cultural, or ethnic backgrounds of its residents (Oakes 1995: 6).

Of course, such a radical reframing of educational rights would require a broad-based political will to fight for inclusive, equitable, and high-quality education that is difficult to imagine, politically, in the current era (Stone et al. 2001). Indeed, as a number of school reform scholars have recently noted, the extent to which such political resolve is possible depends critically on the involvement, leadership, and mobilization of those who are most marginalized and who have the most to lose in the current system and the most to gain in a new one (Fennimore 2004; Noguera 2004; Orfield and Lee 2006).

Such leadership is not unthinkable, however, particularly in light of the increasingly well-documented successes of low-income communities of color to effectively mobilize for stronger school accountability, even in contexts where educational systems have long been controlled by White, middle-class residents and their privilege-protecting interests (see, for example, Noguera 2004; Mediratta, Shaw, and McAlister 2009; Shirley 2002; Warren 2005; and Chapter 7 of this book).

The Mobilization of Latino Communities for Equal Schooling

While relatively little research has been done on the more recent struggles of Mexican American communities to sustain or protect desegregated schools,[14] there is a burgeoning literature on Latino political mobilization for school improvement and increased school accountability that is of relevance here. Much of this research has attempted to understand the relative success of Latino mobilizations for school reform in terms of the conceptual framework of social capital (see, for example, Noguera 2004; Shirley 2002; Warren 2005).[15] In this work, attention has generally been given to two primary and distinction forms of community capacity-building activities—those related to the creation of *bonding*, or *horizontal* social capital—described as the strong and meaningful ties *among* local, working-class residents of color that can serve as the basis for solidarity and collective, grassroots action—and *bridging*, or *intersectoral* social capital, defined as relationships of cooperation and strategic coalition-building *between* distinct groups, sometimes across lines of significant social difference, where less enfranchised groups are connected to institutions and individuals with access to political influence and money (Fox 1996; Noguera 2004). Examples of positive outcomes associated with bonding social capital have included the mobilization of working-class Latino parents and youth, through intentional processes of leadership development and political education, to serve as school-community liaisons and strong advocates for equal access to such resources as high-quality instruction, fair disciplinary practices and a culturally relevant curricula (see, for example, Delgado-Gaitan 1996; Warren et al. 2011). Successful outcomes associated with bridging or intersectoral social capital building have included such things as the establishment of expansive coalitions linking emergent Latino parent/youth leadership groups with broader civic organizations (e.g., gender, labor, civil, and human rights groups) with a common commitment to issues of equity, fairness, and justice and who collectively undertake school-by-school outreach campaigns to promote and implement more justice-driven, school-based models, programs, and commitments (see Shirley 2002; Warren et al. 2011).[16] In each of these cases the process of building power has tended to operate through "organizing groups" that sponsor intentional relationship-building activities, leadership development, political education, and public engagement opportunities in a manner that combines confrontational tactics with strategic efforts at collaboration and institutional development (Warren 2005: 152).[17]

Notwithstanding these documented successes, it bears recognizing that the mobilization of Latino populations to actively participate in the contentious fight for equal education comes with unique challenges, particularly when it involves immigrant, migrant, and undocumented residents for whom a sense of entitlement to society's resources may not be easily rooted in national or legal citizenship status. The willingness of Latino (im-)migrant parents and youth to speak up against educational institutions from which they may feel disconnected or alienated can be restricted by a lack of a sense of a "right to have rights" to such basic entitlements as exercising a critical voice in local schooling politics. It is for these reasons that successful campaigns to politically empower U.S. Latinos—particularly Mexican immigrants—have often been rooted in assertions to "cultural citizenship," that is, rights to belong in the U.S. contingent not on formal citizenship status but on essential human rights to dignity, well-being, and respect (Flores and Benmayor 1997; Rosaldo, Flores, and Silvestrini 1994). Such organizing strategies necessarily engage cultural struggle and power as key elements in the community mobilization process, given the need for strong and collective moral support against ongoing, popular campaigns of exclusion, marginalization, and disenfranchisement (Trueba et al. 1993).[18] The importance of organizing around cultural experience and struggle is the context it provides for developing a sense of resiliency and mutual support to collectively navigate cultural, linguistic, and institutional borders in ways that allow residents to participate in community politics with a sense of power and in ways that sustained them as cultural beings (Dyrness 2011).

Educational ethnographers, in particular, have emphasized the importance of such strategies for empowering immigrant Latina/o parents to become active participants in schooling politics, including the need to create spaces for parents to tell their stories and engage in a political process of "becoming and belonging," which allows them to meet their own goals of self-realization and transformation rather than expecting them to simply "get involved" in existing school site activities that may be perceived as hostile or alienating (Dyrness 2008: 193; see also Delgado-Gaitan 1996; Villenas 2001; Villenas and Deyhle 1999). The availability of such relatively segregated "safe spaces"[19]—often favorably located outside formal institutional settings where normative forces of class/race privilege and entitlement can limit critical conversations—allows a context for socially and politically marginalized citizens to engage in a process of mutual dialogue that may include examining experiences of oppression, cultivating a critical awareness of the larger political system in which their lives are located along with the skills and voice to participate in it, and developing new leadership skills, knowledge, and aspirations, "as well as norms of collective deliberation that enable communities to mobilize social capital for shared goals" (Mediratta, Shah, and McAlister 2009: 140). As organizing contexts, such spaces allow room for Latino participants to understand power, learn public speaking and organizing skills, and "collectively create counter-hegemonic narratives of dignity and cultural pride" that contest the normative societal discourses of deficiency and lack by which their communities and children are often defined (Villenas and Deyhle 1999: 437; Foley 1997),[20] and permit a questioning and reframing of the prevalent logics of educational merit and entitlement that have tended historically to distribute high-quality schooling experiences and opportunities differentially and unequally along lines of race, class, and culture.

Challenges to School Reform Organizing for Integrated Education

A distinct challenge for organizing efforts aimed specifically at protecting high-quality integrated education is that even with substantial capacity building and mobilization of residents from within working-class Latino communities, success is unlikely without support from a significant cross-section of residents from White middle-class communities as well. The prospect of enlisting significant support from White middle-class residents relies on the existence of widely shared convictions about the usefulness and viability of integrated schooling, including a belief among parents that they are not being asked to choose between "diversity" and "excellence" because there are compelling academic and social benefits associated with integrated education (Orfield, Frankenberg, and Siegel-Hawley 2010). From a grass-roots mobilization perspective, it requires the ability to craft a collective action frame broad enough to permit a shared understanding of high-quality, integrated education as both a desirable option (rather than a threatening imposition) and a moral imperative (Oakes and Lipton 2002), so as to attract a critical mass of middle-class White parents as well.

Yet the task of establishing and then sustaining such a social movement frame is difficult when conflict, contention, and cultural struggle are taken as important crucibles for building power and civic capacity for educational change (as they have been with Latino school reform organizing efforts), and when the focus of activity is to challenge normative logics that have long favored affluent White suburbanites. Despite such obstacles, however, organizing in support of shared, high-quality schooling is possible, as Chapter 7 will explore. Here, Latino-led groups in Pleasanton Valley successfully built a broad-based collective action frame that portrayed high-quality integrated education as a fundamental right for all citizens, suggesting there is still some hope for establishing a level of political will sufficient to support integrated schools. Whether or not such popular will can be sustained and translated into structural change at the district and school site levels—against existent political and normative forces of resistance *and* in a way that sustains a critical mass of supporters from the White residential community—remains to be seen.

Summary

In this chapter, I have tried to account for how processes of school resegregation are occurring despite the nation's commitment in principle to racial and socioeconomic justice, equal citizenship, and equal opportunity in the educational realm. Ultimately, school segregation remains a significant barrier to equal educational opportunity not because of some intangible psychological burden, but because of the way in which it isolates whole communities of color in "schools of concentrated disadvantage" for which even campaigns to equalize school funding and enhance teacher training can be expected to have limited impact. Nevertheless, there is a clear divestment in school integration as an equity-based reform measure in the United States, due in significant part to the sustained influence of a particular set of normative assumptions about the "nature" of educational problems in public schools and how they should best be resolved. These assumptions fail, in general, to appreciate the importance of social, economic, and political contexts on students' learning process; instead, they portray "multicultural" schools in the United States as largely neutral institutions that provide equal opportunity for all through a technical, skills-based literacy program that assesses student performance based on very specific (and limited) understandings of what constitutes—and indeed, permits—educational success for diverse learners. The hegemonic assumptions underlying current schooling policy and practice have served to further condone a refusal to view linguistic, cultural, and class experiences as important resources to be engaged in the educational process, reducing them instead to explanations of why students fail.

The retreat from integration and the growth of school resegregation in U.S. suburban areas is not, of course, a simple product of shifting educational discourses; there are clear material interests at play. The ability of White, middle-class suburban residents to renegotiate the terms and possibilities of shared schooling has been made increasingly possible by the prevalent neoliberalism and the growth of an increasingly suburbanized and privatized nation-state.

I would argue, nevertheless, that there is some reason for hope about the future of shared, high-quality education, but only if equity-based school reform efforts can move beyond a primary focus on technical innovations within schools and classrooms—for example, the creation of new, more inclusive educational curricular programs and enhancements of teacher training—to encompass more *popular* efforts to "confront the non-technical (social, political, cultural) dimensions of change that must occur within our schools and across society before the promise of *Brown* can be fulfilled" (Rogers and Oakes 2005: 2195). To this end, social movement activism provides a promising route, particularly when organizing energy and network building is put toward developing and articulating alternative visions of entitlement to "quality education" that challenge the highly normative assumptions and processes that make conditions of segregation so unquestioned within our current educational system. Establishing and sustaining the political will to pursue and put into practice such alternative visions will likely rely heavily on the leadership of working-class communities of color who have the most to lose in the current system and the most to gain in a new one.

The discussion in this chapter, while providing a broad context for understanding the proliferation of citizen-led school secession campaigns, does not fully account for the manner in which such campaigns take root and find justification locally. School resegregation campaigns are, ultimately, local and regional productions that take shape in relation to specific histories of social group encounters, and the impact of these encounters on the development of schooling practices, structures, and patterns of engagement in schooling politics. This local/regional historical process is the focus of the next chapter, as I introduce cultural politics of place and schooling in Pleasanton Valley.

CHAPTER 2

Historicizing Educational Politics in Pleasanton Valley

The Politics of Place and Belonging at Allenstown High School

The first buses appear at the gated entrance of Allenstown High School just before 7 a.m., beginning their winding quarter-mile journey up to the center of the campus. The hilly ascent provides views of well-groomed athletic fields and an expansive, naturally terraced forest of redwood and juniper that rises around the campus on three sides. Passing through a series of staff and visitor parking lots, the bus dips briefly into a canopy of eucalyptus before stopping at the flagpole that decorates the roundabout just short of central campus quadrangle. As the doors swing open, it is mostly brown faces that descend, some having awoken as early as 5:30 a.m. to take the crowded, ten-mile ride from their homes in Farmingville to the Allenstown area high school.

By 7:45 a.m., hundreds more students have arrived on campus, streaming in from the student parking lots rising up along the north side of campus, moving instinctively down toward the central "Quad" area. The Quad is a fishbowl-style courtyard, lined with concrete and dotted with newt trees, that offers an assortment of painted metal picnic tables and wood benches around which students socialize between classes and before and after school. With the exception of the primary entrance from the bus roundabout, the Quad is largely an enclosed area, buffeted on the right side by an elevated cafeteria and on the left by the recessed gymnasium. In the very back of the courtyard is a narrow staircase that leads to a secondary terrace of classroom buildings. Even at this early hour, the Quad is thick with activity as students mingle on benches, gather around tables, sit cross-legged on the concrete ground, or occupy one of the multiple staircases that surround the enclosure on each side.

Student peer groups and networks spread across the Quad in a discernible social matrix that students can map in astounding detail.[1] The broad staircase that descends from the cafeteria is reserved as the exclusive domain of the junior and senior male "Jocks." Below them, in the interior of the courtyard, one finds the "Preps," a fairly equal mix of fashionably dressed girls and boys who sit in small groups on the ground or congregate around picnic tables to talk, eat, or finish homework assignments. Lounging against a wire fence that stretches around to the back of the gymnasium are the so-called "Dirts," who, despite their disparaging namesake, are a colorful coalition of coed peers that manages to incorporate a diverse and outwardly eclectic mix of nonconformist, punk, Goth, trench coat, and neo-hippie styles and attitudes. Near the front entrance to the gymnasium, flanking the soda machines, are the male "Surfer" and "Skater" groups, who can often be identified by their Quicksilver sweatshirts, spiked or shaved hair, and occasional skateboard in tow. On the front side of the courtyard and spilling across the driveway into the interior of the bus roundabout are the self-proclaimed "normal girls" who take pride in their tasteful yet understated fashion style and their well-groomed but generally low-maintenance appearance. Students' social locations in the Quad tend to be remarkably permanent, as most students return to the same spaces before and after school and at nearly every break, some for their entire high school careers.

At first glance, the central Quad area at AHS would seem to provide space for a remarkably diverse cross-section of student identity and status groups at the high school. Yet, among the several hundred students who settle in and mill through the area, one would be hard pressed to ever find more than a very small handful of Mexican-descent students. Even then, they are likely to be individuals or pairs scattered in the larger social groups. Despite making up nearly half the Allenstown High population, Mexican-descent students are almost entirely absent from the Quad area and the central campus region generally. Instead, they can be found dispersed across the more peripheral areas of campus. For example, groupings of primarily English-speaking Latino students congregate on the far sides of the "G" and "H" classroom buildings, two temporary modular units on the front side of the campus. Groups of more recently arrived Mexican immigrants meet outside the ESL classrooms in the high terrace building beyond the Quad; migrant student peer groups congregate near the "I" building, also on the front side of campus, which houses the MEP office and language arts classes such as "Spanish for Spanish Speakers." The largest grouping of Mexican-descent students—a rather diverse mix of first- and second-generation Mexican immigrant youth—hang out along the more remote, multipurpose athletic courts that extend beyond the backside of the gymnasium. The only Mexican-descent students who maintain a close proximity to the central Quad area are those found inside the school cafeteria, a situation most attributable to the fact that they—along with a wider representation of the working-class Latino on the campus—tend to rely on the free or reduced price meals made possible by the National School Lunch Program.

"This Big Ole' Wall That Nobody Can Ever Cross"

The sociospatial marginalization of Mexican-descent students on the Allenstown High campus is not a simple consequence of student preferences. Sonia, a sophomore and Mexican migrant student from Farmingville, describes the anxiety and discomfort she experiences—and that many of her peers would claim to share—when moving through central spaces like the Quad:

> You feel like you don't fit in, just by walking [or] passing through the Quad. When you pass through there . . . they don't even notice you. And it's like you don't belong there. It's weird, and I don't know how to explain it but it's just the *feeling* you have.

Beatrice, a sophomore and third-generation Mexican American, explains why she chooses to avoid the Quad area:

> You see all the White people there? Some of them are really cool to be with. But then there's the little things they say, like when you pass by, they are like "Oh look, there goes another Mexican." So now we started hanging out by the library. We just stick in our little corner.

Ana, a junior female and second-generation Mexican immigrant, asked if she believed the feeling of discomfort and displacement she experienced might be the result of active forces of discrimination at play on the campus, responds:

> I don't know, but it seems that Mexicans are always denied from certain things. Like they hang out in places where they're not seen. The whole Quad is full of different races except for Mexicans, and it does not feel so cool like that. I think it's because, I'm not sure, but there's too many Whites and it seems like they dominate the whole school, and the Mexicans can't do anything.

Jennie, an Anglo-American junior from Allenstown, recognizes as well the anxiety that seems to accompany the spatial segregation of White and Mexican-descent students on the campus, and she is quick to express her sense of disappointment about the general racial and class divisions that characterize student interactions:

> My good friend is Mexican, and I've never been raised to be prejudiced like that. And it was kind of like it was just forced upon you. In classes, you know, they [Mexican-descent students] would be incredibly friendly and very cool. A lot of times they were more down to my level than a lot of other [White] kids that go to this school because they can be kind of rich and snobby and fed with a silver spoon and never had to want for anything. And then once [class] breaks come along, there was like *this big old wall that no one could ever cross* [emphasis added]. Like if you went over there they would all go, "Oh, the White person!" and if one came to us it would be like "Oh, the Mexican." But it goes both ways. I think it's hard because a majority of the Mexicans are really poor . . . we blame a lot of our problems on them and it's not fair. So a lot of times they have resentment toward us and I see why, but it shouldn't be that way.

Mia, a female junior from Allenstown, and one of three African American students at the school, expressed her perspective on the segregated campus environment in the following way:

> It [Allenstown High] is really separated. Like in the "I" building, there's the Hispanic people. Over there is a bunch of "Skaters" . . .

then over here is the weird [White] people who wear scary clothes and pierce everything. And then over—they aren't "Mexicans"—there's a few Hispanic people, but they would be considered "sell-outs" because they don't speak Spanish and they are just Hispanic ethnicity. It's all separated like that. Like all my friends who hang out over there by the tree, they're all White. There's not really a lot of interracial mixing because there's only two types of races, that's White and Hispanic.

These student narratives highlight the complex, disturbingly essentialized, and highly oppositional nature of racial and ethnic relations on the AHS campus. High levels of separation and distrust fuel the development of damaging racial co-constructions and stereotypes, to the point that even students who refuse to align themselves with one category or the other risk being criticized or ostracized by peers from either "side." For example, an assistant principal admitted, "even those Mexican students who have been able to cross over and join some of the White-dominated clubs and friendship groups on the campus have to be okay with being White." By this, she referred to their willingness to assimilate to styles, norms, and behaviors thought to be characteristic of White students (English language, dress, similar preferences for music, leisure activities, etc.) and to minimize expression or behaviors that might be associated with "Mexican-ness," including regular associations with other groups of Mexican-descent students on campus.

One such a "border crosser" was Veronica, a 1.5 generation (one parent foreign-born and the other U.S.-born) Mexican immigrant female from Farmingville who, during my second year of research, was elected vice president of her sophomore class. Asked how she ended up participating in student government despite the fact that so few Latino students were involved in the school's mainstream activities, she spoke of the difficult transformation she had to make after arriving at the high school from Farmingville:

Well, last year, at the beginning of my freshman year, me and my best friend from Rolling Meadows [a "feeder" middle school located in Farmingville] didn't know anybody. So we got to know new people and we like, *left*, we kind of like *stayed away* from our old friends. We *moved on* and we met new people. [emphasis added]

CH: Why did you feel you had to leave your middle school friends to get involved in activities here?

V: Well, when we came, we *did* actually hang out with them. But I would want to go to meetings and stuff and they'd be like, "We don't want to go." And I'd be, like, 'Come on, let's go.' So we just like slowly kept on getting away, because they never wanted to do anything.

CH: How come they didn't like to do that stuff?

V: They were just—well, they were Mexican so, it's like, I don't know. Like those girls that I used to hang around with are still with the same crowd. And it's like, we moved on. And they see how much I've improved and stuff, and I still say Hi and everything. But they're still with the same friends from Rolling Meadows.

For Veronica, the route to engagement and belonging at Allenstown High meant "staying away" from her former Farmingville friends. Her explanation for why they failed to get involved in school activities—because "they were just, they were Mexican"—suggests a skewed social orientation as well as the internalization of a damaging stereotype about her ethnic peers, leaving her to feel that she had to "get away" by "leaving" them in order to "improve" herself. Asked if she felt comfortable and enjoyed being at Allenstown High, Veronica immediately nodded in excitement and smiled: "Yes. It's cool. I love it! I ran for vice president and I won. I know a lot of people [now]. So every day is like—I want to come to school every day in the morning!"

Veronica's story of disassociation above, along with the wider sampling of student narratives collected through the Peers Project research, suggest the way that being "White" or "Mexican" in the school is marked by particular statuses, where being "White" or "American" tends to be associated with enfranchisement (inhabiting central spaces and predominating in high-status school contexts and activities) and entitlement (defining and directing these activities), while being "Mexican" seems to signal disenfranchisement (less involvement or active participation in high-status contexts and activities) and marginality (a sense of not-belonging and a feeling of unequal status in curricular and co-curricular schooling activities). In other words, local beliefs about what it means to be "Mexican" or "White" are linked not simply to skin color or national origin, but to assimilationist expectations and students' willingness—or in some cases, ability—to demonstrate behavioral norms that signal their affiliation with either "American-ness" (defined by norms signaling "White" status) or "Mexican-ness." While school officials acknowledge these dynamics and find them troublesome, many seem as mystified by the situation as anything. Ultimately, their lack of intentionality and initiative to transform the dynamics on the campus has ensured that they have remained somewhat normal and natural among students.

The "nature" of student social relations at AHS plays a significant role in structuring the systematic separation of White and Mexican-descent students in nearly all contexts of the school. Mexican-descent students are highly underrepresented in the school's many curricular, co-curricular, and extracurricular activities, including clubs and sports (with a few exceptions), the frequent student-organized "spirit" activities, and various honors and advanced placement classes. Each of these contexts tends to be dominated, numerically and organizationally, by White students. This underrepresentation has generated negative social and academic consequences for Mexican-descent students, particularly given that active participation in such schooling contexts is known to anchor students to school and connect them to informational and human resources and networks of social capital that aid in social adjustment and facilitate academic success (Gibson and Bejínez 2002; Stanton-Salazar, Vásquez, and Mehan 2000). Given the academic and linguistic needs of many of Hillside High's Mexican-descent students—with nearly 60 percent classified as Migrant students at the time of the study[2]—it is precisely the kind of access and participation they need most but, unfortunately, experience the least.

The essentialized and oppositional nature of racial and ethnic differences at Allenstown High—while viewed as relatively immutable by students and nearly impossible to overcome by school staff—are of course neither natural nor inevitable. Nor are the differential levels of school engagement to which they tend, as will be explored more deeply in Chapters 3 and 6. The racial sensibilities that permeate AHS cannot be explained away as the ordinary product of students' associational preferences, nor as the to-be-expected result of everyday forms of identity construction in secondary schools that function to reproduce broader ethnic and racial distinctions. While the racial and cultural separations that characterize White and Mexican-descent student peer groupings at AHS are given shape in everyday encounters on the campus, they are also deeply historical and rooted in relationships that go far beyond the school context. The very nature of the local racial imaginary is embedded in broader processes of racialization and place-making in the Pleasanton Valley region that, over time, have conditioned social relationships and encounters in such ways as to make possible the kinds of unequal racial and cultural relationships experienced by students at Allenstown High.

The remainder of this chapter engages a broader ethnoracial history of Pleasanton Valley, with primary attention to the patterns of interaction between White and Latino residents. Such a regional politico-historical approach is necessary, I argue, to make sense of the dominant and educationally damaging constructions of racial categories that inform residents' "racial sensibilities" and serve as frames for interpretation and behavior within and around area schools. Centering attention on the political exercise of community in the region will help to better contextualize the relationships and discourses that have helped generate the disproportionate distribution of educational rights and entitlements between citizens in the Valley's two major residential communities and that have produced a long-term failure to establish equal schooling opportunities between local White and Mexican-descent students.

Historicizing Racial Difference and Inequality in Pleasanton Valley

An oft-heard contention among those wishing to make a strong case for the "disfunctionality" of Pleasanton Valley School District as a means of justifying the attempt to split it, is that the communities of Allenstown and Farmingville are two physically separate residential communities with distinct histories and identities that were indiscriminately "thrown together" into a consolidated school district in the late 1960s under the false pretense of financial and organizational efficiency.[3] Yet to describe the two communities as geographically distinct does little to account for how, despite their close proximity, they developed into such distinct social, cultural, and socioeconomic "places" in the region, with such dissimilar social and cultural identities.

As Doreen Massey has argued, the nature and identity of any specific community is always constituted by a wider set of social relations, such that what is perceived as "local" often draws as much from relationships outside the area than from those within (see Gupta and Ferguson 1992; Massey 1994b; Stewart 1996). In this sense, appreciating the particular nature and identity of any "place" requires attention to the specific social relations that have historically intersected at that location along with "what people make of those relations in their interpretations and in their lived practice" (Massey 1994a: 117). This is to say that places are fundamentally political rather than simply geographic, and by seeing communities as *particular historical intersections of social relations* renders struggles of the present—including the antagonisms that constitute them and the political cultures from which they are waged—intelligible. In the case of Pleasanton Valley, paying attention to residential "place-making"—including historical processes of racialization, economic development, and immigrant incorporation—is essential to understanding more contemporary ethnoracial realities as well as existing distinctions related to socioeconomic status, political power, and—particularly relevant in this case—the felt-entitlement of residents in Allenstown to "locally controlled" schools.

Early Racialization Process in Pleasanton Valley—Diversity Structured in Inequality

Farmingville has long been described as a quintessential immigrant town. That its current residential population is nearly 80 percent Latino—the vast majority Mexican Americans who arrived since the mid-1950s—is enough to confirm that status. Farmingville's historic willingness to incorporate and welcome immigrants—which have included, over the last century and a half, waves from Europe and Asia as well as Latin America—is often invoked as a matter of civic pride, particularly by organizations such as the local chamber of commerce and regional historical society. Less acknowledged in recitations of this fabled history, however, is the manner in which the town's diversity has long been structured in inequality and why, until the early 1990s, the town remained controlled politically by a White elite.

Understanding how race has functioned in the configuration of political power in Pleasanton Valley, even to the present day, requires going back at least to the early nineteenth century when Mexico, following its independence from Spain, gained control of the series of Catholic missions along what was to become coastal California (Almaguer 1994; Takaki 1993). When the Mexican government secularized the mission system in 1834, it offered vast expanses of land surrounding the missions to select Mexican soldiers and their children. It is in this way that nearly all of what is currently Pleasanton Valley came under the control of just a few Mexican Californio (mestizo) families (Donato 1987; Lydon 1998). Americans and Western European immigrants, most of them men, did not begin to arrive in increasing numbers until the 1840s. The landowning Californio "Dons" in Pleasanton Valley were said to be rather generous with arriving "Yankees," leasing or bartering their properties for rights to hunting and trapping, cattle grazing, and in some cases industrial and commercial development (e.g., general stores, sawmills, hotels). However, when the territory transitioned to the United States following the U.S.-Mexico War in 1848, violent conflicts over entitlements to land and natural resources emerged throughout California. By the mid-1850s, four-fifths of land holdings titled to Mexican Californio families had been transferred to White Americans as a result of U.S. federal court decisions, legal chicanery, and the forceful takeover of lands by White "squatters." Ideologies of "Manifest Destiny"—along with a strong symbolic association between Mexican "culture" and precapitalist economic formations—justified widespread acquisitions of Californio land holdings. The "culturalizing" of Mexican inferiority reinforced White racial entitlement and further justified taking possession of Mexican-owned land by any means, including nefarious ones (Almaguer 1994).

As regional historian Sandy Lydon (1998) has pointed out, the dispossession of Californios in Pleasanton Valley was said to be less dubious than in other parts of the state, due to the fact that the agricultural potential of the land had yet to be fully realized. However, as the cattle industry began to decline in the mid-1800s, many of the valley's Californio families sold off large portions of their land to wealthy Whites who developed it for profitable industry. The subsequent Gold Rush period (1848–1855) harkened an era of widespread discrimination against non-White Americans and immigrants of color in the region, particularly those with identifiable markers of racial, cultural, or linguistic difference. Lydon (1998) and Takaki (1993) have explored how gold prospecting created the first sites of extreme economic competition in California, and how the northern mining areas became locations within which enhanced feelings of White entitlement and White racial superiority were allowed full development. In Pleasanton Valley, post-Gold Rush settlement brought a "new element" of Whites to the area whose "sharply honed notions about race, culture, land titles, and due process made such niceties of assimilation and understanding impossible" (Lydon 1998: 9).

By the late 1800s, the agricultural potential of Pleasanton Valley was fully realized, and export-based agricultural production grew as a significant economic enterprise with products like sugar, timber, and fruit reaching markets throughout the United States and Europe. With the growth of a vibrant agriculture economy came the emergence of an elite group of local growers who sought to ensure high profit margins and the most competitive prices on the open market by employing seasonal, low-wage laborers, many contracted from foreign countries, who were willing to work for less. As a result, Pleasanton Valley—with Farmingville as its center point—became a bastion of emigration for low-paid laborers supplying the agricultural economy. Native Americans, in an extension of the mission system, provided labor for the earliest agricultural crops. The Chinese entered the area in the 1860s as a consequence of the Gold Rush and began replacing Native Americans as field workers. Though the Chinese were the first sizable group of non-White immigrants to arrive in the Valley, few were able to settle permanently because of the several federal Chinese Exclusion Acts limiting their rights to immigrate, own land, and apply for citizenship. As a result, Chinese immigrants could not be depended on as a renewable source of cheap labor for local farmers, affording an opportunity for eastern European (Slavic) and Japanese immigrants who began arriving in the Valley as contracted laborers in the early 1900s.

Within a decade (1900–1910), Slavic immigrants came to control the entire fruit industry in Pleasanton Valley—from growing to packing to transporting—at a time when the Valley became the primary apple-growing region of the world. The remarkable success of the "Slavonians" (as they were called locally) enabled them to invest economic capital in various small and large business enterprises. This accumulated economic power was accompanied by an ascending political power as well as an acceptance by the existing establishment of White growers in the region and by the public in general. Like their Slavic contemporaries, the Japanese arrived in the Valley lacking significant financial capital and were also able to achieve early economic success as farmers. However, as historian Ruben Donato (1987) has pointed out, while the local community embraced Slavic immigrants for their industriousness, they responded to the success of the Japanese in a largely contradictory manner. In the decade that saw the Slavonians' ascendance to local power, anti-Japanese sentiment grew significantly. The Japanese became perceived as a dangerous presence, partly for the way in which they threatened to unbalance the economic relationship that had depended on an employer exploitation of (non-White) employees. Local White growers began to prohibit Japanese farmers from further buying and leasing land while anti-Japanese sentiment blossomed more broadly across the state, fueling the passage of the federal Gentlemen's Agreement of 1908 that restricted Japanese immigration, and the Alien Land Law of 1920, a California referendum measure that legally prohibited Japanese from buying land in the state. The federal government further validated anti-Japanese sentiment with its passage of the Immigration Act of 1924 where "aliens ineligible for citizenship" (essentially, the Japanese and Chinese) were not allowed quotas. Despite this discrimination, many Japanese farmers in Pleasanton Valley endured local xenophobic pressures and found ways around restrictions on purchasing land. In fact, Japanese maintained significant land holdings in the Farmingville area until the beginning of World War II.

The distinct experience of Slavic and Japanese immigrants in Pleasanton Valley highlights the extent to which racial ideologies structured the early political, economic, and cultural development in the region. As non-English-speaking foreigners, Slavic immigrants were not immune to discrimination in the Valley; however, their acceptance was made possible by a local perception that their accomplishments demonstrated an active striving to become "true Americans." While the Japanese shared Slavic immigrants' industriousness and political acumen, these qualities drew suspicion and positioned them as a dangerous foreign presence rather than as model citizens (Donato 1987). While both groups arrived in Pleasanton Valley as contracted labor, the Japanese—like the Chinese before them and the Mexicans who would follow—were given living quarters separate from that of Whites, either in labor camps near the agricultural fields or in separate neighborhoods. For the Japanese, their racial phenotype along with the coupling of their "race" with their "foreignness"—a foreignness always easily identified by the particularity of their cultural practices, dress, and language—exposed them to accusations of being "unassimilable" and maintaining a self-imposed otherness considered un-American and dangerous, particularly in a rural conservative area like Farmingville. They were therefore treated as "outsiders" and chastised for only supporting "their own kind."[4]

Whereas in the case of the Mexican Californios, racist discourses of "laziness" were employed to justify the takeover of their land, sentiment against the Japanese relied on a contrary representation; it was their astuteness and industriousness that provoked fear and signaled a lack of trustworthiness, illustrating the shifting and contradictory nature of racist discourses in the region. What is common in both situations is the way in which racist sentiment was mobilized through discourses that cast non-White residents as unworthy of equal entitlement—whether because inferior or dangerous—to justify an exploitative *economic* relationship that was simultaneously (and sometimes, alternatively) social, racial, cultural, and political. Furthermore, in each case, the mobilization of racist sentiment was not simply a local phenomenon; local happenings reflected and fed popular sentiment and political struggles on the state and national levels regarding the "place" of foreigners of color—for example, painting them as a "cancer," as unable to share power, as undeserving, dangerous, and untrustworthy due to their "unassimilable" nature. In this way, fears of "takeover" worked together with fears of "unassimiliablity" to create a popular discourse of danger and an anxiety that racial "others" would steal what "Americans" are entitled to. Entitlement in this case refers to the maintenance of both a particular economic relationship—between racialized worker and White employer—and a particular character of community based on European American norms and privilege.

The immigrant incorporation process at play in Pleasanton Valley during the late nineteenth and early twentieth centuries mirrored, to a significant extent, that across the Southwest United States (see Acuña 1972; Barrera 1979; Takaki 1993). Sociologist Tomás Almaguer (1994), in a comparative analysis of the experience of Chinese, Japanese, and Mexican immigrant groups of color entering California during this period, explores how each group was racialized in unique ways and came to represent for Whites a specific kind of obstacle to their future prosperity. In the case of Mexican immigrants, Almaguer shows how periods of heavy migration—particularly of impoverished immigrants—have led to a series of social, economic, and cultural encounters in which Mexican immigrants have been portrayed as threatening the social and economic entitlements of Anglo-American citizens, leading to a resurgent nationalism that each time has "contributed to a major reinscription of the popular image and representation of Mexicans in the state" (1994: 54). This resurgent image-making during periods of heavy migration or economic instability has led in each instance to an "elective affinity" between the material interest of Whites at different class levels—including later-generation White nationals and more recent European immigrants—resulting in Anglo unification and various attempts to promote selective, discriminatory legislation intended to exclude immigrants and minorities of color and to preserve and create the superior social positions of Anglo-Americans in the state. Ultimately, Almaguer illustrates how emergent hierarchies of class and racial inequality in the U.S. Southwest, particularly California, were mutually constituted through an arrogant sense of White entitlement that "relied on Euro-centric cultural criteria to evaluate and racialize the various cultural groups they contended with" (8).

Almaguer's analysis is supported by that of a number of postcolonial scholars who have identified the ways in which modern processes of globalization and transnationality—of which human migration is a part—have led to the strengthening of local identities among dominant racial/ethnic groups and mobilization to enact measures against the threat of "alien others" in their midst, resulting from a fantastic fear bound up historically in discourses of race and "otherness" as well as in a rhetoric of national identity rooted in an invented nostalgia for a mythic, racially pure national character (Morrison 1992; Said 1979; Taussig 1987). This approach helps make sense of the more historically recent exclusionary referendum measures in California that have served to unite Anglo populations across class lines, including the denial of medical and educational rights to undocumented workers (Prop. 187), "English-only" laws (Prop. 63), and the virtual outlawing of bilingual education (Prop. 227).

The Post-World War II "Mexicanization" of Farmingville

In the early 1940s, Japanese residents in Pleasanton Valley constituted the lion's share of the region's farm laborers. The Japanese attack on Pearl Harbor changed things considerably. Anti-Japanese sentiment in the Valley rose significantly, and after a number of federal mandates to evacuate foreign aliens from the coastal areas, the U.S. government announced Executive Order 9066 calling for the mass internment of Japanese Americans. These proclamations led to the forced removal of an entire community of citizens from Pleasanton Valley, a community that would never return in large numbers. Their departure, complicated by the Selective Service drain on farm labor, led to critical labor shortages in the agricultural and railroad industries, compelling the United States to negotiate an agreement with the Mexican government to import Mexican nationals on temporary work contracts. This agreement, which would come to be known popularly as the Bracero Program, was initiated in summer 1942.

The Bracero Program was, in many ways, custom-made for areas like Pleasanton Valley. Men were contracted from Mexico and set up in labor camps near the agricultural fields. As a Farmingville social service worker at the time noted, the men were brought over with "no relatives here, no children here, nobody hanging on them in any way. They were just delivered, just the way you'd deliver troops."[5] By the late 1950s, the bulk of farm labor in Pleasanton Valley was performed by Mexican braceros. Providing low wages for what was essentially dispensable labor, the Bracero Program generated huge profits for growers in Pleasanton Valley. From the early 1950s to the 1970s, Farmingville maintained its status as a prosperous farming town highly dependent on a labor force that was essentially isolated from its social life and largely banned from sharing in its prosperity. The majority of braceros were single men living in labor camps near the fields and on the outskirts of the town, kept only as long as they were needed, typically the March to September harvesting and processing season. Since they were prohibited from bringing their families and did not have children in schools, braceros were not considered "public charges." And since farmers were entrusted with taking care of these workers, the town did not have to commit funds for schooling or other social service programs. Throughout the 1950s, however, men did leave the camp (so-called "skips") and moved into boarding-type housing or rental units in the downtown area of Farmingville or along the river floodplain to the south of town. By the late 1950s, there were a growing number of Mexican and Mexican American families living in the downtown area, with children beginning to attend area schools.

Designed not to exceed the war period, the Bracero Program continued for an additional twenty years before it was eventually discontinued in 1964. The long-term extension was justified, in part, by the realization that ending the program would put agricultural growers in a tough position. Not only had they, and the larger agricultural economy in California, reaped great benefits from the Bracero Program, but developments in agro-technology—including advances in pesticides and fertilizers and a growing local frozen fruit and vegetables industry—generated the need for a more permanent, year-round labor force. Furthermore, growers were not the only ones concerned with ending the program; White residents in communities across the state understood that the growers would continue to hire Mexican workers for low-wage labor and feared an "invasion" from the South.

When the Bracero agreement was finally discontinued, the U.S. government attempted to ease the transition by allowing growers to offer green cards (U.S. residence permits) to foreign workers they needed to maintain their basic operations. Although the majority of the braceros in Pleasanton

Valley were required to return to Mexico, many left knowing, in no uncertain terms, that employment opportunities remained for them in the region. In the months and years that followed, Mexican workers would return to the area—many with their families—as both documented and undocumented immigrants.

Economic Growth, Mexican Immigration, and Deepening Poverty in Farmingville

Between 1970 and 2000, Farmingville nearly doubled in size, from approximately 15,000 to 44,250 residents, with Latinos representing 98 percent of that increase. The Latino population—overwhelmingly of Mexican descent—increased from 17 percent in 1960 to nearly 75 percent in 2000. At the same time, non-Latino population growth slowed significantly in the 1980s and transformed into a mass exodus in the 1990s.[6] Furthermore, U.S. corporate interests in maintaining a cheap labor stream, accompanied by the Immigration Act of 1964 offering amnesty for the purposes of family reunification, supported a large and relatively unregulated in migration from Mexico. The continuous and sustained nature of such immigration was facilitated by transnational circuits (Rouse 1992, 1991) that have connected and continue to connect Farmingville to particular communities in Mexico, particularly rural *ranchos* in the provinces of Michoacán and Jalisco. These circuits facilitate international travel, the securing of a place to stay in the United States, and the pre- and post-travel arrangement of employment opportunities.

Although the demographic shift in Pleasanton Valley had much to do with the availability of low-wage employment opportunities in the local agricultural economy, a diverse range of "push" factors fueled the large scale of immigration from Mexico. This included (1) increased rural poverty in Mexico brought on by years of U.S.-backed capital-intensive industrialization at the expense of rural land reform and development, (2) Mexico's economic failures in connection to the World Bank-financed Green Revolution and (3) the country's 1982 debt crisis and the economic downturn it precipitated (Takash 1990).

The post-Bracero period marked a significant transformation in the social, cultural, and educational landscape of the Farmingville area. The town lacked, and failed to develop in due time, the public resources and social services—particularly in the areas of education, housing, and health services—necessary to accommodate the new immigrants and their families. Schools became overcrowded and lacked the materials and resources to educate a growing, predominantly non-English-speaking student body. Some local Whites, rather than acknowledging the town's lack of resources and initiative, blamed the Mexican immigrants themselves for having "screwed up" the town, reinforcing racist sentiment in the area. This scapegoating perspective—which still exists to some extent in the area—fails to appreciate that it was Mexican laborers who created the prosperity of the town beginning in the mid-1940s and who had long been systematically excluded from its affluence. Racist attitudes tended to be rooted in the understanding that working-class Mexican immigrants were primarily "guest workers" whose value to local public life rested in their role as low-wage laborers. As they began to settle permanently in the area, they were accused of becoming "public charges" and further resented for taking their earnings back to Mexico.

During the twenty-plus year existence of the Bracero Program, farm worker wages in Pleasanton Valley remained relatively stagnant. In the 1970s, however, an increase in the availability of permanent, year-round jobs (due to the growth of the vegetable and fruit freezing industry), accompanied by a powerful unionization movement, improved the wages and working conditions for both strawberry workers (United Farm Workers) and cannery and frozen fruit workers, nearly all of whom were Mexican (im-)migrants or Mexican Americans.[7] The union strength in the area was short-lived, however. Beginning in the late 1970s, the few major corporations controlling the Valley's canning and frozen fruit industries responded to the gains of labor by relocating their operations south of the border to Mexico, where farm labor, land, and capital were cheaper. By the late 1980s, nearly 50 percent of frozen vegetable production in Mexico was sold under U.S. brand name companies. Between 1978 and 1996, canning and frozen fruit facilities in Farmingville began to shut down or merge, causing a loss of an estimated 4,000 union jobs with benefits (Zavella and Borrego 1999: 6). As the canning and frozen fruit industry declined through the 1980s, labor-intensive berry and nursery plant cultivation increased, providing additional opportunities in minimum wage service work. The berry industry, requiring labor for a seven- to eight-month work cycle, contributed to a more settled workforce in the area. This development, accompanied by a heavy drop in real wages in the area, led to an increasing level of poverty for Latino workers and the need for more family members to seek work in order to survive economically. Latino family income in Farmingville, which was 82 percent of the county median in 1970, fell to less than 60 percent by 1990 (Gomez and Wong 1998: 8). By 1994, Farmingville was experiencing an "economic meltdown" as unemployment levels reached 16 percent, a rate twice that of the county and nearly three times that of the state (Zavella and Borrego (1999: 6).

The labor crisis facing Mexican immigrants from the 1990s and into the 2000s was accompanied by a crisis of housing as well. As a Farmingville resident and local historian (Bardacke 1994: 85) has put it:

> In the mere 20 years that I have lived around here, I have seen progress and poverty grow apace. Farmingville and the Pleasanton Valley are both richer and poorer than they were in 1970. A higher percentage of people live in what once were called mansions and a growing number live in garages and made-over chicken coops. Every year the agricultural commissioner reports higher gross receipts from the Pleasanton Valley, while the number of poor farm workers increases. In one possible (probable?) future, Farmingville will have moved, in a single generation, from a moderately prosperous working class town to an increasingly popular California combination on the menu: a wealthy bedroom community sitting next to a Mexican slum.

Today, the Farmingville residential landscape is varied but characterized primarily by densely populated "pockets" of residential developments ranging from mobile home and trailer parks to family apartments to townhouses to single-family homes. Latino home ownership in Farmingville remains less than 30 percent. Some of the poorest and highest-density neighborhoods are found along the river floodplain, which in the pre-World War II period housed a vibrant Japantown but now consists largely of trailer parks and small adobe or wood single-family homes stacked closely together and surrounded by locally owned small businesses like cabinet shops, auto repair and body shops, and industrial warehouses. On the opposite side of town, near the sloughs that branch in from the ocean, are apartment complexes within a larger warehouse district that suffers from high levels of youth gang activity. Just east of town is a pocket of relatively newly constructed single family homes built close together and separated with high fences, known as "Little Mexico" for the way it has been made to resemble the immigrant-sending communities in rural Michoacán and Jalisco. Here, one might find chickens and occasionally goats wandering across streets lined with custom vans and SUVs whose stylistic decals express migrant residents' allegiances to their home communities in Mexico. In the winter, these vehicles are often used to transport large families as they return "home" during the break in the agricultural season.

Farmingville's residential housing has remained highly segregated by race, with the majority of city's White population (22 percent of the total) residing in three predominantly White, middle-class neighborhoods.[8] Until the 1980s, Farmingville contained nearly two dozen small-scale migrant labor camps, many of them crudely constructed near the agricultural fields. A crackdown by city health officials saw the demise of many of these, and there now exist two major housing complexes in the Farmingville area designated specifically for migrant farm workers. One is a publicly managed facility that serves about one hundred families; the other is a forty-plus-unit, privately run facility that was updated in the early 2000s. While the private facility is open year-round, the public complex operates on a seven-month cycle—typically from the beginning of May to the end of November—with an interim during which all residents are expected to leave. While a good number of the camp residents return to Mexico or follow the availability of seasonal agricultural work to southern California, some simply move in with extended family members locally. The cyclical closing of the camp has significant impacts on migrant families with school-aged children, as the mandate to migrate (a required condition to reenter the camp in May) often means that their children will miss a month or more in the local schools. Families typically enroll their children for a short time in schools in Mexico (or Southern California), and they are forced to play academic "catch up" when they return. To avoid these complexities, some youth move in with extended family members (aunts or uncles) locally, instead of traveling with their families. The resulting high-density living arrangement comes with its own problems, of course, including in many cases lack of personal space for such activities as doing homework or sustaining a strong focus on academic studies.

A World Apart: Allenstown and the Politics of Isolation

Traveling north from Farmingville on the state highway, the valley floor narrows considerably and the mountain foothills begin to rise up more sharply against the Pacific Coast. The sprawling commercial agricultural fields that surround the town of Farmingville give way to a more rustic setting characterized by groves of redwood, juniper, and eucalyptus that separate relatively dense residential subdivisions located along or near the coast. A series of narrow roads branch up into the mountain foothills, speckled intermittently with homes of various sizes and elegance. This area, known as Allenstown, has long been described as a bedroom community, given that it serves as the midway point between Farmingville and a relatively wealthy coastal tourist town. Although it boasts a small historic town village, it lacks any distinct social center or "downtown" area. The closest thing to a central meeting place is a commercial strip mall complex featuring a major chain supermarket, drug store, hardware store, movie theater, and a handful of smaller, locally owned businesses.

Allenstown is residential in nature with no significant industry. Its population is predominantly White and white-collar despite its relatively close proximity to Farmingville (approximately ten miles between town centers). With a sizable population of over 20,000 residents, Allenstown is relatively new; only 5 percent of its housing construction predates 1940. However, like Farmingville, the history that is alleged to define its "character" reaches back to the nineteenth century. From the beginning of European settlement in Pleasanton Valley, Allenstown was marketed to be an exclusive resort community for the wealthy.

While Farmingville developed into a central agricultural hub in the late 1800s, the coastal land which is currently Allenstown remained for the most part thousands of acres of timber, grazing, and farmland owned by two wealthy German businessmen. In the early 1920s, the land was sold to a Los Angeles millionaire land speculator who promptly resold it to a number of associated development companies that managed and developed the coastal area through the 1920s and early 1930s. By 1926, there were five new subdivisions and over 2,000 subdivided residential parcels for sale, with a country club-style clubhouse serving as the real estate office. In 1928, the Allenstown coastal development area was renamed "River-by-the-Sea," a name that has stuck to this day.

While the original intent was to construct and populate Allenstown as a resort community and exclusive beach club for the wealthy, a number of historical interruptions deferred that vision, including the Great Depression and the two world wars. In 1955, the River-by-the-Sea beach club was sold to the state, and a year later a golf course—abandoned for fourteen years—was reconstructed and reopened just south of the River-by-the-Sea residential area. To this day, Allenstown's coastal area operates in a split-use manner: as a popular state beach facility and as a "members-only" country club and golf course, the latter bolstered in the mid-1990s with the construction of an exclusive resort and conference center along the bluffs near the golf course.

The early historical development of River-by-the-Sea is significant in that it established Allenstown as a desirable place for well-off Whites to live. By the mid-1950s, the population in Allenstown was growing substantially, and subdivisions planned in the prewar period were built out and occupied. The quick rate of growth was due to a number of factors, including the increased trend toward suburbanization in general, increasing White flight from Farmingville, the establishment of a community college and state university in the county, and the arrival of wealthy Whites from a nearby corporate center for which Allenstown increasing served as a bedroom community. The fact that virtually all new arrivals to the Allenstown area were White—and that the area remained relatively unwelcoming for potential non-White buyers—was not a simple product of local racist sentiment. However, the reality was that many of the ownership deeds for the River-by-the-Sea properties included racial covenants stating that property could only be leased, rented, or sold to those who were White (Lydon 1996). At the same time, the federal government, until the mid-1950s, actively and systematically promoted racial segregation in suburban settlement patterns through the criteria it used to set standards for home loan program assistantship, promoting racial covenants, and refusing to lend money to people of color (see Chapter 1).

Because Allenstown had maintained an image as an exclusive residential community for the well-off, and because other areas in the Valley by the 1960s were experiencing a rapid growth in Mexican immigrant population, Allenstown increasingly became a place where Whites who did not want to live in a "transitional" community settled. This included many Whites from the Farmingville area. By the 1970s, population began to increase rapidly in the Pleasanton Valley region, causing real estate prices in Allenstown to skyrocket. The tremendous increase of land value in Allenstown during the 1970s—concurrent with the increase of Mexican immigration to the south in Farmingville—effectively put Allenstown housing out of the reach of low- to middle-wage working families, including the majority of Mexican immigrants and even later-generation Mexican Americans. At the same time, Allenstown managed to successfully resist the construction of affordable housing units in the area despite the passage of California's Measure J (a growth management measure), which included a provision that 15 percent of all housing built in a county's unincorporated areas must be affordable housing. This active avoidance was made possible by a handful of developers who controlled local housing construction and chose to build up their market rate units in more plush communities like Allenstown while fulfilling their affordable housing obligations in more peripheral pockets of less expensive land.

De Facto Government by HOA and Early Calls for "Local Control"

While the arriving population in Allenstown through the 1980s was almost without exception White and middle class, the community was not politically or economically homogeneous in any strict sense. There were various gradations between middle-class and more financially secure residents, with settlement patterns generating a kind of neighborhood provincialism whereby different subdivisions became associated with particular kinds of politics and social strata. However, as an unincorporated town that lacked a city council or local planning commission, Allenstown politics were dominated by five major homeowner associations—named "improvement associations"—representing the coastal subdivisions. This assured that the cadre of political leadership in the community remained rather conservative and isolationist despite some broader level of political diversity.

Improvement associations in Allenstown were originally established to oversee and assure infrastructural soundness in their particular jurisdictions—including the maintenance of local roads, water systems, and so on. However, the River-by-the-Sea Improvement Association (RBSIA)—which quickly became the most visible, vocal, and powerful of the associations—assumed the additional responsibility of assuring residential integrity within its neighborhoods in order to "hold the high quality and standards of the community" and to ward against rooming-house situations and the "moral turpitude" that might accompany it.[9] RBSIA board members traditionally included those heavily invested in local real estate and therefore interested in preserving desirable rural characteristics that would keep land values high. The effort of RBSIA to keep River-by-the-Sea "the same paradise that old-timers remember" meant at times waging a sort of preservationist politics that included political campaigns seeking zoning ordinances to defend against efforts to develop the coastal area as an attraction for popular, working-class tourism. In the early 1980s, RBSIA went as far as to press its influence on local schooling affairs, bemoaning lowering test scores and demanding change from what they perceived to be the declining quality of local schools, claiming that "administrators and teachers are not getting the job done."[10]

Sustained efforts to maintain the distinct character of Allenstown included struggles to obtain cityhood status as well. Allenstown incorporation efforts began in the early 1960s and recurred regularly until the mid-1990s. Early campaigns for incorporation, led by various improvement associations, were motivated by a desire to promote and enforce zoning regulations that would permit Allenstown to control its own residential and commercial development. Given the shifting socioeconomic and racial demographics, as well as encroaching suburban commercialization in Pleasanton Valley, Allenstown leaders felt increasingly less secure that the county government would be responsive to their desire to remain an unmolested, "quaint" enclave. However, Allenstown city incorporation efforts failed to mobilize widespread support well into the 1990s, largely because neighborhood provincialism had made it difficult to find enough common ground to compel residents to give up their relatively ungoverned state. Allenstown city incorporation initiatives lacked, in the words of a long-time local supporter, the "one single crisis" that could mobilize the public in a way that would make the issue a top community priority. It was not until 1995, one year after a final, failed bid for cityhood, that a citizen group in Allenstown—facing Latino demands for improved educational resources at AHS—began their campaign to secede from the Pleasanton Valley School District. This community mobilization around the issue of school district secession can be seen as an alternative way of obtaining "local control" when cityhood incorporation was no longer seen as viable. In the end, the desire for local control of schooling became that "one single crisis" that did much to bind many residents in the Allenstown community together.

The Birth of a Challenged School District

The public vote to merge Farmingville and Allenstown schools into the Pleasanton Valley Unified School District (PVUSD) in 1967 was a very close one. In many ways, unification was an astonishing accomplishment. Farmingville had effectively resisted school consolidation efforts for nearly two decades, and community leaders in Allenstown had remained recalcitrant against the growing unification movement ever since serious talk about a merger with Farmingville began in the late 1950s. However, a number of factors conspired in the late 1960s to make consolidation appear inescapable. Growing enrollments had begun to make consolidation seem more financially and organizationally attractive. At the same time, consolidation promised to provide a coordinated and consistent K-12 program and curriculum, a fixed tax rate to support all schools, more efficient spending of funds, and an equalization of educational opportunity to children of various socioeconomic backgrounds (Donato 1987). While the demographic changes brought about by increased Mexican immigration had begun to transform the region by 1965, they did not immediately precipitate broad-based resistance to school consolidation. From the Farmingville perspective, this was because the arena of public politics—of which the educational system was a part—remained largely uncontested at that time; the town remained politically dominated by a White elite. That the majority in Allenstown (53 percent) voted in favor of consolidation in 1967 suggests a few things. First, it implies that perhaps the stridently isolationist leadership in Allenstown did not necessarily reflect its larger constituency. More significant, however, was the fact that consolidation promised to have little impact on Allenstown's separate, suburban school structure. In the end, what limited more broad-based resistance in Allenstown was the fact that consolidation would bring little change to how they managed their schooling affairs; Allenstown children would remain in neighborhood schools.

Resisting Integration in the PVUSD

In late 1973, soon after the Supreme Court *Keyes* decision in which Mexican Americans were provided the status of an "identifiable ethnic-minority group" with a right to integrated education, the PVUSD received its first mandate from the State of California to submit a desegregation report explaining how it was going to eliminate racial imbalances in its schools. State criteria for defining a "racially imbalanced" school included any whose minority enrollments fell 15 percent above or below the district average. By this definition, eleven of twenty-two schools in the PVUSD qualified as "racially imbalanced." In 1974, an investigation by the HEW Office for Civil Rights cited the PVUSD as "racially isolated" and in violation of federal desegregation laws. Among their findings were that classrooms in predominantly Hispanic schools were in significantly worse condition than those in mostly White schools, that affirmative action in the hiring of ethnic minority teachers and administrators had not been adequately pursued, and that the district lacked a sufficient bilingual, bicultural curriculum for limited and non-English speaking students (a requisite under *Lau v. Nichols*). In 1976, a U.S. District Court judge ordered the PVUSD to comply with federal desegregation laws within three months by devising a preliminary "reasonably feasible" plan to eliminate its racial imbalances, or risk losing access to federal education funds. Under pressure, the school district offices submitted a provisional plan that suggested, among other things, the possibility of limited busing. The district's submission constituted a "good faith" acknowledgment of its need to institute a comprehensive plan, not a binding agreement to take immediate action on such a plan.

The district's "good faith" plan drew strong anger from Allenstown parents and civic leaders, compelling the district superintendent to concede that busing would only be considered as a "last resort." The PVUSD school board's more favorable alternative would be to close down smaller, racially isolated schools in Farmingville, build new schools in the area, or redesignate students to larger, existing ones in ways that might draw Mexican-descent and White students together. However, given that Mexican-descent enrollments in district schools had reached almost 50 percent by the mid-1970s—nearly all attending the district's southern schools in Farmingville—it was clear that simply moving kids around Farmingville would do little to eliminate segregation across the district, and that any real commitment to school integration would have to include the Allenstown area.

The substantial resistance voiced by Allenstown residents against desegregation was articulated, unambiguously, as an aversion to the possibility of having their children bused to Farmingville. The intensity of this resistance was tested early when the district suggested the possibility of busing fewer than one hundred elementary school students between the two communities. Leaders of Allenstown's RBSIA called it "absolutely outrageous to move children around like pawns on a chessboard," explaining that "many homeowners bought property in *River-by-the-Sea* expressedly for the privilege of sending their kids to the local elementary school." One school board member remarked presciently in the late 1970s that, should Allenstown parents be told that their kids would be sent to school in Farmingville, "their first reaction would be to break away and form their own district."

In early 1979, a school board-appointed Desegregation Advisory Committee (DAC) consisting of thirty-three community members, teachers, and students (considered to be "one of the most integrated groups ever assembled in the PVUSD"[11]) released a preliminary report recommending that the district revise its own working definition of a "racially imbalanced school" to mirror existing state criteria, with one central difference: the designation would apply only to the number of *minorities* attending a school, excluding majority-isolated schools from consideration. With this proposed criterion, nine of the district's twenty-two schools—all in the southern region of Farmingville—would be designated as "segregated." In practical terms, desegregation would require that nearly five hundred students be moved out of affected schools in the Farmingville area. Advisory Committee members defended the plan as the most appropriate and practical option given that "there is no way to move equal numbers of kids without long distance busing, and the community is so opposed to this."

Allenstown residents' opposition to desegregation was expressed not as a fear of ethnic mixing in general, but a fear that mandatory busing could force their children out of Allenstown to schools in Farmingville. As one female parent warned the committee, "you'd better consider the number of parents in this audience who won't have their kids in any of these [Farmingville area] schools." Another resident suggested that given the geographic realities in the Valley, it would make sense to break into two districts, an idea that was said to receive "loud and prolonged applause from his Allenstown neighbors." Not all Allenstown parents were resistant, however. Some recognized that desegregation was important because local Latino students were not "getting a fair shake," with one White parent from Allenstown suggesting that perhaps her own children would benefit from a better cultural mix in the school system.

White residents in Allenstown were not the only ones at the time who opposed busing and felt wary of desegregation; Mexican American parents from Farmingville were also worried about ethnic mixing, particular if it meant their children having to be bused to White-dominant schools in Allenstown. They were less concerned about their children having to leave the community per se than about the mistreatment they worried their children might receive in Allenstown schools. Francisco Mendez, a Mexican American parent and member of the DAC at that time, recalled in a 2003 interview his feelings of ambivalence about helping craft the district's desegregation plan:

> [Desegregation] was most difficult on our [Mexican-descent] kids. There were times when I would personally visit some of the classes in Allenstown schools and would see how badly they were treated by their peers. And, well, you had cliques, you had groups, all of these kinds of things going on, and now to be a person that is forced into a school where they are not wanted? It made it even worse. So a lot of us [on the committee] felt like, "God, why are we pushing this desegregation thing," you know? . . . I think that was the bottom line; a lot of us saw who was really suffering from all of this, and that was the young kids. There were going through this, and they still are. I'm not happy with what we do with the K-12 education. Kids are still ostracized because they are brown.

Although Francisco was willing to consider short-distance busing if it was necessary to satisfy the state, he strongly objected to any proposed measure that would bus *only* Mexican-descent children to schools in Allenstown. "I would rather not bus anyone than bus just Mexican kids," he explained.

For both White and Mexican-descent parents who opposed "long-distance" busing in the PVUSD, it was clear that the actual mass transportation of students was not their primary concern. By 1979, over 62 percent of students in the district were *already being bused*. This reality compelled one parent to remark: "When kids ride a bus to school where their classmates are the same color, that's called transportation. When kids ride a bus to a school where many of their classmates are another color, that's called busing."

In late 1979, the DAC released a desegregation plan that proposed closing two minority-impacted elementary schools in Farmingville and suggested a limited busing arrangement for Latino students. Children in Allenstown would remain in neighborhood schools while Mexican-descent students in Farmingville would be moved. In the end, however, the DAC plan constituted only an advisory recommendation for PVUSD trustees, and the trustees ultimately chose not to act on it. "The school board decided to put it on the shelf," a former DAC member explained to me, "as they typically did with controversial issues, and let it sit." Consequently, the state deadline for a desegregation proposal came and went without the district committing to any kind of "reasonably feasible" plan.

By 1980, the PVUSD was one of the few school districts in the state of California that had failed to submit a desegregation plan. In March, federal investigators from the HEW Office of Civil Rights visited two schools in the Farmingville area and determined that the district's bilingual education program failed to meet federal requirements, leading to the denial of several hundred thousand dollars of Emergency School Aid Act (ESAA) funds to district schools. The denial was a clear indication that the district was under the scrutiny by both federal and state authorities, and that continued inaction to develop a "reasonably feasible" desegregation would produce further negative consequences. In response, two of the school board's more pro-integration trustees—one White and one Latino—advocated for a limited, two-way busing proposal, including the movement of two hundred Allenstown students to Farmingville, pushing the district in the direction of bilateral integration. One school board member, anticipating "an explosion" from his Allenstown constituents, voiced vehement opposition to the idea, stating that "when it comes to busing across the district, I think we'd rather go to court and fight it." Pointing out the difference between satisfying the law and moving toward full integration, he remarked: "I feel we have to do something [to obey the law], but I feel we can do a lot less and get away with it." Overwhelming opposition from civic leaders and parents in Allenstown compelled the school board to set up a special "informal" session in Allenstown that drew over 150 residents (largely parents) and a "flood of emotions on the issue." Most voiced anger and stoic resistance against the idea of having their children bused to Farmingville schools. As one Allenstown parent explained, the idea of busing children between the two communities "overlooked the social reality . . . the district is an abstract category linking two distant communities. We are not a single community . . . this is an abstract law being applied to a realistic situation in which the law does not apply. We must redefine the law!" Another parent remarked that "if you force children on the buses, you will lose parent support." Yet another parent—referring to the state desegregation mandate—reminded the board that "there is not one word that says we have to bus anyone—there is not one word that says *thou shalt bus*." In a similar but more aggressive commentary, one mother admonished that: "the idea busing will eventually be put on us stinks. . . . You have no assurance kids will get on the bus to study freeway flowers. Parents will find alternative forms of education." Frank Amos, an Allenstown parent and private practice attorney, suggested an alternative approach that would shift the focus away from busing and toward improving the quality of education in those schools with high-minority enrollments:

> What we are talking about is substandard education. But if we don't have substandard education, what the hell are we doing? . . . We should tell the state that we aren't going to bus. I'm familiar with *de jure* and *de facto* and the rest of the garbage you want to lay out. When the state tells us we don't have a plan [and attempts to remove our funding] we'll slap a restraining order on them.

Amos, well known for his strong antibusing views and his persuasive legal rhetoric, was elected as a PVUSD school board member just a few months later.

The only person attending the special meeting in Allenstown who spoke in favor of the busing plan was Claudia Morales, a Mexican-descent mother who had two children in the school district and also served as a member of the district's Bilingual Advisory Committee. Attending the meeting with a fellow parent from Farmingville, she admitted to favoring integration:

> Personally, I'm for it. As we drove up here, we said "how nice." Facilities in Farmingville do not compare to facilities in this area. I believe that children in the south county need to mingle with White children. It seems to me that you want to keep us separate, and I want to know why.

When I spoke with her years later about the meeting, she vividly recalled what took place:

> I listened to parent after parent after parent oppose the busing of students from Farmingville to Allenstown High School. And I remember in my stomach, how it just kept going round and round because they were talking about the students—my son—that they didn't want him over there. So after about—I think the [public] testimony period went on for over two hours—and 3 minutes before the end, I stood up. And I was the only person that said "this is a good thing." And I looked out at the audience and I asked: "why don't you want my son here, why don't you want *us* here?"

Despite a visit to the PVUSD by the chief counsel to the State Board of Education urging the district "to move ahead in good faith" or risk a court mandate to initiate cross-district busing, the school board ultimately decided to produce an entirely *voluntary* desegregation plan that called for the establishment of two magnet schools in the district and the closing of two racially isolated elementary schools in the Farmingville area. The plan was inherently limited; its overall effect on segregated schools in the district would be to reduce them from eight to seven. Nevertheless, the proposed plan called for an annual review and evaluation of the voluntary provisions, stating that "if it is determined that the [voluntary] plan has not resulted in a successful desegregation program, it will be the goal of the District to develop alternative strategies, using the public hearing process, which will meet requirements of the State Board of Education, and of state and federal law." However, conservative parents and civic leaders in Allenstown continued to steadfastly oppose the inclusion of any language in the plan that would suggest the district entertain "alternative strategies" should voluntary efforts fail. They refused to support the plan, arguing that "you don't give a voluntary plan a chance with the axe of mandatory busing hanging over our heads." The full PVUSD board remained split on this proposed amendment, some arguing that "we ban the word 'compliance' from our vocabulary" while others argued, on the contrary, that the plan was unfair and did not go far enough. Those supporting a busing strategy claimed it was the only way to comply with the spirit of the law and to be fair to both minority and majority populations. "Education and integration are part and parcel of the same thing," one pro-integration board member proclaimed. "No matter how many hours of reading and writing a child gets, if it takes place in a segregated atmosphere it is not truly educational." On the other side were citizens who maintained that busing not only "exceeds the requirement of the law" but causes "long-lasting harm to the unity of the total community" resulting in "confusion and frustration of children" and "an additional cost to the taxpayer." An Allenstown parent called the idea a terrible "social experiment" where "the tools of these experiments are our children." An Allenstown-area school board trustee concurred, claiming that an integration proposal is "an insult to every brown student in this district, to say that the only way they are going to be educated is by sitting next to a White student" and that such an action would fail "to respect the integrity of each student." Against such opposition, an activist speaking on behalf of a county-level antipoverty program questioned the moral resolve of the board to act on integration, asking them: "How are you going to educate this community when this document infers, by its omission, that you yourself don't believe that cross-cultural exposure is necessary for White children, also?"

The school board's deadlock on desegregation was finally broken in summer 1980 when one of the most stridently "antibusing" trustees from Allenstown realized, on closer examination of the wording of the plan, that forced busing would not be *required* if voluntary measures should fail. His reversal allowed a 4-2 vote in favor of the voluntary integration plan. In the end the state provisionally approved the plan.

"Mandatory" Desegregation Becomes Unlawful Under Desegregation Mandates

A first step of the PVUSD desegregation plan was to institute a series of magnet programs at three elementary school sites in the first year—one in Allenstown and two in Farmingville. Over the next four years, five other schools were to be progressively added, at a total cost of approximately five million dollars. The district's financial plan to support the magnet school idea fell through early, however, when a funding proposal submitted to the federal ESAA ranked 59th of 83 applicants and was rejected. The federal government low rank was justified on the claim that the educational programs for each school site were poorly planned and that the percentage of the district's students who would be moved into the proposed programs (a few hundred of the 12,600 students) was insufficient to rationalize the funds requested. In the end, the PVUSD committed $500,000 of its own funds to establish a limited, pilot magnet school project at two schools.

Concerned that the federal government failure to support its magnet programs meant that the district might soon be pressured into more serious desegregation strategies, leaders in Allenstown began to encourage the school board to drop the desegregation plan altogether and accept a completely voluntary approach to integration. The RBSIA called for the "immediate withdrawal and nullification" of the desegregation plan. Allenstown attorney and school board trustee Frank Amos took the lead in opposing busing as a possible future option, vowing that if mandatory busing were instituted, there would be lawsuits and "I would be at the forefront. Don't push mandatory busing. It's not required by the law. It's not common sense." Given growing political pressure and the election of a new, more conservative group of school board trustees on a wave of backlash against both the bilingual education and desegregation experience in the area, a 5-2 school board vote deleted any language from the desegregation plan that suggested introduction of "alternative strategies" should voluntary integration measures fail. In the plan's adopted version in 1982, all reference to the consideration of ethnic/racial data in reassigning students was dropped. In fact, the revised plan not only mandated completely voluntary integration, it made any nonvoluntary strategies based on balancing racial makeup (including reassignments) against its own desegregation mandates—predating by some twenty years the Supreme Court's similar logic in its 2007 *PICS* decision.

The PVUSD desegregation plan went through various incarnations from the mid-1980s to the mid-1990s, but its basic tenets remained the same: the pursuit of voluntary integration based on the magnet school concept, and later, on a voluntary open enrollment/intradistrict transfer policy. By the mid-1990s, the district—having paid close attention to evolving federal and state laws and court decisions suggesting more flexibility in the administration of desegregation programs—began to more openly articulate that its central concern was to offer parental choice and "provide a quality educational experience for all of its students" rather than to eliminate racial isolation in its schools.

Three major legal developments, beginning in the early 1980s, significantly impacted how California school districts could structure their desegregation programs. The first was the decision of the California Supreme Court in *McKinney v. Board of Trustees* (1982) which argued that the "primary objective" of a desegregation plan is to achieve a "uniformity of educational opportunities for all races by eliminating the detrimental effects of a segregated school system, not to precisely correlate the racial composition of each school with that of the district as a whole." Second, in 1993, the California legislature's passage of AB 1114 provided for parent choice in the transferring/reassigning of their children to other schools within a district. Third, the U.S. Supreme Court's 1991 decision in *Board of Education of Oklahoma Public School v. Dowell* recognized that school districts could return to primarily one-race schools for the asserted purpose of alleviating the financial burden of busing if the patterns of residential segregation that required the busing had resulted from "personal decisions" and "economics" rather than a district's intentional discrimination based on race and ethnicity. The PVUSD legal counsel understood the implication of these decisions on local desegregation requirements and actively shared them with district officials and members of the school board. It is clear that such understandings influenced the way the district designed its desegregation plan.

Integration Without a Mandate: The False Hope of In-Service Training on Equity and Diversity

By 1995, it was clear that the magnet school idea had not taken. The district's five magnet schools had attracted only 152 students, with one school attracting only three students to its program. The ultimate failure of the PVUSD integration efforts revealed the central limitation of the district's desegregation plan from the outset: the belief that integration could reasonably be achieved through a limited, voluntary approach. Yet district officials clung to the claim, throughout the process, that they had a mechanism capable of transforming a "reasonable" voluntary plan into true integration in district schools. This "silver bullet"—which was adopted in the district's original desegregation plan in the early 1980s—was to institute "a comprehensive, District-wide in-service training program relative to school integration, involving staff, students, and parents." This broad-based professional development strategy was to "provide an environment which embraces and unifies the diversity of the community in order to heighten each pupil's individual feeling of identity and self-awareness." In 1990, the district renewed its commitment to such a systematic training by pledging "additional programs and staffing focused on inter-group relations between incoming students, parents, community and receiving staff, students, parents, and communities." By 1995, however, a district-appointed Desegregation Task Force concluded that the PVUSD, as a whole, had developed neither "a defined multicultural curriculum" nor instituted a "curriculum effort in the area of inter-group relations." In other words, in fourteen years under a desegregation plan, the district made little headway on what it claimed to be its primary strategy to move toward integration.

In fairness to the district officials, school board members, and citizen advisory committees who were tasked with the development and implementation of a "reasonably feasible" integration plan in Pleasanton Valley, the challenges they faced were myriad. Beyond significant community resistance to equity-based educational reform efforts—particularly those designed to provide redress for historical inequities along the lines of class, race, and culture—they faced administrative inertia and teacher apathy as well. Carmen Mendez, a second-generation Mexican American from Farmingville and a long time teacher-turned-district-administrator whom I interviewed in 2003, described the challenges to liberal educational reform that have existed—and continue to exist—in Pleasanton Valley schools:

> All the way to two years ago, what didn't happen with desegregation was an [change in] attitude [toward] equity and diversity. The movement to change attitudes was not part of the activities of desegregation or integration. And it still doesn't exist in the district. What I believe is one of the issues that really has to be addressed by the district is that if they are saying that our schools are integrated—and they are *not*—[but] if they are saying they *are*, one of the issues they haven't addressed is equity and diversity. I mean, to my knowledge, not one of the schools has any kind of plan. We were never asked to make any kind of plan of how we were going to address issues of equity and diversity. As an administrator, it took me one year to convince my teachers to even allow me to have a staff development day around these issues. And it was just a one-shot deal: "Ok, we've had enough, we don't need any more." It's was like, you know, it's hard to teach an old dog new tricks, that kind of thing. The talk was there, they just didn't walk it. The new teachers that came in were more open and willing to try new types of strategies and activities in their classrooms, but some of the teachers that have been around for a long, long time are just comfortable in what they are doing. And they could be good teachers. Their heart is there, they really want their students to be successful—it's not like they are malicious people or anything like that. It was hard for them. They are just sort of stuck and not moving.

Conclusion

Historically, resistance to school integration in Pleasanton Valley has been voiced not in terms of racial or class interest, but as a (White, middle-class) fear of losing "local control" over the schooling process and the ability to rule on as local a level as possible. Allenstown citizen groups have framed their struggles as ones meant to sustain the "quality" of schools, to protect community resources, and to maintain local ways of managing their affairs and finances. In this matter, community leaders and citizen activists have achieved significant success in persuading the school board to accept their positions. From the 1960s to the early 1990s, it is clear that politically powerful White residents in Pleasanton Valley took part in what George Lipsitz (1998) has called practices of "resistance, refusal, and renegotiation" in relation to racial integration mandates. While members of the local PVUSD school board and local schooling officials continually dismissed allegations that racial, class, and cultural concerns have impacted how they manage issues of equity and diversity or shape the decisions they make about school policy and practice, they failed historically to comply with federal and state mandates to integrate students and to assure the provision of state-mandated services and resources designed to ensure equal opportunity and service to Latino youth and their families. Beginning in the early 1970s and continuing to the mid-1990s, the PVUSD school board maintained patterns of inaction to state requirements regarding desegregation, even as they continued to incur state sanctions and significant financial penalties for their failure to do so. In cases where mandates were finally met, it was often through conscious strategies to do the minimal possible to conform to the letter of the law rather than the spirit behind it. The school board, often paralyzed by controversy, failed to provide the leadership to assure Latino children's rights to equal and quality desegregated education.

The history of school district decision making from the late 1960s to mid-1990s bears significantly on present schooling realities, particularly as it relates to issues of equity and diversity in school programs. Here it is necessary to consider not only the long-term effects of particular decisions on the availability of educational resources for Latino youth, but how historic patterns of neglect have conditioned the way in which teachers and administrators address, or fail to address, issues of equity and diversity in their schools and classrooms. It also explains how school environments like the one described at Allenstown High at the beginning of this chapter are allowed to develop. The consequences of this historical neglect in Pleasanton Valley schools are highlighted in the following two chapters.

PART II

The Origins and Development of the Allenstown School District Secession Campaign

CHAPTER 3

Latino Empowerment and Institutional Amnesia at Allenstown High

The Growing Political Clout of Latinos in Farmingville

Two events in 1987 marked a significant transformation in the political landscape of Pleasanton Valley. The first was a voting rights lawsuit brought against the city of Farmingville by the Mexican American Legal Defense Fund (MALDEF), challenging the legitimacy of the city's at-large municipal election system which had long favored White candidates for city council. While Latinos had come to constitute about half the city's population by the mid-1980s, no Latino had ever been elected onto Farmingville's city council. In fact, between 1971 and 1985, nine Latino candidates ran for the council without ever winning a seat. Local explanations for Latinos' failure to garner political office included claims that candidates were not sufficiently "qualified" or that the local Latino population simply did not vote in large enough numbers. MALDEF's argument, which the court would eventually endorse, was that an at-large municipal election system, along with a long history of racially polarized voting in the region, had served to dilute the minority vote in a way that unfairly disenfranchised Latinos, leaving them with little encouragement to vote—because they felt they could never win—and little political influence.[1]

The court decision, in favor of MALDEF and the local Latino plaintiffs it represented, mandated the establishment of a district-based election system that divided the city into seven geographical areas where residents could cast votes only for candidates residing in their residential district. Given prevalent residential segregation by race and class, the new election system immediately transformed the voting power of working-class Latinos. In

1989, the first Latino candidate supported by a majority of Latino voters was elected to the city council, a victory directly attributable to the MALDEF lawsuit. By the mid-1990s, the city council would move away from its more conservative stances and better reflect the diverse attitudes and interests of the community of Farmingville. By the early 2000s, Latinos began to consistently hold a majority of city council seats.

The "Integration" of Allenstown High

The year 1987 was also one of important demographic and political transformations in the PVUSD. The rapid growth of the Mexican immigrant population in Farmingville, coupled with the historical failure of district voters to support bond measures for new school construction, led to dire overcrowding in the city's only comprehensive high school. As a consequence—and in the face of nearly two decades of active resistance to school integration mandates—the PVUSD began a modest and limited cross-district busing program, moving about 200 students from Rolling Meadows Middle School, a predominantly Mexican-descent secondary school on the Farmingville's northern periphery, to Allenstown High School. By the early 1990s, Farmingville High had become further impacted by conditions of overcrowding while Allenstown High remained under-enrolled. As a result, district officials were left with few options but to send the entire Rolling Meadows graduating class (about 320 students) to AHS beginning in 1992. By the mid-1990s, and not without some irony given historic efforts to thwart integration mandates, Allenstown became home to the district's first truly desegregated school, with Mexican-descent students from Farmingville making up nearly half the high school's total population of approximately 2,000 students. Nearly 80 percent of these Farmingville students were from families with two immigrant parents, meaning they were either immigrants themselves or first-generation Mexican Americans. About 50 percent arrived at the school with limited skills in academic English.

During the first few years of busing, incidents of interracial conflict were allegedly not widespread. The AHS administration, in counsel with the district, had taken some initial steps to help facilitate the integration of incoming Latino students with the White majority on campus. Their strategies included the creation of a Bilingual Advisory Committee, the institution of a school "homeroom-forum" period that was designed to involve, among other things, "activities to promote social mixing and breaking through cliques" and plans to organize a schoolwide Cinco de Mayo celebration. The school also provided an "activities bus" in the evening that permitted Farmingville students to participate in sports and other afterschool activities without the difficult—and in many cases impossible—task of having to arrange rides home with family and friends. Beyond these accommodations, the school administration offered some level of programming to prepare AHS staff for the sensitive situations that might be expected to arise when students from different backgrounds and communities came together in the high school. Karen, an AHS teacher at the time, discussed the staff development plan:

> To give you an example, we had a professional development day that included a student voices team. It was a workshop—a one-day workshop that we've all been to 800 times in our lives—with all the faculty there, and a team of about four people that facilitated. One activity was a group of students in a circle, of all backgrounds from the school, speaking about how they felt [being] at the school, how they felt they were treated, what worked for them and what didn't work, their perceptions around access at the school, and how kids got along with each other. That was provided with absolute [good] intention.

Unfortunately, this one-shot deal—limited to a few hours during one day of professional development—was not linked to any larger or more comprehensive effort to share strategies for integrating students and communities, or for dispelling the stereotypes that students might have of one another, or that faculty might have of the newly arriving immigrant students and their parents. Joanna, a long-time Spanish teacher at the high school who had been involved in the "conversations" to prepare the school for the increase in Latino students, explained her feelings that the school took some steps but not nearly enough:

> I was on the committee to help integrate those students. My comment when I was involved is, you have *got* to help get [Latino] student leaders mixed in with the White leaders. You have to have students who are Latino mixed in student government and any other phases of decision making that concern students. I said that

> all of our students need role models. Well, the White students had plenty of role models. The Latinos did not have many role models. There were a lot of reasons for that. One is, we don't have very many Latinos as instructors. Back then, everyone was White. So as students came in, they had to be encouraged to be in sports teams, student leadership, other activities, cultural or otherwise. But not much was really organized for those students. I never got the feeling—and I taught a [popular general education] course at the time, so I was around a lot of Latino students—that they really felt at home here. Back then, I would say, "How do you like Allenstown?" They'd be like "uummm . . ." When I came here, it was White, basically. And people's names who were Hernandez (*ear-nán-days*) wanted to be called Hernandez (*her-nan-dez*). I really think this school has done a generally poor job of making the Latino kids feel welcome. Now, that's not true in the area of maybe, sports, or in student government—anyone can sign up. But *it's the feel of the place* [emphasis in original]. I don't believe that enough is offered to create a mix.

This sentiment was echoed by former students as well, including Rebecca Sanchez, who had entered Allenstown High as a freshman in 1991. Born in a small pueblo in the Michoacán province of Mexico, she moved to Farmingville with her migrant farmworker parents in the mid-1980s. When I met her for the first time in 2003, she was in her second year of a Master's degree in education at a California state university. She could recall in vivid detail the feelings she had when she first began attending AHS:

> The word was that Allenstown High was this racist school that didn't want Mexicans. I mean, literally, that's what it was. And I remember my friends kind of teasing me and telling me "you're gonna become White." You know, you are going to become this *gringa* and all this stuff. And it was actually really intimidating because I thought, oh no, what am I getting myself into? And so I remember going into Allenstown High, the first day there, and it was really intimidating. . . . After the first week or so, I could see stuff that was happening. I could see all the Mexican, all the Latino kids, hanging out in a certain area. And then all the White kids hanging out in another area. . . . What else started to become

> apparent to me was that I didn't see any support groups. There weren't any Latino groups—there weren't any groups for Hispanics or Latinos to join. So a lot of the kids didn't. I mean, they went to school, they came home. We lost a lot of our freshman that year. We lost maybe, and I might be exaggerating, like 20% of our class.

In Rebecca's opinion, the perceived lines of racial difference had been drawn even before students entered the school, as a result of the particular histories of racial polarization between the communities and in schooling politics, the existent patterns of residential segregation, and extensive socioeconomic differences. As a consequence, Latino students entered the school with a distrust of the unknown "other" and a sense of nonbelonging. As she noted, this perception could perhaps have been dispelled, but not without active, thoughtful, and organized efforts on the part of local schooling officials.

While AHS pursued some level of well-intentioned strategies to address the shifting demographics at the school—namely, limited curricular changes and the assurance of more equal access to curricular and extracurricular activities—such strategies ultimately proved inadequate. Increasing Mexican-descent students' access to opportunities did little to change the "the feel of the place," to dispel the environment of distrust, or to counter the racist sentiments, stereotypes, and misunderstandings that existed among both students and teachers at the school. While there could be no expectation that the school administration institute comprehensive changes all at once, former students and teachers spoke with unanimity about the lack of any clear and committed agenda to provide intentional spaces or programming opportunities that might allow students to engage with and come to understand one another's situations, backgrounds, and feelings in a manner that would challenge or ward against distanced and often harmful stereotypes.

Thomas Murphy, also a freshman at AHS in 1991, was one of a small percentage of White students who arrived from Rolling Meadows Middle School in the early years of the busing plan. He echoed the perception that that little was done to prepare students for the culture shock they would face at their new high school:

> So my freshman year at Allenstown High School, it was wild and polarized. . . . You had these White seniors who had been there for four years, and now they had to go to school with these Latino

> students from Farmingville, and there was this violent fighting, it seemed like every week. There was one in particular that was just a nasty Mexican-versus-White-football-players kind of battle. It was just very hostile. A lot of anxiety. I think as the years went on, people started getting used to it, but it didn't mean that people came together.

Interracial skirmishes, including the one of which Thomas spoke, were mentioned by all the former students I interviewed who attended the school in the early 1990s. In response to the fights, the school administration brought in a cadre of local police officers to maintain a patrolling presence at the school during a short period of unrest. One former student shared with me a powerful image from his 1991 yearbook: a picture showing a group of shielded police officers in riot gear lined up along the high school's central quad. The militarized image attested to the degree of racial tension on campus, and unfortunately, it became the school's preferred manner of responding to racial conflict. In light of recurring incidents of violence—and the perceived threat of continuing violence—the school elected to hire permanent, private security personnel to patrol campus. At the same time, due to budget cuts, the school released its counselors and opted to hire fewer, less qualified "guidance techs" to take their place. In 1992, two guidance techs served more than 1,800 students at the school.

Allenstown High teachers were not entirely apathetic or inattentive to the crisis at the time. In an effort to help Latino students develop a sense of belonging at the school, a student club called Tiberones Unidos (United Sharks) was formed. Advised by one of the school's only bilingual Mexican-descent teachers, the club supported students' efforts to organize cultural events like Cinco de Mayo and helped arrange university visits and other special events for club members. The intention of the club was to recruit both White and Latino students together, but the club tended in practice to mainly attract Latino students, with a few exceptions. The students I interviewed believed Tiberones Unidos was successful in providing a limited number of Latino students with leadership aspirations and a feeling of belonging at the school—among them, Rebecca Sanchez—who would successfully run for the ASB vice presidency three years later. Unfortunately, though, it was the only club at the school with such a mission. A former female student—and one of only two White students who consistently participated in club activities at the time—spoke about how Tiberones Unidos served as an effective but inherently limited strategy to transform relationships at the school:

> Nora [the club advisor] was actually really good about [helping Latino students feel like they belong]. She took a group of the students from Tiberones Unidos, including me and four or five other Latino kids, to hear Paolo Freire speak. . . . But then, she was the only person during that time [who was doing such things], and it wasn't even revolutionary. Sure, Paolo Freire is, but it's not like we came back and started educating other students about what Paolo Freire said. It was just for our benefit. It wasn't revolutionary like creating a huge agenda for change.

Thomas, too, recalled the school's lack of initiative to develop a broader agenda for change that might bring students together at the school:

> The thing I remember about the administration is that they did *nothing* at all to bring people together. There were no assemblies addressing this new situation. There were no activities to have both sets of people interact with each other. They ignored it, or just pretended that there wasn't a problem. And it just carried on for years and years, *until eventually something had to give* [my emphasis]. It was a very tragic thing, because as leaders of the school, they also had the opportunity to do something. But they weren't there for us.

While school officials may have lacked broad knowledge about evidence-based models for promoting mutual understanding and respect for students across lines of racial, cultural, and socioeconomic difference, it was clear that ignorance alone did not explain the failure to institute a longer-range plan for high-quality integrated education. Kenneth Reed, a local educational consultant specializing in intercultural communication who was working with the district at the time, provided his take on the situation:

> I had the opportunity to tell the school four years before the busing program began that they needed to start to change their culture *now* and not wait until the people got there. But they didn't. And that's what happened: the school became 50/50 Mexican

> American/White and didn't have an infrastructure, a consciousness, a willingness, a conversation of any depth, meaning, intelligence, or insight—there was no study, research, whatever. They were just going to put these people here together.

Proposition 187 and the Return of "Chicano" Politics

By the early 1990s, growing backlash to Mexican immigration across the U.S. Southwest helped fuel a virulent, xenophobic nationalistic politics—particularly in the state of California—which included a range of proposed state referendum measures whose explicit intent was to protect the rights and entitlements of "Americans" against what was perceived to be a menacing outside threat from Mexico. The most iniquitous of the referenda measures was Proposition 187 (a.k.a. the "Save Our State" initiative), designed to outlaw all basic social services (medical, health, and educational) to illegal immigrants and their children. While the primary intent was to cripple the rights of undocumented workers and their families, the proposed method of enforcement was to require educators, health care workers, and social workers to report to local law enforcement authorities anyone whom they "reasonably suspected" of being illegal immigrants, or children of suspected illegal immigrants. In this way, the proposed measure would serve to justify the harassment and intimidation of both Latino immigrant and nonimmigrant youth and their families, whether documented or undocumented.

Mexican-descent youth, because of their visibility, became a central target of many of the anti-immigration state referendum measures put forth by citizen groups anxious about the economic and cultural changes they believed to be transforming and undermining the health of the state. In California, a series of initiatives spanning from the late 1980s through the 1990s including Propositions 187, 209, and 227—each of which was passed into law by a majority of California voters—specifically targeted minority and immigrant youth and children.

When California's Proposition 187 was formally proposed in early 1994, Latino populations across the Southwest, particularly Mexican-descent youth and those who would speak with them, were quick to condemn the injustice and the spirit of intolerance underlying the measure. Mass mobilization against the ballot measure took place in regions across the state with sizable Latino populations, signaling a renaissance of political awareness and "Chicano" activism that included a network of coordinated organizing campaigns in which regional and statewide dialogues informed local strategies of direct action. Such mobilization led to numerous student school walkouts across the state, from the elementary to the university level. In April 1994, over 1,000 Latino junior high and high school students walked out of twelve schools in Oakland, California. On September 16 (Mexican Independence Day), over 4,000 students walked out of schools in San Francisco, Oakland, Berkeley, San Jose, and Gilroy. Later, a coordinated "blowout" was orchestrated that included participation of thirty schools in Northern California. As Elizabeth Martínez (1998) has explained, the reasons for the "blowouts" were diverse. They were the result not only of anger and frustration over the scapegoating of immigrants for the deepening economic crisis in the state, but also the product of a growing awareness of the underrepresentation of Latino teachers in California public schools; the recurrence of racist incidents between teachers and Latino students; the continued low retention levels of Latino students statewide; and continued popular attacks on bilingualism and affirmative action. Secondary school walkouts across the state could be linked to increased organizing activity among college-level Latino students that produced, in 1993 alone, two highly publicized actions: the student sit in to protest the threat to Ethnic Studies at UC Berkeley, and the hunger strike to win departmental status for Chicano Studies at UC Los Angeles. However, as Martínez importantly notes, the walkouts of grade-school youth throughout California were not simply an extension of college student organizing; though youth "may have received information, ideas, contacts, resources, tips on security, and other help from college students and experienced organizers . . . in the end, they did it themselves" (1998: 215). This was certainly the case for students in Pleasanton Valley.

Latino Student Empowerment and School Walkouts in Pleasanton Valley

In May 1994, several hundred Latino students walked out of Farmingville High School in protest of governor Pete Wilson's support for Proposition 187. Student leaders who coordinated the walkout, counseled by a newly reborn chapter of the Brown Berets[2] in Farmingville (see Chapter 7), took the opportunity to demand the creation of classes in Chicano Studies and permission to form a MEChA[3] group on the high school campus. The day after the walkout at Farmingville High, over one hundred students at Allenstown High—mostly Latino students, with a handful of White allies—left classes as well to participate in a nearly eight-mile march from the high school to downtown Farmingville. Proposition 187 hit very close to home for a number of AHS Latino students, many of whom were children of immigrant or migrant parents or were (im)migrants themselves.

While the walkout at AHS sent shock waves across the campus, it failed to generate overwhelming concern in the larger Allenstown community. Because the walkout was perceived to be a relatively isolated and spontaneous incident involving primarily Mexican-descent youth from Farmingville, with relatively little impact on the education of the children living in Allenstown, it did not produce substantial alarm. Also, because the walkout took place at the end of the school year, it was assumed that students' passion and anger would prove fickle and dissipate during the summer recess.

However, early in the next academic year, with polls showing 2-1 voter support for Proposition 187, student demonstrations again broke out across the state, including a walkout of over 70,000 students in Los Angeles. By this time, the PVUSD school board had joined an increasing number of civic organizations throughout the state in publicly opposing the proposition by passing a unanimous resolution against it. Yet on November 2, several hundred AHS students—the vast majority of them Mexican-descent—staged another school walkout and again made the long trek to downtown Farmingville. Their action was followed by multiple student walkouts in schools throughout Farmingville. These relatively peaceful marches and rallies transformed, on some occurrences, into more intense encounters between students and law enforcement officials, and sometimes between some Latino youth groups themselves. Despite the limited nature of the confrontations, the idea that the marches had "turned violent" became highly politicized in the local press and was widely circulated in popular discourse about the walkouts.

Reactions to the Walkouts at Allenstown High

The Proposition 187-inspired walkouts at Allenstown, while providing a positive venue of expression for a number of more disenfranchised Mexican-descent students, managed to animate underlying racial tensions and contested views about who and what kinds of behaviors "belonged" at the high school. One controversy revolved around Mexican-descent students who chose to bring Mexican flags to the high school to demonstrate pride in their Mexican heritage. On various occasions of protest, Mexican-descent students would congregate at the entrance to campus and wave Mexican flags as cars entered. A teacher's recollection of the situation highlights the tension and polarization that resulted:

> During the walkouts, it was pretty tense. You'd show up here in the morning and kids were waving Mexican flags and that sort of thing. But other kids were walking around with—they started going around with the American flag flashing them in people's faces, and it got ugly. And it got to the point that they would stick American flags—not like after 9/11. After 9/11, it was more of a patriotic thing. But at that time, it had nothing to do with patriotism, it was all about a "This is America, and you are not welcome" kind of message. And I would find flag stickers everywhere. People would put flags on their backpacks. And it wasn't like "I'm proud to be an American;" it was more like "This is America, quit wearing your [inaudible]." They [Latino students] would flash flags too: "It's all about Mexico!" and that kind of thing. Then American kids would go: "No, it's all about the U.S.!" So it got really ugly. . . . There was wrongdoing on both sides. There was just a lot of mistrust at that time.

My own efforts to engage former teachers and administrators in discussion about these events and associated tensions at the high school were often met with expressive sighs and recollections of that "difficult," "confused," and "emotional" period about which—even in retrospect—they struggled to find words to describe and give meaning. And the reactions of AHS teachers varied considerably. Some thought the walkouts were a good thing, others were disturbed for having lost class time, and yet others were bothered because they felt only a small minority of Latino students really cared about the issues, while the others were just "bandwagoners" using it as an excuse to leave class. Although some teachers expressed sympathy for Latino students' feelings, many teachers disagreed with—and, when possible, actively discouraged—direct action as a way of dealing with the situation. For example, a White, long-time math teacher at the school who worked closely with Latino students recalled his position on what was happening at the time:

> I don't think that most of the kids had a real sense of what was going on politically with the 187. I don't think they really knew—I don't think *anyone* really knew—the ramifications of this whole thing. And a lot of these kids—many of these kids—were not very good students. And they were just doing it to like—"Oh, there seems to be a little chaos going on, blah, blah." Other kids really understood, had political ideas that were very different, maybe not exactly in the mainstream, you know. But many of the people who were directly involved in the walkouts, and showing the flag and everything, they didn't quite know exactly why they were doing it. "Because we are *Mexicanos*!" [they would say] and I'm like, okay, but why are you going to walk out of the school? "Because this school has done nothing for us!" And I'm like, who told you this? I said, wait a minute, you guys are all receiving your education free and good. But, the students would say, how many Mexican teachers are in this school? And at that time, you know, we didn't have a whole lot. There were some but there was really a low percentage. But I said, Hey look, you want them in here? You go out and become one and then you will do it! Here is another example, I said: What about "Spanish for Spanish Speakers?" [a course offering at Allenstown High at the time] Can you imagine an "English-for-Gringo speakers" class in Mexico? Do you think they are going to accommodate the Americans over there and make a whole new class for free? This is a pretty nice thing here. "Well, yeah," they'd say, "but . . ." Their whole thing was that this school has nothing for them, and they alluded to embedded racism. And I was wondering, now, I'm not sure exactly where you see that embedded racism, you know. I know that there is a lot of racism everywhere and that people have biases. But from what I saw here, I didn't see any of the things that happened here as the result of outright racism.

The assumptions in this narrative—which were expressed in various forms from several teachers I interviewed—deserve some unpacking. First, while it may be true that Latino students were not equally informed about the complex politics inspiring the walkouts, the assumption that "most of the kids" walked out simply to skip class and cause trouble serves to criminalize the majority of these youth and to discredit the varying levels of disillusionment and disenfranchisement they may have felt from both the school and from the larger society. Equally problematic are the claims that Mexican-descent children living in the United States are "lucky" to have "free" education at all, portraying public education as a privilege rather than a right, and that classes such as "Spanish for Spanish Speakers" are "special" accommodations for foreigners rather than legitimate academic classes that productively build on students' existing linguistic skills and strengths to facilitate and enhance their learning. Third, the reliance on a "bootstrap" model of ethnic behavior as a way to bring about social change—that is, "play by the rules and you will slowly but surely glide into equality"—neglects the reality that those invested in maintaining the status quo of schooling in Pleasanton Valley have historically conceded little without a challenge or demand. Finally, limiting legitimate claims of racism to those of "outright" personal bias excludes historically engendered forms of institutional racism like—as this teacher mentions—the lack of Spanish-speaking administrators and teachers at the school.

Racist sentiments and stereotypes among teachers did, in fact, exist at the time. A former teacher recalled an interaction he had with a colleague after the first faculty meeting following the walkouts. Referring to those students who participated in the walkout, a teacher allegedly said: "Let 'em go. They're like the sewer in San Diego. Let 'em go downstream." In another incident, one of the AHS football coaches said publicly that he had taken "a count of all those [Latino] students who had walked and took an average of their GPA and it is 2 point something. Let them walk out!" This statement—besides erroneously linking students' worth and educational rights to their grade point average—was disturbing in the sense that the coach would have access to all students' records for this purpose. Another AHS teacher elaborated on attitudes among teachers: at the time:

> As far as the discussions with other teachers [after the walkouts], some of the teachers at our school are racist. Some of them think that the Mexicans are lazy. They see them as wearing *sombreros* and sleeping under a tree, with a burro tied around the trunk of the tree. Faculty meetings were rather volatile in that sense. People would not come right out and express it, but you could tell by the tone and their especially chosen words that they weren't happy with a lot of

> the things that were going on on campus. Things like the Latinos asking for more classes. Things like Latinos wanting a club. . . . You know, it was always: "That's a Mexican thing, we're in America now." And I heard that from a lot of teachers.

From the perspective of the school and district level administration, the walkout could be viewed in a productive light—an opportunity to focus attention on the need to integrate the campus and pay more attention to issues of Latino enfranchisement—or it could be taken as a counterproductive conflict, an unraveling of the school brought about by an unruly group of Latino students intent on creating problems and promoting lawlessness at Allenstown High. The AHS administration's response ultimately fell somewhere in-between. According to former students and teachers I spoke with, the administration chose a more "hands-off" approach. Andrew, an AHS literature teacher at the time, explained his view of the response:

> There was some concern, but there was kind of a feeling of helplessness. One time I went to the principal and said "Hey man, what's going on with these kids that keep causing trouble?" And he said: "Andy, there is nothing we can do. This is all we can do and there is nothing else we can do." And I was like, what? They were just as helpless, it seemed, as we were. Not a lot of ideas for change. Not a lot of innovation. I think they just weren't—I'm not sure they were actively seeking solutions. Maybe they were and things weren't working. So that was the atmosphere here. It wasn't very pleasant.

Some former teachers and students were inclined to pin blame for the walkouts on the Allenstown High principal, Don Stevenson. Thomas Murphy, who served as the student editor of the high school newspaper at the time, offered his own take on why the principal and his staff failed to pursue a more positive and proactive response to the walkouts:

> I think he [Stevenson] made absolutely no effort to ever bridge the community . . . I think there was also this threat, because they were voicing out their opinions and holding walkouts and protests—oh my gosh, the riot police are here at Allenstown High, disrupting this smooth community that we have always had.

In Thomas's narrative—as in others that shifted at least some blame toward the school's principal—there was an implicit understanding that his actions were tempered by the watchful eye of parents and community leaders in Allenstown who were concerned with protecting their children and schools from the threat of perceived violence and gang activity they often associated with the Farmingville area.

MEChA and the Emergence of Latino Student Leadership

The student walkouts constituted a political awakening of Latino students at AHS. Thomas vividly recalled his excitement about the transformation:

> It was a beautiful thing coming out of Prop. 187, because the students initially felt so [inaudible] and unappreciated, you know, like they just got the crap beat out of them. And then all of a sudden they just found the strength. Coming out of that, they found their voices and strength and a unity and a pride that I didn't see before. In terms of culture, they started celebrating culture at school and [being] a lot more active . . . they felt comfortable enough to be themselves.

The walkouts were organized not by more enfranchised or assimilated Latino students, but by a handful of working-class, Mexican-descent immigrant students who had remained largely outside the social and academic mainstream at the school. They had begun to meet together soon after the first student walkouts in March. Lacking any voice in the school, segregated class-wise, and feeling uncomfortable socially on the campus, this group resolved to take the issue of enfranchisement into their own hands. Following the March walkouts, they followed Farmingville High student leaders' lead in forming a MEChA club, writing up a constitution and pursuing all the formalities necessary to establish a club on campus. By the November walkouts, the MEChA group had already held a few meetings.

Because some of the students in MEChA were among those who had helped orchestrate the walkouts, the club was viewed suspiciously by many teachers and administrators who were concerned about what they perceived to be its radical, revolutionary, and separatist nature. Others believed MEChA students were being controlled by radical "outsider agitators" like the Brown Berets in Farmingville, and they feared that the group was not simply pro-Latino, but anti-Anglo. Teachers recalled—and some still maintain—their fears and ambivalences about the group. Referring to her interpretation of the college version of the MEChA constitution, a former White AHS Spanish language teacher explained:

> MEChA is a college movement, I know. And MEChA as a word means the thing you put before the bomb—the fuse. And their thing is, an [inaudible] with a fuse about to go into a bomb. It's not a very peaceful thing.

However, such characterizations of MEChA overlooked the specific purpose and conditions that led to the formation of the group at AHS. It was designed to promote cultural identity and political awareness, not to be a radical or separatist group. As former members and supporters maintain, MEChA was not brought in by outside agitators to "control" students, it was born of a lack of resources and adult role models at the school who were willing to listen sympathetically to Latino leaders' concerns and help them think through tangible ways of improving their situation within the school. These students felt themselves without anyone in the student government to represent their interests and ideas or any teacher or administrator willing to advocate for them.

Rebecca Sanchez, who became one of the original founders of the AHS MEChA group, spoke to me about how the club offered Latino students a creative space at the high school that had not formerly been provided:

> What really happened is that we started talking to people about the Brown Berets in Farmingville. Because we were feeling like our voices weren't being heard about certain things. We didn't see any Latinos in student government. We wanted a Cinco de Mayo celebration and Dieciséis de Septiembre [Mexican Independence Day] but were having a hard time trying to organize it and get it done because we weren't part of the student government. And the student government did this kind of stuff. . . . We started finding some faculty that thought this was a good idea. And we started finding students that wanted to do this. And then we started finding students that wanted a Chicano club on campus, that wanted something they could affiliate or feel at home with. We would have

> sections or meetings where we would teach the history of the Aztecs because we didn't get that in the classroom, because Chicano history in the classroom is like this paragraph in U.S. history. So we started to be mad. That was the whole purpose of MEChA on campus. It didn't become so much political until Proposition 187. It was more of an educational thing. I remember one day we walked in and 187 was a hot issue of the meeting, and we talked about maybe doing something political. And the next day, before I know it, we were all getting ready to walk out. And a lot of people did it. And it was mainly Latino students. And it was very organized because they had microphones and Diego [a MEChA student] was carrying a bullhorn and telling people—Come on, let's do this, and this is *why* we're doing this.

When the MEChA group supported the first walkout in November, they did so without having a single AHS teacher or administrator on their side. When MEChA students first began to suggest organizing a student walkout in response to Proposition 187, their faculty advisor at the time, a second-generation Mexican-descent male social studies teacher, resigned from his post and distanced himself from the group. Yet school administrators and teachers recognized the club's influence among students, so much so that, on the day after Proposition 187 was passed by voter referendum, and when student walkouts were being planned across the county, the Allenstown High school administration enlisted MEChA leaders to encourage students *not* to walk out. Addressing students over the loudspeaker system at 7:45 in the morning, MEChA leaders urged their angry peers instead to attend a voluntary assembly that would be hosted by the principal in the cafeteria during a late-morning tutorial period. Hundreds of students jammed into the cafeteria—the majority of them Mexican-descent students, but also a small but significant number of Anglo students and student government representatives. Many voiced their anger and frustrations, while a few used the occasion to make accusations of racism against the school administration.

Among those in attendance at the assembly was Luis Sandoval, an Allenstown High social studies teacher and a Latino of Cuban-descent. During a schoolwide assembly that had taken place several days earlier, Sandoval had publicly criticized Allenstown High administrators for their neglect to address issues of integration and equity among students at the school. In a speech that was eventually published in the school newspaper, Sandoval suggested a number of concrete steps that the school could take to improve the social conditions for Latino students. Among them were that the administration take leadership in offering training on culture and diversity to school staff, that teachers voluntarily reach out and try to understand the situation of Latino students, and that the Booster Club consider funding nonathletic activities to help integrate the school. In his closing statement, Luis challenged students to "ORGANIZE, because if the adults won't do it, then you will have to do it on your own. . . . But in all that you do, do it with organization and non-violence." Immediately after the morning assembly, the student leaders of MEChA asked Sandoval to serve as their advisor, which he accepted.

At the time, Sandoval was a well-liked and respected teacher among both the Latino and White students with whom he worked. Among the several classes he taught was an AP History course, made up mostly of White students, during which he would facilitate dialogues about the transformations taking place at the high school. He engaged students in debates and allowed them a forum to discuss the tensions and difficult issues at play in the school—an opportunity students claim was largely unavailable in their other classes. Many students found Sandoval's convictions and sense of social justice compelling. Some students I spoke with professed that it was their engagements in his class that provided them with a more profound understanding of the actions and behaviors of Latino students at the school. A handful of these White students—many of whom were involved in student clubs and extracurricular activities like the student government and school newspaper—came to share the Latino leader's vision of making Allenstown High a more welcoming place for students of all backgrounds.

Sandoval was quick to clarify that his willingness to serve as advisor of the MEChA club was not in order to take the group in a radical direction, as some would later argue, but to assure that these students stayed in school without walking out, dropping out, or feeling "pushed out." As the only strong supporter of the MEChA club among the high school's teachers and administrators, Sandoval became as much an advocate for the club as an advisor. Soon after taking on the advisor role, he circulated a memo to school staff that was intended to mitigate their fears about the radical and seemingly separatist nature of the club, and to dispel the myth that those who had participated in the walkouts were largely Mexican "gangsters" using the political situation as a convenient excuse to skip class. In the memo,

Sandoval related the feelings and thoughtful vision of the MEChA students, which included their sincere desire to create unity and facilitate positive change at the high school:

> Here at Allenstown High, the students of MEChA are the reason we have not had any walkouts this last week. They feel people are listening. They feel that people care about their pain and fears. I don't want to lose this opportunity to make reciprocal camaraderie grow. Some of the MEChA students are angry. But they *want* an education. They *want* to stop gangs. If you sit down and think about it—what they want is what we want. The last few days at MEChA meetings we have had 50 plus students. They are sitting on the floor and spilling out into the hallways. They are looking for connection. They are saddened, fearful, upset. Their own leaders are providing the infrastructure. We need to hear them and respond.

Although Sandoval supported MEChA students' convictions about the injustices they felt Latinos faced in the school and the larger society, he would often temper students' statements about rights and demands of "La Raza" by emphasizing instead the rights of "la raza humana" (the human race) so as to encourage students to envision a more inclusive frame for political action. MEChA students appreciated Sandoval for "being there" and for his proactive concern for Latino students, as well as for making himself and his room available at a time when other staff members did not.

Claiming to welcome all students at Allenstown High, MEChA developed an ambitious platform to create unity on the campus. Their campaign would include running student candidates for political office, organizing a forty-foot mural for the school gymnasium, instituting an elective course on Chicano studies, and overseeing an intervention program to talk with gang members and "wannabes" about "putting aside their colors."

Although the events surrounding Proposition 187 produced distrust and hostility, they also produced a sense of hope for many students—Latino and White alike—that perhaps this was the moment when AHS would move toward becoming a more welcoming environment for all students and for a variety of expressions. This sense was clearly reflected in election campaigns for the Associated Student Body that began shortly after the walkouts. The recurring theme in each candidate's platform was an interest in fostering integration and breaking down racial barriers to improve the tense conditions and racial polarization that characterized the school environment. Typically, student body elections at Allenstown High—as is the case with many public schools—did not command the attention of a wide range of students. They had been viewed by those less involved as a social club for the enfranchised, providing something nice to put on one's work résumé or college application. The 1995 elections, however, were different. The MEChA club—made up of students with no previous experience or connection to the student government or any other high status club/activity on campus—prepared to run a slate of candidates for all major student government positions, including president, vice president, secretary, and treasurer. Rebecca Sanchez, running for ASB vice president, recalls the excitement, ethic, and planning process for the MEChA group:

> Yeah, we ran someone for each position. And then it just happened. People [in MEChA] started nominating people. And we decided who was going to run for what. And then we would meet, the four of us. And we would think about the stuff we wanted to campaign for. We would talk about *how* [to do it] because most of us had no idea. We would practice speaking in public. We would practice speaking into a microphone because that kind of stuff we didn't know, we had never been exposed to. And so it was really important work. And we had campaign managers, and people who would campaign for us in the classrooms and during lunch. And it became this big whole campaign thing at Allenstown High.

The campaign required bureaucratic processes as well. The MEChA leaders were disadvantaged from the outset because their campaign had begun late, and they had missed a deadline for required paperwork, including the necessary petitions of student support and signatures of teacher sponsors. A White female and former student I interviewed who was an ASB officer at the time recalled that, given the distrust toward MEChA, their candidates received little support from the current ASB members or faculty advisor:

> There was a whole process to able to run for a position at the election convention. Of course, none of the students in MEChA, or the students that were running, or Mr. Sandoval, knew about this process, because they didn't even have any friends who had ever run

> for these positions or who were in the ASB. . . . There was a lot of distrust and there wasn't a lot of support from the ASB advisor. From my recollection, [the ASB advisor] never went out of his way to kind of include—"Oh, you want to run, this is great! Let me show you how it works." Because they obviously had no prior knowledge of how it worked. And the administration wasn't very supportive. So I would go to some of their meetings to kind of talk them through the process. Ok, you have to get this many signatures, and then you'll be put on the ballot, and this is how the election convention works, and you are going to be asked questions, kind of explain the whole process.

While MEChA's paperwork was accepted by the ASB campaign manager, the question arose as to whether MEChA, as a student club, should even be permitted to "sponsor" candidates for the election. In the eleventh hour of the election campaign, the acting ASB president issued a change of rules/constitutional amendment regarding elections, mandating that no club could sponsor a candidate for office. All the signs showing MEChA support for particular candidates had to be taken down. Despite these obstacles, MEChA candidates moved forward on their campaign.

Daniel, a White student enrolled in AP classes at the time, remembered "Election Day 1995" at Allenstown High and the compelling speeches given by both Rebecca and the presidential candidate, Diego Omán:

> I remember that day at the election convention, they [the MEChA candidates] were speaking, and just really changing people's minds about who they were and who this population of students were, and what they could do and accomplish.

In the end, Rebecca won the vice-presidency by a landslide, while Diego, MEChA's candidate for president, won a battle decided by fewer than two percentage points. The two became the first Latino students slated by Latinos to hold top offices in the Allenstown High ASB. The election results, though disappointing to some, provided hope for the students and teachers who were uncomfortable and concerned about the lack of unity and mutual respect that had come to exist the school.

Diego, the new ASB president, was a senior from Farmingville, and a first-generation immigrant from Mexico. He had created a name for himself as the outspoken leader of the student walkouts. "He wanted to be a Cesar Chavez," claimed one teacher who worked closely with Diego. Considered a "Chicano radical" by many at the school, Diego was known above all as an uncompromising promoter and spokesperson of the rights of "Chicano" students at the school, a role that had given him legitimacy among Latino as well as some progressive White students on campus. In the words of one former student, Diego "seemed passionate about something that mattered, and I think that meant a lot to a lot of people." According to Rebecca, Diego's participation and leadership in the walkouts and in MEChA had changed his life:

> Diego had a history of being a rebel kid. So MEChA really brought him together and gave him a leadership role. And a bunch of us thought like, whoa, Diego has really got it together. He was doing good in class. He was really active. And I think what started happening is that he had started hanging out with a lot us [in MEChA].

During and after the walkouts, Diego served as motivator and spokesperson for the cause, expressing strong political opinions that included unapologetic criticisms of school authorities based on what he perceived to be the discriminatory treatment of Latino students, and neglect to pursue reform measures that would ensure all students felt a sense of belonging at the school. Diego also worked actively with gang-affiliated students at the school, among whom he had some legitimacy, encouraging them to "tone down their colors" and unite as one *Raza* (a term of ethnic or racial pride). What was perhaps Diego's greatest strength as a leader was his eloquence and presence as a public speaker. His rhetorical strategies stressed Chicano unity and "Brown Pride," convictions he appropriated at least in part from his friendships and involvement with local Brown Beret leaders and his attendance at regional gatherings with other MEChA leaders. One teacher's impression of Diego at the time of the elections describes his rare ability to simultaneously make people uncomfortable and persuade them to believe in the sense of social justice that informed his convictions:

> I think what Diego did was to try to get a sense of inclusion in our school. To try and offer things for the Latino kids to make them

> feel like it was also their school. I think when Diego came in, he was also wanting to bring up the Latino image at the school, to make them more of a presence . . . Diego was a very interesting person. I think he was a little bit of—I want to say a radical—but there was a general feeling on Diego's part that some things, by goodness, were going to happen . . . I would liken him to Malcolm X in a way. I think he said: "We are not going to take this anymore, and I'm going to do something about it." He wasn't the Martin Luther King, he was the Malcolm X who says, "I'm not just going to go peacefully into the night because this ain't happening . . ."

In the case of the ASB election, Diego's talent as a speaker and motivator, and his unwavering commitment to social justice, outweighed the negative reception he received for some of his more controversial statements. As a teacher at the time explained:

> You see, Diego got those kids totally enthusiastic about voting for him. I bet every single brown face voted [for him]. Because they really believed in him. Like when we used to go to assemblies, and he'd get up in front of the assemblies, he had a real presence. And I know there were teachers who didn't care for him because they knew a different side of him. Maybe he was a slacker in a class, or maybe this or that happened. But he had a presence, and he would get up, and he could just galvanize a group.

Diego believed that some of the largest obstacles to the involvement and academic success of Latinos at the school were the stereotypes they endured and the treatment they received from the AHS administration. In a public statement just before the elections, Diego asserted:

> It's not a good school. The students are good but the adults, the administration, they don't treat us the way we should be treated. It's just the way they treat us, you know, by the remarks that are said. When they refer to Mexicans, they say "gangsters."

Diego's running-mate, Rebecca, had also served as a leader in MEChA and in the walkouts. Her agenda, above all, was to bring some sense of unity and common cause to the student body:

> [My campaign] was really about being united, about being one Allenstown High, and really filling that hole. I knew that when I filled that hole, everybody else who was Latino, everybody else who was Asian, everybody else who was Black or White would feel like they belonged. And so that was my whole thing.

Rebecca recalls that when the election campaign began, she felt she and Diego were working toward the same goals: "We had the same ideologies, we had the same platform—we were at the same level." Yet while Diego was committed to addressing racial divisions on campus, he was just as concerned—if not more so—with breaking down gang rivalries among his Latino peers. Of central concern to him was unity among Latinos—a unity made difficult by gang oppositions that led to social separation in the community and on campus, as well as territorial markings and the constant fear or threat of violence. Diego understood that fostering unity among Latino students was in some ways a precondition of the integration of Whites and Latinos at the school. This focus on Latino unity did not mean that he was not also concerned with creating an environment of mutual respect and unity among all students on campus—Brown and White. As time went on, however, Diego's efforts tended to prioritize the former over the latter. This manner of prioritizing was not, however, the consequence of a blind adherence to a "Chicano nationalist" posture—as some teachers and administrators would later argue; rather, his actions were tempered by a series of events that followed his election as ASB president. In the end, it was Diego's and Rebecca's different tendencies—Diego toward a protection of Chicano dignity at all costs, and Rebecca toward an interracial cooperative posture—that would lead them not necessarily in opposite directions, but toward different kinds of obstacles and pressures, ones that would ultimately unravel their partnership along with the fragile unity among Latino students at the school.

"Is It a Crime to Be a Chicano or Does It Just Make You Suspect?"

In early December, just two school days after winning the ASB election, president-elect Diego was called into Principal Stevenson's office for a personal meeting. The night before, a drive-by shooting had occurred in a nearby college town. Three Farmingville teens were shot, two of them Allenstown High students. The following draft passage, written by a student reporter from the AHS student newspaper who had spoken with Diego immediately after the meeting, related what (allegedly) transpired:

> The next morning, ASB President-Elect Diego Omán found himself in the inner-sanctum of Principal Stevenson's office, surrounded by a phalanx of Narcs. [Diego said]: "[The principal] had all the Narcs there. They took pictures. A Narc asked me: 'Did you know there was a shooting last night?' He showed me their pictures and then Mr. Stevenson came in and asked them to leave . . . and he was telling me that I better watch what I'm doing and watch what I say because important people are watching me. When we finished with everything he told me to stay out of trouble, and don't bring any more weapons to school. Look at all I've been doing! You can't all of a sudden assume that I would bring a gun. He made it seem like I did it [the shootings]."

This awkward meeting and its remarkable content, once public, enhanced the controversy and finger pointing about racial discrimination and constituted another act in the larger theater of media spectacle. Diego and those close to him considered this incident a classic case of intimidation. One Latino parent at the time queried: "Don't cops usually follow up their own tips when it involves possible felonies?" while another implored, "Is it a crime to be a Chicano or does it just make you suspect?" The event itself became the subject of endless speculation, particularly since there was no certainty as to what had in fact taken place in the meeting. The student newspaper interview above was pulled before being published, a censorship many perceived to be a directive of the principal. The incident brought a complaint from Diego's parents who, accompanied by a lawyer, arranged a private meeting with Stevenson and school district officials.

Although Stevenson admitted to some misunderstanding and apologized to both Diego and his family, he could not dodge a windfall of criticism that descended on him from several directions. For Diego, it served to fuel his already distrustful stance toward the administration and intensified his feeling of being the object of racist targeting. As he related at the time: "He [Stevenson] knows that once a Chicano student rises up and tries to change himself for the better, people are not used to seeing that stuff so they consider us a threat; I think he considered me a threat and pulled me in for questioning."

Further enhancing the controversy was a letter to the editor that appeared in Farmingville's daily newspaper, written by a former ASB president at AHS who had graduated the previous year. The student claimed that he, too, had been intimidated by Stevenson while serving as student body president. This student's favorable reputation commanded respect among many parents, teachers, and students, which made Diego's claims of discrimination more difficult to dismiss as those of a Chicano radical "playing the race card."

The Camps Develop

The infamous meeting between Diego and Principal Stevenson, along with additional accusations of misconduct and bad leadership against the principal, brought about an investigation by the American Civil Liberties Union. While a number of school staff and community leaders came to Stevenson's side and supported the decisions he had made as principal, others—including social studies teacher and MEChA advisor Luis Sandoval—questioned Stevenson's conduct and leadership. It was around this set of issues that "camps" among school staff began to take form, further enhancing distrust and polarization within the school. On one side were those supporting Stevenson—including teachers, staff, and parents—who believed he was the target of sensational journalism and an overbearing sensitivity about race. On the other side were Sandoval and a smaller group of teachers and parents, including the Farmingville-based Migrant Parent Advisory Committee (MPAC), who were concerned by what they saw as Stevenson's arrogance and his inappropriate—and for some, racist—behavior. The development of these camps precipitated a significant breakdown in communication between key staff at the school, producing multiple incidents in which people on one side would accuse the other of harassment and slander. Several incidents required mediation by the district, while some ended up as legal battles in local courts.

The conflicts among staff did not go unnoticed by students, particularly Latino student leaders. In December, a group of Latino student leaders sent a letter to PVUSD board members "demanding an end to the harassment of any student or teacher involved with the great and positive changes that are occurring at Allenstown High."

Despite the divisiveness and a sense of distrust that characterized relations among some students, faculty, administrators at AHS, the students I interviewed recalled that the ASB class—under the leadership of Diego and Rebecca—was home to heated but generally productive discussions about culture and class entitlement, racial privilege, and how to work productively through differences while maintaining a shared vision. Although not everyone in the ASB agreed on all issues—for example,there were animated discussions about the need for a Chicano Studies course—the ASB class offered a rare space for dialogue and planning by a diverse group of students addressing the complex issues dividing the campus. An activity coordinator at the time explained what he saw happening in the meetings:

> It was real interesting. When we would take votes, they would be fascinating because Diego would get as many Anglo votes as Hispanics, and the opposite side would do the same. The voting on issues was not all the Hispanics voting one way and all the Anglos the other. It didn't happen that way, although people may portray it that way. There was disagreement . . . one Hispanic would say something, and the [Latino] guy next to him would say "I don't agree with that." So it wasn't like they represented a block. Anybody who thought that did not see what was going on.

Kenneth Reed, a consultant hired by the district in February of 1995 to help mediate the conflicts at the high school, expressed his feeling that the ASB class seemed to be the one place on campus where fears about racial and class difference were engaged, and where talk about dissipating these fears was actively pursued by student leaders:

> I was very impressed with a number of the young people there. That group was very disappointed with people blaming the school's problems on Diego and knew that it wasn't true, and was trying to empower itself and talk about: "it's us, we're all responsible." Several young White kids—I mean, I was more impressed with them than any of the administrators who were there most of the time, or the parents. That's why I kept saying that if we could support the

> students in a plan that they come up with, then it increases the likelihood that it will happen. Because it is about them, they are *in* it, they've got to do something. And they were up for it in that leadership class. The Anglo student didn't know what was going happen, but they figured the journey was worth it.

In early February, the ASB organized a lunchtime "unity event" in the Quad. Typically the domain of White students at the high school, the Quad was outfitted with an amplified stereo system that played a broad and inclusive range of music from modern pop rock to Mexican *ranchero*. With Diego and Rebecca taking the lead, members of the ASB sought out partners from other racial groups and invited them to dance. A White student remembered the event:

> It was really interesting because they'd come out and they'd dance. And I don't really like *banda* music but I love to watch them dance. And I thought that it was kinda cool that they could be the center of attention and not in a negative way, for once.

Although by some measures a token activity, teachers and administrators in both camps saw the event as a good first step—a spectacle of cooperation where cultural and racial difference was engaged without being politicized.

Unfortunately, the ASB class was not entirely immune to the divisiveness and distrust that had developed between AHS teachers and between teachers and administrators. Problems in the ASB began shortly after the student elections when Diego and Rebecca met with their then-ASB faculty advisor, Gary Simmons. In my interview with Simmons, he recalled his skepticism after this first meeting where, he alleged, Rebecca and Diego came to him with a "script." Instead of seeking suggestions and advice about what direction the ASB might take, Simmons felt the students "told me the way it was going to be and what they were going to do." A second, equally frustrating incident for Simmons was when, a short time later, Diego failed to meet with him to discuss the formation of commissions to recruit students for the ASB leadership class. In this case, Diego said that his "other advisors" had told him not to meet with Simmons on this issue. Diego's dilemma was that he did in fact have two advisors—Simmons and Sandoval (both clubs in which he served as president)—and communication between the two teachers had become severely strained. This antagonism manifested itself as a sense of distrust between the students in the two extracurricular groups. For example, a handful of students within MEChA claimed that the ASB was sending "spies" to MEChA meetings, a perception seemingly redeemed when an ASB member who had attended a MEChA meeting was quoted in the school newspaper as saying the meeting was "anti-Anglo" and that a MEChA member had made some "anti-White, racist" comments.

The Quest for Chicano Studies

As Diego was facilitating ASB meetings under an increasingly strained relationship with the club's advisor, he was also busy leading another hotly contested battle on the campus: a campaign for a Chicano Studies course. The desire for such a course had first been expressed by MEChA representatives during the Proposition 187 walkouts. In fact, in December, Diego and a group of Latino student leaders had met privately with select PVUSD school board members to discuss whether such a course could possibly be offered at the school. The school board members had given their tentative backing for the class, assuming there was a broad enough demand, but they had also encouraged student leaders to seek the support of the Allenstown High's Social Studies Department and the school's administration. The students approached the AHS administration, whose response was that they could not promise to offer the course for fear that the school lacked sufficient funds to finance it. The Social Studies Department met to discuss the possibility of offering a Chicano Studies course in late December but failed to produce a course outline by the district's early February deadline for new course proposals. Moreover, the department claimed it lacked personnel who would or could effectively teach such a course. The best candidates were social studies teachers Sandoval or Joel Borrego, the former MEChA advisor. However, Sandoval was not committed to remaining at Allenstown High the following year and Borrego claimed to already have a full load of classes. A third Social Studies teacher, a White female, did not consider herself a strong enough candidate to teach the class.

The group of students who had sought support for the course felt that they were being "stonewalled" despite having followed the necessary channels to facilitate its approval. As a response, Diego and others organized a walkout for Chicano studies in late February. The walkout—the first since walkouts opposing Proposition 187 the previous November—included nearly 150 Latino students. That evening, after the walkout, Latino student leaders attended a PVUSD school board meeting where, in a tearful testimony, Diego presented a petition "demanding" a Chicano studies course at AHS. Principal Stevenson claimed to be surprised by the walkouts, casting blame on "outside organizations" that he believed were controlling the unruly behavior of these students—including a Farmingville chapter of the Brown Berets.

Diego, for his own part, was receiving less and less sympathy from AHS staff and administration and became increasingly viewed as a renegade whose "demands," statements, and actions bordered on insubordination. The day following the Chicano Studies walkout, Diego was invited to attend a meeting with the Social Studies Department faculty to discuss the situation. What transpired in this meeting provides a good illustration of the state of distrust and division that had developed among AHS teachers, and between some teachers and ASB president Diego. Before the meeting even began, an argument over a procedural issue sparked an angry exchange between social studies teacher Sandoval and department chair Janette Cummings, an outspoken supporter of Principal Stevenson. After this inauspicious beginning, Diego was interrogated intensely by Cummings about why he had organized a student walkout without having pursued a direct dialogue with the Social Studies Department or the school administration. Faced with this hostility, Diego stated that he had "gotten what he wanted" from the school board already and added that he and a group of students would have the final approval over the content and material of the Chicano studies course. Borrego took offense to Diego's suggestion that students would dare dictate the content of teachers' curriculum, arguing that he "did not study for years to be a content area specialist to be told what he would teach in his course." In the days following this meeting, Diego wrote a letter to the Social Studies Department, thanking them for the invitation to the meeting but expressing his resentment "for being dragged into your department problems that concern your department members and not us as students."

The "Unity Mural" Project

One of MEChA's primary endeavors to build mutual understanding and respect on campus was to sponsor the creation of a "Unity Mural." The mural, approved by the administration soon after the walkouts, was to be painted on the outer wall of the school gymnasium under the coordination of a locally renowned Latino muralist. The theme and content of the mural were to be collectively agreed on by an advisory committee made up of AHS students and teachers. Sandoval, as MEChA's advisor, took a leadership role in overseeing the mural. He assured those skeptical of the project that the group would not produce a "Chicano," "racial," or "politically correct" mural; instead they would design an inclusive, "humanly correct mural which will embrace ALL who study, work, and dream of making this campus in Allenstown a better place." The mural committee was made up of a small group of teachers (including one who donated $1,000 of her own money to the cause) and a deliberately chosen group of both White and Latino students. Working with the muralist, the students on the committee designed a provisional sketch that included four ethnically and racially distinctive characters crossing the ocean in a boat. The figures were of an Aztec warrior, an African goddess, an ancient Greek, and a Chinese woman, each donning a "folkloric" wardrobe. The story behind the images was one of travelers embarking on a transformative journey from a condemned, divisive "old world" to a new land of harmony and unity. The "new land" was represented as the bountiful Pleasanton Valley, replete with images of agricultural cultivation and the like. The boat was given the name *Xantlot*, an Aztec word meaning "coming together." Sandoval had agreed to help develop a story for the mural that would link the wayward travelers to Chinese, Greek, African, and Aztec mythologies.

When the sketch of the mural was made public, it created immediate controversy. Several school staff and Allenstown parents saw the imagery as too exclusively Latino, lacking proper representative of either White students or the larger Allenstown community in general. Others condemned the strange inclusion of a "skateboarder flying over the boat from the land of discontent," an image, it seems, that was added later under pressure to make the mural more inclusive. Yet others opposed the design for its emphasis on "an Aztec style" that they felt would only exacerbate racial polarization on the campus; they argued, instead, that symbols of race and culture should be deemphasized. A former ASB student offered her feelings about what was likely behind the resistance of some in Allenstown:

> I think it was threatening to people. Because they had these powerful images of Chicano students, and they wanted these

> powerful images of Chicano students up on this mural. This really kind of like raised Chicano culture and lifestyle. And I don't think people were comfortable with that, because they had never seen that before.

Yet people in the area *had* seen this kind of mural before; they existed in the majority of schools in Farmingville. These large murals—with their "ethnic" symbols, their political and cultural representations of Mexican history, and their powerful images of Latinos—were seen as typically a Farmingville thing, not an Allenstown thing. The proposed mural not only failed to present strong images of the White community in Allenstown, but it seemed to have very little to do with Allenstown. Furthermore, the mural's Latino iconography was seen by some to constitute a sort of symbolic "invasion" of the high school. A district administrator at the time offered this interpretation:

> I think a mural was considered too controversial. There was a sense that, for some faction in the Allenstown community, "we are not going to do one of *those* murals here, we don't want one of *those* murals on our campus." . . . My guess is that there was pressure on the administration at that point to not do it. Maybe somehow with all the other activities going on, that would be viewed as something that would just heighten them up again.

A teacher centrally involved in the mural project provided another perspective on the controversy, and her narrative highlights the fact that the "real" battle over the mural seemed to have more to do with contesting interest groups within and outside the school than the actual merit of the project itself:

> T: We had a group of teachers—Luis and his group—who were really pushing to see some changes and meet some of the demands that the students were making. And then there were the teachers and part of the community that did not want to see it happen, such as the mural. And so these parents stomped around . . . they saw the mural as divisive. . . . And other teachers did, too. And Luis worked his tail off. He created the stories and he thought it would be good to teach the stories . . . I went to meetings about that, and we looked

at drawings and tried to involve students here. Then finally, some of the very vocal White parents said "Over my dead body, you're not putting any mural up there."

CH: So what were some of the general contentions they had? Was it the Aztec symbols? How did they justify their dislike of it?

T: It was veiled. All their comments were veiled. They said putting that up right now during [Proposition] 187, and all this upheaval at our school, was something that will further divide the school. But my feeling was that they really thought: "This ain't going in our White school."

What further generated resistance to the mural was the fact that it was being overseen by Sandoval. Given his role in questioning Stevenson's leadership, his support of Diego and the MEChA group, and his emerging communication with MPAC—some of whom were voicing a growing distrust and dislike for the principal—Sandoval was increasingly perceived by the principal and his supporters as having his "own agenda" and the interest of Latino students—rather than all of Allenstown High—at heart. When, in May, Sandoval claimed that the majority of AHS staff had voted in support of the proposed mural design, Stevenson demanded to see the ballots as well as a list of the students who were still involved in the project, claiming he had "heard rumors that most, if not all of the students had dropped out of the process some time ago." He also accused Sandoval of dismissing recommendations for changes that had been submitted by some AHS staff. Making things worse, ASB advisor Simmons, who had initially given his backing to the project, changed his mind after seeing the sketch and withdrew his support.

As the end of the school year neared, the mural project had all but died out. Despite the energy and enthusiasm that had been invested in the project, a host of factors eventually killed it. Among them were Sandoval's increasing alienation, the growing anger about Diego's leadership style, an increasing disillusionment and disinterest of students involved in the project, and some Allenstown parents' and community leaders' ambivalence or outright resistance toward the mural design. And, as a former teacher recalled, the district did its best to stay out of the fray:

You can tell when a project isn't moving. And it wasn't moving for many reasons. You need energy, you need administrative help,

> you need district help to make something like that happen. It's like nobody wanted to get their feet wet. And it was like "hands off" because the district had to deal with all these parents over here. They have to accommodate two separate populations. . . . And so people did kind of drop off, and I think [because] they saw that [they] weren't getting the support from higher up. And we started seeing the handwriting on the wall. They had done everything here—the sketches Luis passed out, the sketches faculty and people voted on. It really went through quite a process. And then it was pretty much killed because I think people got afraid and weren't willing to support something that they either didn't quite understand or they didn't like it, period. It was very disappointing because a lot of work had gone into it.

Students Try to Make Sense of the Racial Polarization at the School

Despite the sincere campaigns of ASB and the MEChA club to promote integration and draw attention to issues of racial inequality at the school, a number of AHS students remained ambivalent and uncomfortable about the developments. This sense of discomfort was expressed well in the following editorial from a White male student from Allenstown that appeared in the school newspaper:

> It used to feel good walking down the halls. Now I feel a tension, like everyone's radar is on over-watch, waiting to react to the tiny click of the pin that signals the grenades explosion . . . We've grown hypersensitive to issues of race on campus, and this hypersensitivity is what's coming between us. . . . As it is, efforts to heal the wound only antagonize it further, mainly because they try to make us look unified but do nothing to make us feel unified; we become overly aware of our differences. . . . How can we ever be unified when our differences are always pointed out in the same breath with which we preach unity? . . . The student walkouts for Chicano studies did nothing to help the problem; it made things worse. . . . Unfortunately,

> if you're part of the minority—for instance, someone who doesn't support Chicano studies—you will be judged anti-unity and therefore racist! . . . [Prop. 187 has brought about] an abominable destruction of objective instruction and freedom of speech on campus . . . [because] teachers passed onto students their opinions of Prop. 187, never pointing out the other side of the coin. There was an underground group of people who supported 187 but were afraid—AFRAID—to voice their opinion, for fear of the majority's reaction. This is not true democracy. This is mob rule. Prop. 187 aggravated the issue of race and set into motion the hypersensitivity we face. Now we are afraid to be ourselves.

According to this student, it was those "hypersensitive" about issues of race who were responsible for further antagonizing the conditions of polarization that divided the campus. In his view, "racist" was being applied to anyone anxious about integration or uneasy with the agenda for integration that students were spearheading. Reacting to the way that the significance of race seemed to be overdetermined in the school, the author saw anti-Proposition 187 rhetoric as a kind of "political correctness" masquerading as a form of thought control. At the same time, he grieved that there seemed to be no neutral language or any safe place from which to debate both sides of the issues surrounding the proposition. While admitting that the school lacked spaces to discuss these issues, he tended to cast blame on those students who continue to "make a big deal" about race issues. He was unable to imagine any way in which "we can ever be unified when our differences are always pointed out in the same breath that we preach unity."

This student's inability to imagine a kind of unity that values diversity and respects and engages difference, further illustrates the negative impact of the lack of a broad and reasonable discussion about what multiculturalism means and what it might offer within the school. Inclusive, schoolwide discussions of this kind might have been able to engage the stereotypes and notions of social and redistributive justice informing people's stands on the propositions. As well, they might have enlightened students about the multiple relations of power, privilege, and interest that serve to create, maintain, and reproduce differences along racial lines. Moreover, fostering these sorts of discussions might have helped elucidate the origin and continuing existence of the social conditions at Allenstown High that prompted Latino student activism in the first place.

Diego's Undoing

As the school year went on, Diego became increasingly isolated within the school due to the rising backlash he faced for his aggressive campaigns for change and for his public questioning of administrative leadership. His dual roles as president of ASB and MEChA had proved difficult to reconcile given the divisive environment at AHS. He had lost most of his allies among the administration and faculty—except perhaps Sandoval who was himself consumed by his own conflicts with the administration and, increasingly, within his own department. The pressure and hostility building up on Diego—to which he responded with an increasingly defensive and unapologetic posture—began to impinge on his ability to maintain an inclusive leadership style in the student government. As a fellow ASB representative explained:

> Diego did some good work as president in the beginning and along the way. As time when on, though, he became worse at running the meetings. He went from going around the room and seeing that everyone could speak, to speaking his mind and not letting others share their opinions. Students would come up to me after class and say, "I had something to say but never had a chance to say it."

As things began to unravel in the second semester, ASB advisor Simmons explained to me that he was committed to doing what was necessary to "get control back" from Diego because he "would not yield the gavel [and] would not be conciliatory." In early May, Diego was accused of pulling a fire alarm on campus. Although his culpability was never confirmed, the incident—along with a burgeoning resentment of Diego's uncompromising political strategies like that of "demanding" Chicano Studies—led to a direct questioning of his competence as a student leader. Proceedings began within the ASB to remove Diego from his position as president. Simmons recalled the impeachment process:

> The impeachment vote was to determine if students in ASB felt he was worthy to have in this office. You are accusing him not necessarily of pulling the alarm, but of creating an atmosphere where he is no longer going to be a capable leader. . . . And the vote had to go to the Student Senate. You [ASB] are only choosing for the Senate to vote on it, which was seen as necessary to clear the air and go on by having a full hearing at the Senate, [and the ASB vote was] pretty much unanimous. Now, there were people who believed he should stay on as President, but they also believe that his case should be heard by the Senate. Their vote to impeach was not to get rid of him, but to clear the air . . . Then the senate voted to get rid of Diego. . . . They voted for a replacement, and they picked Rebecca Sanchez. That is how the year ended.

Over the course of the school year, there was a growing split between the virtue of what Diego was trying to do and the way his actions were being received and interpreted in the school and the larger Allenstown community. In a few months, he had gone from the status of bold leader to that of deviant "gangster."[4] Diego's behaviors were increasingly fit into a negative stereotype of the Chicano activist—an anti-authoritarian, militant, "rabble-rouser" not concerned with academics—reflecting a common-sense misconception about the behavior of Mexican male youth in general. What remains unaddressed in these sorts of characterizations is an attempt to understand *why* Diego challenged the administration in the uncompromising way that he did, or why he might have refused at times to go through the "proper channels" to pursue reform at the school. His efforts, however imperfectly pursued, sought to transform public memory and heighten the political agency of his Latinos peers in a way that might empower them to invest in restructuring the organization and culture of the school. At the same time, Diego was committed to addressing the political dimensions of how power, resources, and opportunities were negotiated at the school, believing that in all such negotiations, a high value ought to be given to promoting justice and fairness for Latino students. His campaign of direct action demonstrated his unwillingness to postpone progressive and seemingly reasonable demands for things like a "Unity Mural" and a class in Chicano Studies.

Unfortunately, Diego's strategies for bringing about social change were viewed by others as requiring an unworkable expense—that is, a radical alteration of existing schooling organization and practice. In the opinion of one White ASB student at the time, the school just was simply "not ready" for Diego and his political rhetoric of "Chicano" empowerment. However, this same student also believed that the inability of many other students to accept or even engage with Diego's ideas had perhaps more to do with the lack of dialogue within the school than the "radical" nature of his beliefs:

> Part of [Diego's] rhetoric was, really, part of the Brown Pride movement. Taken straight from the 1960s and 1970s dialogue: "take back, this is our land," that kind of thing. Which I am not—I totally see where that comes from and I'm not even disagreeing with it, but I don't think our school was ready for that kind of dialogue. Because there was never any meaningful dialogue outside of ASB or outside of MEChA to educate other students on it. Because other teachers avoided it and never talked about it. And I still think you see that a lot in high schools. You don't talk about race that much.

The reactionary anger of some school staff and parents, and the foot-dragging on controversial issues like Chicano Studies, would have required Diego to take a more compromising, "slow change" approach that—given his conflicting loyalties, the hostile school environment, and his strained relationship with key school staff—he was unwilling or perhaps personally unable to take. However, the interest in my analysis is not to dwell on the psychology of Diego, largely because the unrest at Allenstown High has been portrayed in the popular press, and in the minds of many I spoke with, as the "Diego Omán story"—the story of the radical who went too far and ruined something good that might have happened at the school. Such a simplistic rendering of complex events provides a convenient scapegoat that avoids having to engage with the dimensions of shared responsibility. A district administrator I interviewed put it this way:

> Diego was set up in a very, very difficult situation, and then he "acted out" in some way or another, and all of that has its varying degrees of authenticity and accuracy. But it wouldn't surprise me, given the hostile environment in which he became the target for people's hostility. Instead of me taking any responsibility for my role in it, I target people, which is a common experience in our culture. And then if I can demonize the target, then I can justify doing

> anything. And the community is already there for it. So that built up—that tension and pressure built up to where Diego blew it. They created enough heat for him to blow up, and they could say "see," and then they went back into denial. That's the way it went. It blew up, they accused him of some wrong-doing—"see, we told you, blah, blah, blah." And then they were able to go back down to the district, [and] the leadership didn't do anything to keep it going. That superintendent moved on. And the other one comes in and starts the whole planning process again.

The focus on Diego as the main problem at AHS enabled the construction of other claims about the roots and sources of troubles at the high school. These claims, when circulated within the larger contexts of school and community, invested Latino militancy and distrust with a particular agency of its own. By not working through the system and by not taking the opportunities available to them, Diego and other Latino students supporting his various campaigns for change were seen as demonstrating behaviors not befitting of proper citizens, resulting in their portrayal as having "bad attitudes" and of exhibiting a disinterest in academics. In this sense, Latino activism and anger were reduced to a moral issue—Latino students, in their campaigns of direct action, demonstrated a moral deficiency in their unwillingness to pursue the proper course of action required of good students and citizens. The case of Diego became the perfect example for why critical multicultural education does not work—all students must be willing to "work through the system" to create change, otherwise they serve only to exacerbate the problems.

Institutional Co-optation and Breach of the Latino Partnership

While it is reasonable to believe that Diego received unjust treatment by some school administrators and teachers, his own uncompromising and unapologetic politics—though providing a sense of inclusion for some Latino students—promoted a sense of exclusion for others, alienating real and potential allies among both Latino and White students. As time went on, for example, Rebecca Sanchez—Diego's partner in both MEChA and the ASB—was forced to confront how Diego's behavior was being interpreted by other school staff and students. Diego had begun to embody a stigmatized definition of "Chicano" from which she wished to distance herself, not simply because of what others thought, but because his uncompromising politics were at odds with her willingness to maintain dialogues with the other factions and authorities within the school. As a result, Rebecca felt compelled to reposition herself more favorably against the growing backlash and souring representation of the Latino leadership as characterized in the actions and rhetoric of Diego and his supporters. This meant, at one point, distancing herself from the MEChA club that she had helped create. As she explained:

> I know that it got to the point for me that MEChA had become too radical for Allenstown High, had become too radical for me—for who I was. Because I ran under a different platform. I didn't run under a MEChA/Chicana platform, although they did sponsor us, or whatever. But you know my whole thing was that now we were going against that . . . I think when it initially got started, we had a lot of support from people. And when it started becoming radical we had lost the whole purpose of everything, so people didn't believe in us anymore. And it happened with Latino students, it happened with Anglo students, and we were getting criticized. And MEChA had become a really negative thing when it had started off to be something really good for the Latino students and for the campus as a whole.

Diego and Rebecca's increasingly divergent ideas about how to transform the social environment at Allenstown High became clearest in their differing approaches to the campaign for Chicano Studies. Although both were committed to seeing a course instituted at the high school, Rebecca felt that—given their privileged positions as student leaders and the particularities of the environment at Allenstown High—walking out was no longer a necessary, nor a particularly effective strategy for bringing about change:

> [In the walkout for Chicano Studies] I remember Diego coming up to me that morning and telling me: "We're walking out." And he looked at me and *told* me we are walking out. He didn't ask me. And I thought, No we are not. We are officers now. You and I can do things. We can sit down and talk. We don't have to walk out anymore. We walked out because we didn't have any decision-

> making power. We weren't really anyone at Allenstown High. No one really knew us. But people know us now. . . . And my whole thing was that there are other ways of resolving things, of dealing with things. [Prop.] 187 was really, really big. And I think people needed to walk out, because we needed some activism. But I didn't want to be walking out for every single thing that came up. And I didn't want people to think that that's how we were going to address everything—that Latino students were just going to walk out every time something happened. . . . My whole concern was that people had already been talking, "Oh, they walked out because they didn't want to go to school." And so I thought: let's not do it again. And I told him, Let's do a rally, whatever you want to do, but let's not miss school for this. And he had another thing [already planned].

This difference of opinion reflected a growing separation between the two that turned bitter when impeachment proceedings began within the ASB. Rebecca recalls that when Diego was removed from office, he expected her to step down with him:

> When Diego got impeached, the constitution states that the Vice President takes over. And so I took over. There was this whole voting process, and I ended up becoming president. He didn't like the fact that I had accepted the presidency after he had left. Because we were united—you know, us, because of MEChA. And he thought that I should step down because, you know, in the name of MEChA . . . And I thought, No, this is my chance to do what I've dreamed to do at Allenstown High. And I had a lot of people supporting me. I mean I'm really—I know some people stereotyped me because I was in MEChA, and because I was Diego's friend and they probably thought, Oh no, it's going to be the same story all over again. But I think I did a very good job of not being what they thought I was going to be.

Replacing Diego as the leader of the ASB, Rebecca found herself embraced by the school staff as well as the more enfranchised students on campus because of what they perceived to be her much more moderate approach. Yet her choice not to stand by Diego—along with the way she fell into the favor of more enfranchised White students, staff, and the larger Allenstown community—positioned her unfavorably in the eyes of some of the more disenfranchised Latino students who had supported Diego. They saw her as being coopted in a conscious campaign by the AHS administration to further isolate Diego and to undermine his campaign to secure rights for Latino students on the campus. In this sense, Rebecca's enfranchisement and success was viewed as a "selling out" and a betrayal of her *Raza*, an accusation that she says still haunts her to this day:

> I have had Latino students say that to me, who call me a "sell out." And say that I had been turning White because I was ASB president, because I had White friends. Because I eventually started to know a lot of people and some of my very good friends were White people. Because I got to know them, and they were people I could relate to. It had nothing to do with the color of their skin. And it started to become that there was a group of students who thought the people in ASB that were Latinos were there because they were "whitewashed." Which I didn't understand because I thought, here we are trying to do all this stuff for you and for everybody else. Here we are doing Cinco de Mayo and Dieciséis de Septiembre, representing your culture and you're calling us sellouts! And I went through it. I had people tell me that I had turned white.

Here, Rebecca's willingness to lead the ASB after Diego's fall was viewed by some of her Mexican-descent peers as acculturating to dominant, Anglo norms of language and behavior.[5] Such questioning of her racial authenticity and loyalty to her Mexican heritage perplexed Rebecca because she did not believe she had assimilated—as some do—to an "American" status by way of "leaving culture at the door" and disowning their "Mexicana" heritage. Nevertheless, these accusations made her take a long, hard look at herself:

> I remember one of the first times I heard it, I thought—I kind of checked myself again. You kind of check yourself and think, Wait, am I really turning White? And I thought, No, I'm doing this for the right reasons and no one really knows me from inside and what I feel inside when I do this kind of stuff. I am one of the most cultural people you will ever meet. I am really into my language, and into my background. And I felt like I didn't have to justify it to

anyone, I didn't have to prove that to anyone. . . . So at first of course it hurt me. Because they were talking about something that was really dear to me—culture. It's a thing that I don't ever want to lose, that I am really worried about losing. Because I think that eventually my kids might lose it or their kids might lose it and it really becomes a fear. And so I kind of just ignored it.

Though she ignored the accusations, she did not dismiss them outright. She tried to empathize with her peers, understanding that despite differences of opinion, maybe they shared the same fear:

> I really tried to—I'm the kind of person who really tries to understand people instead of judging them and saying, Oh, they're dumb or whatever. And I felt like, Why would they do this to me? Why would they? And I think maybe it is fear that we are losing our culture. And maybe they saw me being involved and mingling with White people, and they weren't, and so they thought: "That is a White person. She must be White." And maybe it does become a fear that your people are losing their culture. And so that kind of makes you mad and defensive.

The rift that grew between Diego and Rebecca—and the accusation of betrayal that Rebecca eventually faced—highlight the ongoing struggle within the Latino community in Pleasanton Valley over political and cultural loyalties, between an Americanized model based on Euro-American cultural practices and norms of behavior and the desire to be considered "authentically" Mexican. In this case, the negotiation over loyalties, and the labels used to mark them, were central to how students positioned themselves to one another as well as how they oriented themselves to schooling activities. Yet the accusations of "acting White" that befell Rebecca for her decision to remain involved in school leadership are not an inevitable byproduct of the encounter between White and Mexican-descent youth. Nor should the phenomenon be viewed as one that derives from "Mexican culture"; instead, censorship against "acting white" must be understood in relation to a host of local factors, including the local conditions of segregation within school and community, the severity of socioeconomic inequalities between White and Mexican-descent residents, the leadership opportunities available for Mexican-descent youth in the school, and the relative awareness of school staff about the larger political issues that informed Latino student and community activism. In other words, it depends a great deal on the community and school context. Moreover, "acting White" is a phenomenon more likely to manifest itself in subtractive schooling environments (Valenzuela 1999) where expectations that students divest in their "Mexican" cultural and linguistic heritage are high, and where practices, structures, and discourses of exclusion are widespread.

What Diego and Rebecca *shared* in their divergent political strategies was a common desire to see the extension of rights of first-class citizenship to Latino youth in a schooling and larger community context that "relegates cultural group members to static and disparaged ethnic, racial, gender, and class identities" (Zentella 1997: 36). Perhaps Rebecca's decision to part with Diego should be understood less as a move toward whiteness than as a desire to avoid a more exclusivist [masculine] "Chicano" rhetoric that tended—and has tended historically—to marginalize diverse and dissenting voices and to limit conversation about the possibilities of pursuing progressive change.[6]

Looking Back

An AHS teacher commented insightfully to me that the 1994–1995 school year at Allenstown High was "an aberration in very positive ways. It actually gave kids an opportunity to come together in ways that they hadn't come together before." She continued:

> At first, it was, YEAH! 187 has happened and things are unhappy and let's fix it. Pretty soon it was, I don't want to fix it, I'm going to go to my own camp, and you to your own camp. For different reasons.

Certainly, things could have happened differently. The situation seemed to turn into a "problem" when the AHS administration initially proved unable to pull in the new Latino leaders such as Diego, Rebecca, and their supporters. Without the ability to communicate with the frustrated Latino students, and unable to see the conflict as an educable moment, the principal demonstrated neither the skills nor the vision to defuse the situation. In the end, the administration never bought into students' vision of what they wanted. Lacking such "buy-in," the campaign had little chance of success. Making things worse was that the principal—rather than setting out to guide and encourage the new student leadership—chose to eye the new Latino president with suspicion, subjecting him to interrogation and intimidation. Another significant obstacle for the new Latino leadership was a lack of allies among school staff from the very beginning. The handful of AHS staff willing to advocate for these students and to support some of their demands faced campaigns of marginalization and demonization for their involvement in the students' activism. This was particularly true for Luis Sandoval. A former student from his AP History class explained the extent of Sandoval's isolation at the time:

> Mr. Sandoval really had very few allies within the school. Nobody. He had so few allies or other teachers that wanted to work with him and say like, "What you are doing is cool, you are really trying to help the Latino students at our campus feel more involved in the school and give them a voice." Nobody was really there to support him . . . I'm pretty sure that most teachers wanted to stay out of it. They wanted to stay out of it because they didn't want to get involved in this controversy. And when I think about it, if more teachers would have supported what Mr. Sandoval was trying to do, then things probably would have turned out differently. Because if you are the only one wanting to do it—you know. So now that I look back on that, I feel bad for him that he never had that.

As Sandoval got caught up in the divisive politics of distrust that developed in the school—over MEChA, between MEChA and the ASB, over the school newspaper censorship, Stevenson's leadership, and the mural—some of the students who had originally felt empowered by Sandoval to transform the school environment began to resent being increasingly drawn into the larger battles among administrators, teachers, and parents. As one of these former students related to me, "I think initially the students who felt very empowered, by the end of it were starting to feel like, This is not our show." According to some students, Sandoval's personal entanglement with other school staff eventually translated back into his classroom in unconstructive ways, particularly in his AP History class:

> We started calling our AP history class "AP MEChA" because basically what he [Sandoval] would do, starting in November when

> the whole everything really started happening, all he would do is come to class and talk to us about what was happening in MEChA and all the trouble the administration was giving him, and the harassment he was getting from other teachers, and the harassment Diego and Rebecca were getting, and all we talked about was that stuff. So basically, the students in the class started calling it AP MEChA. And at times we were like, "Oh, we don't have to do work." But hardly any of us passed the AP class at the end of the year. There was resentment.

Nevertheless, another student from that AP History class who—like Rebecca—has recently entered a Master's degree program in education at a prestigious university, admitted that she remained thankful for the conversations that were allowed to take place in Sandoval's classroom. She saw these conversations as significantly impacting her life direction, whether or not the class had ultimately helped her prepare for a test:

> Now I think back about it, I could care less that I didn't pass the AP History test. It really has had little meaning in my life. And the kind of dialogue—even though at the time it didn't seem meaningful, now when I look back on it, I'm like, that was probably more meaningful for us to talk about race, to talk about the politics of what was happening at our high school, and having us start to think about it critically, than [being taught for] the test.

Conclusion

In recounting the mid-1990s controversy at Allenstown High, I have tried to complicate the popular portrayal of the unrest as various versions of the "The Diego Omán Story." Clearly, the leadership choices the ASB president made played a role in how events played out at the school. However, in important ways, Diego became the target/object of blame for the unrest at the school in a way that drew attention from the way the environment at the high school had historically been unwelcoming for Latino students from Farmingville. With Diego as the target, the need for the AHS administration to consider how schooling practices, structures, and ways of socially organizing students might be contributing to these unwelcoming conditions was minimized. An interesting question is whether any sort of empowerment of Latino students could have happened without someone like Diego willing to take a strong and uncompromising stand against the treatment of Latinos at the school and not be coopted into a "slow change" approach to school reform and transformation. History in the area has shown that significant transformation of the status quo of schooling relations to more equally serve minority students has required individuals or groups to speak up—regardless of being positioned as the "real problem"—to assert claims of rights and entitlements and to petition outside support to assure that such changes are instituted. History has also shown that it is rarely the case that the "demands" emanating from the Latino community are, in fact, unfair or concessionary; they are often demands for rights already guaranteed by law but that have long been resisted, overlooked, or insincerely committed to. Unfortunately, Latino demands that do acquire acceptance, sometimes with help or the mandate of a higher authority, often do so without significant support among middle-class Whites in the local community, meaning that changes are often tentative, short-lived, or highly conditional, and sometimes eventually revoked or ignored.

There is a great deal of rhetoric and "lip service" given to efforts pushing "multicultural education" and "education for diversity." Yet the way in which educational institutions claim to support equality and diversity while cultivating little (or no) space for discussion about how dynamics of inequality are established—even within their own confines—risk naturalizing the exclusions that some students feel, and are perhaps *made* to feel, in that context. I argue that this was the case—and to some extent remains the case—at Allenstown High, and it was an important reason why the events following Proposition 187 took the unfortunate course that they did. The further implications of this lack of open discussion are considered in the following chapter, where I look at the contemporary conditions at the high school and explore the extent to which it has improved the services and opportunities it provides for Mexican-descent students to participate as equals in schooling activities.

CHAPTER 4

The Road from Dissent to Secession

Constructing White Victimhood and the "Problem" of Mexicans in Farmingville

The Proposition 187-inspired student walkouts across Pleasanton Valley schools precipitated a series of negative responses from citizens in both Farmingville and Allenstown. Included was an animation of latent anger among some White residents in Farmingville who expressed, publicly and in no uncertain terms, their resentment of the growing Mexican-descent population in the region. In a series of local newspaper editorials, long-time Farmingville residents—positioning themselves as "taxpaying citizens"—spoke of being "fed up" with the "intolerable" behavior of "questionable citizens." They instructed dissatisfied Mexican immigrant youth and their families to "go back to Mexico and fight for reforms in your own country." They also chided school and law enforcement officials for not "nipping this illegal march in the bud." The citizen narratives presented an elaborate discourse about the nature and danger of the "illegal alien," as exemplified in the following excerpt from an editorial in the *Farmingville Register*:

> Proposition 187 will sever the umbilical cord to a myriad of FREE social services and jobs, leaving little incentive for freeloading, sneak-in bandits to muscle their way across our borders. It will curtail fraud and theft by illegal aliens who sweep through the system scooping up our tax dollars with the equivalent efficiency of a flea comb. . . . In short, why should we be their scapegoat?

Here, the term "illegal alien" refers not simply to a working resident without legal citizenship but to a deviant and demonizable Other who, it is assumed, is unwilling to pay taxes or abide by laws—in other words, a criminal free-loader who has "reaped the benefit of free education, medical care, and housing and food assistance." This construction of "the illegal" provides a benevolent us (U.S. citizens) versus a threatening them (undocumented worker) dichotomy in which the Mexican-descent worker becomes the primary culprit for the socioeconomic and moral ills plaguing the region and state. This inversion of "playing the victim" represents the (White) American worker as vulnerable and potentially violable, and endorses a defensive "taking up of arms" against a dangerous and illegitimate alien presence.

Some of the most outspoken residents faced accusations of "racism" for expressing their feelings about the dangerousness of the immigrant presence. Many remained unrepentant, however, claiming it was precisely Whites' fear of being perceived as racist that had historically deterred civic action that could have prevented Mexicans from "ruining" the valley in the first place. As one Farmingville resident wrote:

> The city of Farmingville [has been] held to its knees by the Mexican population, legal and illegal. Everyone is afraid to speak out for fear of being called a racist, and we all sit on our cans and watch this happen. . . . Farmingville has become a city of illegals, gangs, shootings, rampant drug dealing, and young Mexicans driving expensive cars that you can't buy working at McDonald's. Wake up.

Here, fearful constructions of Mexican "otherness" are linked to rising levels of criminality and utilized to justify a denial of basic rights and services to undocumented immigrants. Yet as George Lipsitz (1998) has pointed out, such a rhetoric of aggressive scapegoating obscures, whether as a matter of ignorance or convenience, a host of associated factors that have stimulated the inflow of undocumented workers to the Southwest and have produced the economic recessions that historically fueled anti-immigrant sentiment. These factors include the role of corporate capital in aiding the process of "illegal" immigration, the assaults on regional labor through anti-union activities and corporate "outsourcing" (as explored in Chapter 2), the historical willingness of local businesses and private individuals to hire immigrant workers at low wages, and the reality that corporate welfare constitutes as significant a drain on federal tax dollars as the relatively meager social services made available for undocumented workers. As well, the representation of undocumented immigrants as criminally dangerous overlooks the reality that immigrants' tenuous situation and fear of deportation makes them among the least likely of U.S. residents to participate in criminal activity. As border crossers, many undocumented immigrants are much more at risk of being the victim of crimes (e.g., by border police) or of harassment (sometimes violent) by U.S. citizens with anti-immigrant biases (Rosaldo 1994).

The "Mexican Problem" at Allenstown High

While discourses about the dangerousness of "illegal aliens" influenced some Allenstown residents' interpretations of the conflicts at AHS, a more concrete set of factors fueled assessments that the social unrest at the school was really a "Mexican problem." Rebecca Sanchez recalled the accusations she heard from Allenstown parents:

> I could tell that the parents started becoming really scared of what might happen at Allenstown High. I went to school board meetings, and I left there *so* furious. Because they [some Allenstown parents] had said stuff that I know was not true. They had said that Allenstown High was low on test scores because of all the Mexican students that were there, and that we created all the conflicts at Allenstown High. That there were fights and gangsters because of all the Latinos there.

Among the claims of the fearful Allenstown parents was that juvenile crime has risen sharply in area since the late 1980s, which they attributed directly to the bused-in arrival of Farmingville's Latino youth. County law enforcement officials were quick to dispel this myth, however, pointing out that while juvenile crime had indeed risen in the area, "the crimes occurring in Allenstown are being committed by young adults and juveniles who live in Allenstown," not by Latino youth from Farmingville. A second factor inflaming negative stereotypes of Farmingville Mexican-descent youth at Allenstown High were recurring incidents of "gang-related" activity—including posturing and fighting—at the school. Allenstown parents were centrally concerned about the safety of their children, fearing that they might become targets of gang activity or get "caught in the crossfire."

Gang activity had, in fact, increased in the Farmingville area. This was due in significant part, however, to forces originating from outside of Farmingville's Latino community. The economic meltdown that Farmingville faced in the mid-1980s as a consequence of corporate capital's migration south to Mexico (specifically, the relocation of the frozen fruit and canning industries) and the loss of labor union strength precipitated an intensifying poverty that created a fertile environment for increased gang activity. At the same time, the deepening social inequality in the area—the growth of a wealthy enclave next to what was quickly becoming a semirural "ghetto"—contributed as well. The inability of some youth to reconcile a discourse of democracy and equality with an everyday experience of extreme poverty pushed them toward alternative strategies for establishing integrity, status, power, and means of financial remuneration.[1] Perhaps most important of all, increased gang activity must be seen in relation to the failure of area schools to serve the educational needs of large numbers of Mexican-descent students. The lack or inconsistency of resources and programs to address the needs of English language learners, the lack of qualified teachers who understood the children's language and valued their cultural experience, and conditions of extreme overcrowding in Farmingville area schools all contributed to "push-out" rates where only about one-third of the Mexican-descent youth enrolled in district schools graduated from high school.

Nevertheless, Allenstown parents' fears about the criminality of Latino youth were enhanced further by popular characterizations of Allenstown High's student body president, Diego Omán, as a "rabble rouser" with a "gimme-gimme" attitude—of the same kind, it was assumed, that had "ruined" Farmingville. Diego was seen as responsible for exacerbating racial polarization at the school and undermining thoughtful attempts by administrators and other students to mitigate the social polarization on the campus. Moreover, the fact that Diego seemed to be a respected leader among his peers suggested a more broad-based deviance of Latino youth rather than one limited to just its most marginal (gang) members.

Finally, the perception among Allenstown parents that the Latino students were the "real problem" at the high school was perpetuated by the relative academic attainment of Latino students at the school, demonstrated in their lower score averages on standardized tests and their perceived language "disabilities," including a lack of English fluency and the use of code-switching varieties ("Spanglish"). Some Allenstown parents felt Farmingville Latino youth presence in classes promoted a less challenging curriculum and was bringing down the quality of education available to the generally higher-achieving, English-speaking students in Allenstown. That a number of these same students were "walking out" of classes to oppose Proposition 187 instead of "hitting the books" perplexed and angered many Allenstown residents.

Mexican Migrant Parents' React to the Crisis at Allenstown High

Latino parent groups were compelled to enter the political fray at AHS soon after the principal's controversial meeting with newly elected ASB president Diego Omán. Latino representatives from two district-wide parent organizations—the district's Bilingual Advisory Committee and the Migrant Parent Advisory Committee (MPAC)—submitted a co-signed letter to the PVUSD school board in which they admonished the AHS administration for its failure on several fronts. They criticized the school leadership for their failure to support multicultural projects like the "Unity Mural" and a Chicano Studies course, their lack of initiative in providing multicultural in-service training and workshops for school staff, the harassment of students and teachers by school administrators, the alleged censorship of the school newspaper, the misappropriation of state desegregation funds, and the lack of bilingual information at "back to school" night—among other claims. The parent representatives also reminded district officials of the more enduring, structural obstacles that limited Latino students' equal access to quality education at the school, including the lack of bilingual and bicultural administrators. In 1995, when 45 percent of the approximately 1,800 students were Latino, only one full-time administrator was proficiently bilingual and she was White, not Latina.

"We have to acknowledge our children's alienation on the Allenstown campus," read the letter. "Integration through busing has not worked in light of an administration and staff that has not made the campus a welcome place to go." Demanding accountability, the parents requested that the school board schedule a public hearing for all parents' complaints to be heard. Principal Stevenson was "deeply offended" by the parents' letter and produced a rescinding communication in which he acknowledged the existence of some problems at the school—including a qualified recognition of the troubles with the "school culture"—but distanced himself and his school administration from most of the allegations. He argued that the problems were largely structural and outside the school's control, a consequence of "pay reductions, layoffs, anemic book and supply budgets, and a host of other negative factors." In addition, he deflected claims of alleged discrimination, including the failure to provide support for Latino students, and he vehemently rejected the idea that integration "has not worked" at AHS. He claimed, to the contrary, that the school "continue[d] to offer one of the finest educational programs in the county."

Paradoxically, the letter from Latino parents provided additional fodder for those who saw Farmingville Latinos as the "real problem" at Allenstown High. Here, Latino parents—rather than bringing their concerns directly to the school administration—chose to undermine school leaders by taking their complaints directly to the school board and the press. Like Diego and his supporters at Allenstown High, Latino parents refused to "go through the proper channels" to express their concerns about the school, thereby exacerbating the problems rather than helping to resolve them. This "divisive" strategy added to existing misgivings among some Allenstown parents and school officials who resented the Latino parents' more systematic failure to participate in organizations like the Booster Club and the School Site Council.

Although the Latino parents' letter was highly critical of Stevenson's leadership at the school, the point was made that "what is wrong cannot be blamed on one individual. Rather it is the state of mind that permeates the school." This "state of mind," they argued, found its origin not ultimately in Stevenson's prejudices but in the pressures being applied from parents and political leaders in the Allenstown community. One former student mused, "Principal Stevenson was a little puppet who the [Allenstown] parents controlled." Rebecca Sanchez characterized the principal in the following way:

> Stevenson wasn't a very good principal. He was very good about coming out and saying Hi, but when you really needed his support, he didn't know how to direct that because he had a lot of pressure. You need to understand that we are in Allenstown where parents don't really like the idea of Latino students being bused in. And then, being bused in and holding a political office? And then walking out? It just didn't look very good to them.

Stevenson's reputation in the Allenstown community was solid. His supporters viewed him not only as an educational leader but "one who sees a responsibility to the community." During his four-year tenure as principal, he was successful in soliciting support from a range of influential civic and business leaders, and was able to facilitate a variety of partnerships and alliances between the high school, local businesses, and law enforcement. This commitment assured him a core of loyal supporters among business, real estate, and chamber of commerce leaders who were active in, and centrally concerned about, schooling politics in Allenstown.

These supporters came to Stevenson's defense immediately after the release of the Latino parents representatives' letter. Editorials ran in the major regional newspapers attempting to rescue Stevenson from character assassination and allegations about his lack of professionalism. The stories highlighted commentaries from upstanding Allenstown community leaders and from AHS staff who dismissed charges of racism as "groundless," arguing that Stevenson had "gotten a bad rap," and that perhaps he had been "targeted unfairly by critics and some people carrying a political vendetta." In this vendetta scenario, Stevenson was the victim of a mean-spirited political campaign spearheaded by a group of Latino community leaders, parents, students, and their White allies.

The Origins of Allenstown School Secession: The 1995 Parent Meetings

Moved by growing expressions of anger, fear, and distrust among and between White and Latino parents, the PVUSD school board scheduled a series of private parent meetings that began early in 1995. The purpose of the gatherings was to provide a forum to discuss the complaints raised about the principal as well as to address concerns about racial tension, student safety, school support programs, and disciplinary policy at the high school. Four parent advisory organizations that represented diverse voices within both Allenstown and Farmingville were invited to the meetings. Two of the groups—the School Site Council and Booster Club—were predominantly White, middle- to upper-middle class parent groups from Allenstown. The other two groups—the Bilingual Advisory Committee and MPAC—were largely made up of Latino, working-class residents from Farmingville.

The district hired an African American educational consultant, Kenneth Reed, to mediate the sessions. Reed was a respected facilitator with a long history of providing consultation and in-service training on issues of multiculturalism and diversity in the region. Reed envisioned the meetings as a "safe place for parents to share their humanity" and to recognize commonalities in what they desired for their children. His intent was to shepherd a process of mutual exchange characterized by empathy and a willingness to listen to the concerns of others. This, he believed, would cultivate greater understanding between groups and reduce the existing tensions. The success of the meetings, in Reed's words, depended on a spirit of collaboration in which "the leadership of the entire community will provide a message to the children about whether we welcome diversity and value it . . . or we continue a history of dominating and devaluing it."

Concerns of the Migrant Parents

MPAC in Pleasanton Valley was established in 1982 under the federally funded MEP. MPAC was originally commissioned as a district-wide parent advisory committee responsible for providing active oversight of various aspects of the MEP, including the hiring and reassigning of MEP staff, the review of annual budgets, and the appraisal of program goals and program assessment, among other duties.[2] By the early 1990s, however, the Pleasanton Valley MPAC began to assume an increasingly political role in local schooling affairs by establishing itself as one of the primary district-level advocates for educational equity and the educational rights of Latino students. According to a handful of long-time MPAC members I interviewed, the evolution of the group's political consciousness can be traced back to an early 1980s MEP-sponsored program called Literatura Enfantil, based on the liberatory pedagogy of Paulo Freire. Migrant parents' participation in this family-based literacy program helped them develop and clarify their own sense of political consciousness and social justice, which inspired their commitment to serve on MPAC.

MPAC played the role of watchdog organization within the district, and in that capacity, it enjoyed significant legitimacy within the working-class Latino community. It was a group to which Spanish-speaking parents turned *con confiaza* (with trust and confidence) regarding questions or grievances about equity and fairness, or to help resolve issues surrounding student discipline and expulsions. The group also served as an advocate for Latino parents against district or school administrators in cases where it appeared that parents were being manipulated, ignored, or denied access to information they needed to make informed decisions about their children's schooling.

Over time, MPAC established itself as a formidable presence in district meetings as well as in ad hoc meetings with school staff and principals.

Operating as an advocate for educational equity in a district historically resistant to challenges to its status quo, it is without surprise that the group earned the label among some as a "divisive" organization intent on undermining the best efforts of district administrators. This critique of the MPAC surfaced in relation to the group's response to (and, as some critics argued, their *role* in) the unrest at Allenstown High. This condemnation came not just from Allenstown administrators and parents, but from some Latino school administrators who were more enfranchised in district- and school-level decision-making. Carla, a second-generation Mexican immigrant and county-level administrator who lived in Farmingville, and whom I interviewed in 2003 about the mid-1990s parent meetings, viewed MPAC—and its sponsoring organization, MEP—in a negative light:

> You know, Migrant Ed has always been an enigma to me. And this is very, very important. Migrant Ed has always polarized people. And they were very instrumental in polarizing students [in the unrest at AHS]. I work the other way, I work to resolve problems working *with* the system. The Migrant Ed leaders and the parents were always trying to fight the system and work against it. The students who raised hell and got in trouble got that from the leaders of Migrant Ed. I see migrant parents confronting administrators. I see them confronting teachers. But they don't have the skills—they haven't been *taught* the skills to work within the system. The parents are being polarized, they have no skills to work with the system. . . . Until you become a part of the system, you can't do anything to change it. And I see that with Migrant Ed. They are bitching and complaining all the time instead of asking: How can we help you [and] take an active role in making change?

Carla's narrative highlights not only the diverse and sometimes conflicting political philosophies among Latinas/os active in Pleasanton Valley schooling politics, but also the classed assumptions about what constitutes the "proper" skills to be effective and legitimate players within the local educational bureaucracy.

Against Carla's critique, MPAC representatives argued that they had a rather long and foundational history of experience in local schooling affairs, given that many parents had been serving on the committee for more than five years at the time of the parents meetings. Having begun their service on the committee during their children's early years of schooling, the migrant parents had, in fact, developed a fairly comprehensive understanding of district politics as well as the skills necessary—given the local political landscape—to participate resourcefully in the battle for educational equity and reform. Refuting characterizations like those from Carla, MPAC representatives claimed that when they were actually *invited* to take part in committees and decision-making processes, they willingly offered their assistance. In cases where they were *not* invited, or were actively *excluded* from decision-making processes—or when they felt parents were being denied information or receiving it in biased form—they saw their role as watchdog and whistle-blower. As one representative put it, their group was obliged to "identify inequity and complain about it, which may not be pleasant from an administrative point of view."

When MPAC entered the parent meetings in 1995, they did so with a level of skepticism that owed to the history of empty enthusiasm they had experienced within the district and at Allenstown High in particular. Migrant parents' central concern was that, despite eight years of racial "integration" at AHS, Farmingville's Mexican-descent children remained isolated, unwelcomed, and underappreciated on the campus. While denying that they were in any way "behind the student walkouts" at AHS, MPAC members admitted to understanding students' feelings and the reasons for which they were inspired to act. (All MPAC narratives are translated from Spanish.)

> *Miguel*: When we, the parents, supported our children, we didn't support them in going out and marching or protesting. No. We support them when they are trying to express their way of thinking or when the school tries to discipline them. And when we think it's *unjust*, then that's when we come in, because we want all of them to be treated fairly—the same way that other students are treated.
>
> *Antonio*: Parents have never supported the students in movements they do within the school. Rather, the parents ask: "What are the reasons for why they are starting this movement?" and then they [the parents] may support the reasoning. But they [the parents] didn't support the type of movement that they [the students] were doing. The parents have never said "Do it!" nor have they ever

> encouraged them to do this. What makes the students react in this manner is how the administration acted during that time.

MPAC supported student demands for such things as a Chicano Studies course not simply because they wanted their children to "feel proud of their roots" but for broader political and civic reasons as well. Among the reasons was a desire to improve the educational resources available for Spanish-speaking students at the high school and to promote a more inclusive re-visioning of California history. Such a revisioning would position Mexicanos as active history-makers who have contributed to the state's economic, social, and cultural development, rather than as demonized "border crossers" threatening the quality of life of "true Americans": As Antonio, one of a group of seven former-MPAC members I interviewed in 2003, explained:

> When we asked for Chicano studies classes, it was simply a suggestion. But what we really wanted was for the school to carry Spanish-language books so that the students would learn what they were being taught and so that they could do their homework because the library had nothing. So this is how the idea of Chicano studies was first presented. It was just a suggestion. But in reality, the history of California is linked to Mexican history and to the Spaniards, right, even before the Anglos came. So, this isn't about Mexican history; it's California's history. It's about the history of where we are. We aren't trying to invent or bring in a foreign culture. The history developed here, in this place, before the Anglos came. So, we're not going to teach them a foreign culture, it's the culture of *this* place.

The need to promote such a perspective, in which Mexican-descent residents were positioned as active citizens belonging to California and the state as benefiting from their contributions, was particularly important at Allenstown High given popular representations of Mexican immigrants as primarily "alien outsiders" who arrived under questionable circumstances.

Common and Uncommon Ground at the Parent Meetings

The White parent representatives of the AHS Booster Club and School Site Council entered the meetings with a very different set of concerns than those of the migrant parents from Farmingville. Central among them was a fear about the safety of their children, particularly given the rumors of gang activity and what some expressed as the potential for "race riots" at AHS. Safety issues became, in fact, one of the few points of common agreement among White and Latino parents in the first meeting. As mediator Reed explained:

> The first thing every parent wanted was their kid to be safe, because there was this real tension and there was this stuff in the quad. And everyone had their place, it was segregated. It was like a powder keg waited for sparks to ignite it throughout the day.

The need to ensure "quality education" for all children was a second general point of agreement among parents. However, exactly what constituted "quality education"—and how it could best be achieved—were topics of significant debate, and they were imagined very differently by parents from Allenstown and Farmingville. For example, MPAC member Gloria Rocha was centrally concerned about "quality education" as it related to issues of fairness and equality, particularly that the school be *equally welcoming* to all students:

> What should happen so that schooling is equal for everyone is that the students should all receive the same treatment, the same respect, the same preparation in every one of the schools. To teach or educate the teachers so they know how to treat people of different races. . . . Because if this type of rejection towards the children starts from them [the teachers], the children are going to feel it because they're sensitive, and one knows when one is wanted or not. *So we need quality education, but one that is equal for everyone* [emphasis added]. This is what should happen. In any case, we have confidence in our children. We know that their minds are aware of how important it is to be prepared.

While parents from Allenstown were also concerned about issues of fairness, what many saw as an obstacle to "quality education" was the unchallenging classroom environments they felt their children had to endure. Jake Simmons, a White Allenstown parent and a vocal leader in the parent meetings, claimed that two primary factors contributed to the unchallenging classroom environments. One, which he viewed as a district-level issue, was the "ineffective, misguided" curriculum programs like bilingual education and more "applied" academic offerings like the Interactive Math Program (IMP). He believed these programs "pandered to minorities" by maintaining low expectations and thereby providing "a terrible disservice to all children." Simmons's second contention was that bringing children in from Farmingville, who generally tested at lower standardized achievement levels, resulted in a less academically challenging environment for his children. Anticipating challenges that his convictions might be viewed as racially motivated, he pointed out that the unchallenging classes in the district were "not about race" and were "independent of ethnic makeup." He viewed the problem primarily as a class issue. From his perspective, the situation at Allenstown High illustrated the inherent difficulties of maintaining high-quality education with students from a wide range of socioeconomic backgrounds. The problem for him, which was echoed by a larger group of Allenstown parents at the meetings, was that their better academically prepared children were attending classes with (working-class Latino) children of lower "ability levels" and with differing language needs, diluting the quality of education their children were able to receive and that they deserved. Simmons admitted that students of different backgrounds and abilities could work together and still be challenged, but only with "the right curriculum and talented teachers," which he felt the district lacked:

> I want to believe you can have kids from all different backgrounds and have them challenged in a heterogeneous setting. The problem is that it has to be an exceptional teacher. Right now our children are not being challenged in the classroom. They are bored. . . . The teaching quality—with a few wonderful exceptions—is not what it could be.

Considering Simmons's logic against that of migrant parent Rocha (quoted earlier) brings into sharp relief the distinct imaginings of "quality education" and educational justice that emerged from concerns about what was wrong at Allenstown High. Rocha spoke of fairness in terms of an inclusive, culturally sensitive pedagogy that is "equal for everyone." While agreeing in principle that education should be equal for everyone, Simmons believed the "curricular tragedies" and "unique class experiences" ensured that these conditions of equality did not, and could not, exist in the district.

Believing that the Allenstown community had played no particular role in the unfortunate conditions that gripped the district, he felt his children should not be negatively affected by them. In other words, the blame could be placed largely on a district dominated by the concerns of the Farmingville Latino population, including a special needs curriculum that, in effect, promoted low expectations and achievement for the district's Latino students and provided a lack of challenge for middle-class children from Allenstown.

In Simmons's argument, higher standards and a more rigorous, traditional curriculum should take precedence over a pedagogy centrally concerned with engaging and promoting diversity and intergroup understanding. "Diversity is like breathing," he explained. "It is essential, but like breathing, you shouldn't to have to think about it. If you start to think about things that should be automatic, that's a problem."

Simmons's vision of "quality education"—one that promotes like-ability classrooms, condemns bilingual programs, and prioritizes the promotion of higher standards over comprehensive multicultural pedagogical efforts—was shared by a number of Allenstown parents at the meetings. This perspective led mediator Reed to concede that "the interesting thing is that Allenstown representatives want a quality education for their kids, but I'm not sure they value multiculturalism. If students don't go through the experience of getting to know each other, they're going to be out in an increasingly diverse work world without that education."

In Reed's opinion, the discrediting of multiculturalism stemmed from some Allenstown parents' inability to see the positives that racial and socioeconomic mixture might have for their children. In fact, given the environment of fear inspired by unrest at the high school, Allenstown parents not only perceived little benefit from ethnic mixture but saw primarily negative impacts on their children's current and future academic success. He explicated farther:

> Without any statements that are telling parents: "Hey, there is something in it for me," they see as "It's dragging me down." And a good case can be made for it. [They say:] look at the test scores, look at their varying ability, this affects my kid. . . . So there wasn't a value in it [class/ethnic/racial mixture]. There wasn't a sense that this is going to be an enriching experience that we are going to be challenged by because it is going to change us—that we are going to

> need to learn some things. But if there is no value, then what? "You're a beaner." "What do you got that I need to pay any attention to, or give any respect to?" People had a limited experience with that. . . . They believed this mixture could only hurt them.

In Simmons's case, what was interesting is that he did not deny—nor did he fail to recognize—the potential benefits of racial and class integration for his children. However, for him, these potential benefits needed to be weighed against associated risks—in this case, the risk of a negative influence on his children's college preparation and, ultimately, on their future economic mobility. Rather than deny the value of race and class integration, parents like Simmons simply lacked prevailing convictions about its value.

The Failure of the Parent Meetings

There is little question that Allenstown and Farmingville parents' distinct views about quality education and the nature of social justice in the schooling process limited the ability to establish common ground and identify a set of shared goals to strive toward in the parent meetings. However, such contested views were not the only obstacles that served to undermine the spirit and purpose of the parent meetings. The problem, according to Reed, was that parents entered the meetings with "already preconceived notions, prejudices, stereotypes, that nobody ever talks about. They'd prejudged things before the fact—both sides."

The intensity of distrust and suspicion between the parent groups became evident even before the first meeting began. "When we arrived at that first meeting in Allenstown," recalls MPAC member Elena, "they told us that we couldn't come in. And just like that, they closed the door in our faces." Hector, a fellow MPAC member, provided a more nuanced accounting of the situation:

> The superintendent set up the meetings and organized a committee. But because of our language (as primary Spanish speakers) he didn't want all of us on the committee. The translation of the letter that he sent out said that not all the committee can come. Only one out of the whole committee can show up. But our committee is at a district level. . . . Our children attend schools all over the place.

> Each and every one of us had a right to attend this meeting. They didn't let us go into the meeting. . . . We fought hard against the superintendent. . . . At the meetings that were held in Allenstown, he would never want us there as a group but simply as parents who had kids attending Allenstown.[3]

Elena then recalled that "they finally let us in, but when we first went into this room we felt as if we were on trial. That's how it was, and it feels so horrible and so cold. I think that if they had been able to kill us, they would have done so with their stares."

Despite the mediators' best efforts to keep the meetings focused on points of common agreement and the best interests of all the district's children, a deep sense of distrust and suspicion saturated the first meeting. MPAC representatives could recall, in vivid detail, the visceral and interpersonal dimensions of each of the parent meetings, including what they remember as the accusations, insinuations, and disconnections that Mexican-descent Farmingville parents experienced at the hands of White Allenstown parent representatives. MPAC member Tomas offered his memories of the first meeting:

> [The mediator] asked us what it was that we wanted for the students. We were separated into groups and he asked the other group what they wanted. We all wanted the same thing—quality education, respect—right? This was all we wanted, and it was the one thing we agreed on. Each of us spoke about our fears, and then they [Allenstown representatives] said that they were afraid of us burning down the school. They said that we we're going to burn the [American] flag and that we're going to kick them out of their school. And I said, Why would I want to take over something that is already mine? I always pay my taxes and you say that it is yours but the school is a public school. It's everyone's and I don't know why you feel that it belongs to you. And the worse fear that they felt of us was—they said that we [our children] were savages, gangsters, drug dealers.

In Tomas's view, Allenstown parents failed to entertain the idea that problems at the high school stemmed from "the state of mind that permeates the school"; instead, they shifted blame to Latino parents and their children who were cast as potential criminals and questionable Americans. Contesting insinuations that Latino parents from Farmingville lacked the right to express legitimate complaints about problems in an "Allenstown" school, Tomas asserted an entitlement as taxpayer to equal access to the district's public educational services, regardless of where they were "placed."

Yet it was clear that the unwelcoming stance of Allenstown parents resulted, at least in part, from a sense of resentment over not having full control over issues taking place in "their" community. Latinos from Farmingville were seen as establishing an increasingly dominant voice in district decision making, while Allenstown parents were experiencing a growing sense of powerlessness. If Allenstown parents could not control things at the district level, they were certainly going to be sure they controlled what was happening at their "own" high school. According to one district staff representative who attended the parent meetings, some Allenstown parents went as far as to voice an anxiety about a possible Latino "conspiracy" to take over the district:

> There were accusations being made toward the Mexican American community, with the student body president, some people on the board being Latino, and all the school board meetings happen[ing] in Farmingville. The Allenstown folks were feeling powerlessness and couldn't see how it possibly could be orchestrated with their best intentions in mind.

According to mediator Reed, another factor inspiring the intensity of resentment and level of aggressiveness of some Allenstown participants toward Latino parents was a heated defensiveness against accusations or insinuations that they might be "racist." Reed believed that it was precisely this defensiveness and denial of race as an issue to actively engage with and reflect upon that severely limited the range of concerns that could be addressed and worked through during the meetings:

> To me, there was a level of denial that sabotaged the process from the very beginning, in people working very hard to defend themselves against the accusations that racism is happening. See, that's the underlying elephant in the room. The inequality of power, resource, influence, all of those things—with the Mexican American folks coming from the position of questioning their own worthi-

> ness, their own ability, their own skills in dealing with all of this. So it's tense—what I would call a minefield. With people tip-toeing around, trying not to say what they really feel, or to interact or talk about what is going on with them because they blow up: "I may be called a racist!" which people go nuts over.

After four meetings convened over a two-month period, little was accomplished to quell what one parent called the "horrible discordance" between parents in the district. "We wanted to resolve the problems of the students, but I think we have created a community problem" said Bilingual Advisory Committee member Maria Torres. Paul Reilly, an Allenstown parent, admitted he "attended three of these meetings, and I think I'm in more trouble now that when I started." MPAC member Elena described that her loss of faith in the meetings was not just due to the virulent attacks from members of the Allenstown contingent, but from a feeling that migrant parents were not being listened to and their concerns were not perceived as legitimate:

> It was a very ugly thing, these meetings. Supposedly it was to get to know us better; supposedly it was to know what Mexican or Latino parents wanted, but it had nothing to do with this. It felt like we were so unpleasant to them. Each meeting was like an attack on everyone. And they continued to attack us. All of this was like a rejection to us, and of course, to [our] children, right? More so for them than for us, because we are adults and we can defend ourselves. But if they are offending our kids, then there's no way around it, they have to be there [at the school].

Migrant parents were not the only ones to draw attention to a strong unwillingness among some Allenstown parent representatives to listen to Latino parents' concerns at the meetings. A White district representative in attendance found evidence in the underlying kinesthetic and nonverbal communication that characterized interactions at the meeting, particularly in cases where Latino parent representatives attempted to convey the particularities of their language, cultural, and class experiences:

> One of the things I noticed at the second meeting, that then clicked for me, is that the Allenstown parents never watched the

speaker [when a parent spoke in Spanish]. They always watched the interpreter. . . . After that evening, it became clear: they are not even connecting. Because for me, I understand only a very little bit of Spanish, but the challenge for me is to see if I can get the communication when I don't understand the words. So I am there intently watching the speaker, and then when the speaker says something that is important to them—or impactful or animated, or if there is some nonverbal communication happening—I'm checking out the patterns. And I'm noticing that nobody is looking at the speaker. Some people are reading papers. Some people are in various states of distraction. [They think] "I can't deal with this. I'll wait until it comes from the translator when I can deal with it." And that was the click for me that this was not going to happen, because [Allenstown parents] are not even interested in connecting with you while you are sharing yourself, while you are opening up or you're taking these risks, being vulnerable.

Another instance that seemed to reveal an underlying unwillingness on the part of some Allenstown parents to empathize with the experience of the Farmingville participants came in the third meeting. Here, as Reed recalled, the president of MPAC "created some challenges for the White folks:"

He [the MPAC president] asked them [Allenstown representatives]: "Who do you know? Do you have friends who are Mexican American? Do you know any Mexicans?" The Latino parents have talked about how hard it is for them—"I work all day in the fields"—trying to explain how it is hard for them to be available, and that doesn't mean that they don't care about their kids. Then one of the bolder Allenstown parents who had had enough of the migrant parent representative—a man of stature, passion, and power—was pushed to the place where he just went off and said, "I don't have time for this—these emotional outpourings!"—a characterization demeaning and demoting this guy's authenticity, this guy's invitation for them [middle-class, White parents] to take a look at some of their [Latino parents'] behavior and some of their histories. So I could see those [Latino] parents going home to their kids and

> having those kids say: "They are never going to accept us, why do we need to put out anything? Am I going to put myself out there to get knocked down every day? Am I going to take a risk, am I going to be vulnerable every day to get disenfranchised, de-esteemed?" So, then they cut it off, to protect themselves.

"The truth is," MPAC member Sonia explained, "in the long run these meetings were a waste. They made lists and petitions as if they were magic wands to resolve the problems, and the truth is, if we would have done one thing, with so much wasted time, everything would have been fine. But these meetings were purely . . . well, we got tired of them because what use did it serve us to meet?" An AHS teacher offered a succinct commentary about what she saw happening with Allenstown parents at the time and how this behavior seemed to relate to concerns of race and class:

> Those parents [from Allenstown] who were involved in those original meetings trying to bring peace to our school, their bottom line was: We're different. The north end is different from the south end. And I interpreted that as racist—not hardcore—but nevertheless, and elitist. And I thought this school is really going to suffer with these kids here if they continue to take that feeling.

The Move to Secede

The "we are different" perspective asserted by some Allenstown representatives reflected anxieties about their diminishing voice in district affairs, particularly in relation to the interests of Farmingville area Latinos whose "special needs" programs remained inconsonant with the needs and desires of the Allenstown area parents. However, the perceived threat to the academic achievement of Allenstown children was not the only factor fueling the growing anxiety following the unrest at Allenstown High. There were also concerns about the how the situation might potentially impact the Allenstown area real estate market. The willingness of outspoken Latino children and their parents to challenge Allenstown's manner of organizing its schools and socializing its children posed a threat not only to Allenstown's image of itself, but the image it had for so long marketed to others. As a district official observing the meetings alleged:

> The parents were there because [of] real estate. Ultimately, we were talking about the power of my property values, my image of myself. Allenstown had an historical image of itself that was being threatened to its core, where people would not come there, people would not buy homes here, [so] "We've got to do something about this. Our property! The value is going to go down, right? We can't have it anymore; we've got to have our own thing." Neighborhood control. Community control. . . . And we can't talk about these things here [at the parent meetings].

A similar interpretation was offered by an AHS teacher:

> What you would call "neighborhood control" is code for real estate values, and that is what was going on here. So, they wanted more neighborhood control of the school—right? That is clearly what they mean. And those neighborhoods are segregated. So, if the neighborhood was integrated, it would just be about community. But because we [voicing Allenstown residents] have gone through so much trouble to make this place just for us the way it is, we have to fight for that.

This combination of fear of violence, of unchallenging curriculum, of declining property values, of a community being pulled away from an image of its own unique character, not only provided a juggernaut to the productivity of the parent meetings, it also triggered a separate series of *private parent meetings* that began while the district-sponsored parent meetings were still in progress. In these private meetings, however, there was no cross-section of district parents and school officials present, nor were they talking about how to resolve existing tensions. Instead, the meetings were organized and attended by a group of White Allenstown parents and community leaders extolling the virtues of community control of their schools, a topic not easily breeched at the district-sponsored gatherings. Discussion within this group shifted to talk of leaving the PVUSD and forming their own, separate Allenstown school district.

Interestingly, it was the same core group of Allenstown parents participating in the district-sponsored parent meetings that became the leaders of the new secession campaign. As a long-time educator within the PVUSD characterized it:

> We [voicing the group of Allenstown parents] are tired of going to meetings in Farmingville. We are tired of them setting up the calendar [around] migrant trips back to Mexico instead of our ski season. We are tired of these board members who don't really get it, who don't see that we are deserving of this state of "our way." We can't have it anymore; we've got to have our own thing. Neighborhood control. Community control. So we separate. We've got to separate, that's the only answer. So, they had the usual case. It's been that way. You set up segregated neighborhoods, you have segregated schools, you don't have to look at me. It's just the way it is. And our politics supports it—the integrity of neighborhoods—we want to be sure everyone is safe in their neighborhoods.

As the private Allenstown meetings got underway, it became increasingly clear that the Allenstown parents' continued involvement in the district-sponsored parent meetings was less than sincere. As Kenneth explained:

> So, they [the parent groups] definitely had some points of agreement, but there was the underlying intention on the part of Allenstown parents that "I'm just going through the motions, but it's really not going to change anything." We were having this charade; we were going through the process. And as folks from the Allenstown side were accusing and questioning the motives and the intentions of the Farmingville contingent, they were planning their secession movement. So, we weren't talking about *that.*

Allenstown parents' shift of interest away from resolving the problems at hand to hosting exclusive meetings to discuss forming a new school district further convinced migrant parents that racist motivations seemed to underlie the parents' actions. MPAC representative Elena explained:

> We understood very clearly that it was racism because after everything that we have said, right after, they wanted to get

> separated. They were alleging that by separating themselves, they were going to have a better quality of education for their school, but that was not the truth.

Conclusion

Beginning with the student walkouts and continuing through the district-sponsored parent meetings, it was increasingly clear that Allenstown parents would be expected to share control of their schools with working-class Latino students and their parents from Farmingville. For some Allenstown parents, this meant sharing control with Mexican-descent parents—including migrant parents—who were thought to lack (or be unwilling to exercise) the appropriate skills to participate in school site management and assure high academic expectations for their children. At the same time, it meant sharing control with "other people's children" (Delpit 1995) who seemed to offer little of value to their own children and were viewed by some as both deficient in academic ability and lacking motivation.

In this analysis of the origins of the secession campaign, I portray it as a reactionary movement motivated, in part, by fear of losing control to racial and class others. This approach may matter little to those who favor secession for reasons they do not associate with racist intent or even class-based interest. As well, this approach may be of less significance to county and state government agencies that have their own criteria for assessing the merit of such campaigns. However, how the secession campaign took root certainly matters to those who experienced the campaign from the other side. The fact that migrant parents and their children highlighted the racial dimensions of events surrounding secession was not a simple matter of "playing the race card" to maintain some sort of group advantage; it was because both parents and students could enumerate numerous examples of what they perceived as "out and out racist" actions during the course of the controversy.

But oppression took other, less obvious forms as well. In the way Allenstown school administrators and community residents resisted Latino student endeavors to promote multicultural understanding at Allenstown High was viewed by Latino leaders as a kind of cultural imperialism in which Latinos were seen to have little value to White "Americans," but "[Anglo] American culture" was supposed to have great value to them. At the same time, it was the low value given to multicultural understanding and the need to cultivate mutual respect that both migrant parents and the district-hired mediator perceived as undermining the parent meetings. Here, migrant parents felt a sense of powerlessness in being denied the kind of authority and dignity that permits one to be listened to and *heard* with attention and respect. Instead, they found themselves being called "economically inferior" and perceived to be largely culpable for the blight existing in some of the district's schools.

The parent meetings, by limiting discussions about the problems at Allenstown High to issues of student safety and quality education, elided talk about the impact of past and present institutional racism on schooling conditions within the PVUSD. The absence of talk about race and racism allowed other claims about the nature of the problem at Allenstown High to be articulated and find acceptance in ways that made secession seem reasonable, and to some, necessary. From the perspective of some working-class, Mexican-descent parents and their children, secession was seen as yet another attempt in a series of more or less successful efforts by local Whites to marginalize the Farmingville Latino community from important, quality educational resources as well as from social life among class and racial others. Consequently, both forms of marginalization contributed to the reproduction of schooling conditions unfavorable to Latinos students and their improved rates of academic success. Moreover, such marginalization was *felt* by many Latino students and parents as exclusionary, further reenforcing a sense of nonbelonging and alienation from local schooling structures.

A White former AHS student explained how she believed the events of 1995 affected Latino students at the school:

> I think that the whole series of events during that junior year of my high school and the secession movement immediately following that, sort of made Chicano students a little uninterested in being involved, because they just really felt that nobody cared about them and nobody wanted them to be at that school. Okay, now after 187, you want to split the school district up and bus us back to where we are from, or whatever, you know.

CHAPTER 5

Race and School District Secession: Allenstown's District Reorganization Campaign, 1995–2004

I'm not dead set against the creation of smaller districts. When we started talking about this over a year ago, I wanted to see more than one alternative. That hasn't happened. The boundary lines could be drawn in a way that favors integration. . . . The details of this latest attempt haven't changed since the Allenstown secessionist movement. The plan is essentially the same, with a dividing line that mirrors the Mason-Dixon. This continues to be a movement to separate the rich and the poor, Anglos and Hispanics, high-performing schools against low-performing schools. I'm very disappointed that an educational leader would not stand up for integrated schools. The idea that segregated schools are better for our students is unfathomable to me. I don't see how anyone could remain neutral in this debate.

—Stacey Nevells, PVUSD School Board Member, 2003

School District Secession and the Question of Race

When the Allenstown secession campaign went public in the spring of 1995, it was led primarily by a group of Allenstown parents and concerned citizens rather than any teacher or student groups in the district. Support within the larger Allenstown community was substantial. Within a few weeks, secession leaders had collected over 5,000 signatures backing their proposal. While the announcement followed closely on the heels of the failed parent meetings, the movement's leaders argued that the idea of an Allenstown School District was not new but had in fact "been the talk of Little League sidelines for years."

To what extent can we say racism was at play in the Allenstown secession campaign? Was the issue of race overblown? Alternatively, to what extent might secessionist proponents have used discourses about its "overblown" nature to delegitimize the racial dimensions of their own rhetoric and political action? Is it possible to talk about race, and how it functions, in situations where people do not see themselves as being racist?

I argue that the school secession movement in Pleasanton Valley cannot be collapsed, by any means, into a simple narrative of White racism. Here, a primary focus on intentional racism obscures important distinctions between motivated racist behavior and those less-recognized social and individual attitudes and actions (and even preferences) that have racism as their effect (Omi and Winant 1994; Winant 1998). At the same time, a focus on racism-as-explanation-for-behavior fails to provide an account of the diverse motives and meanings that shape behaviors, attitudes, and social action among people who are often called racists but do not see or understand themselves as being so (Anderson 2003; Hartigan 2001). In the Allenstown secession campaign, discourses perceived to be "racial" or underlying a "racist" agenda are better represented, in the words of John Hartigan, as "multiply inflected, referring to and projecting a host of competing interests and threats, audiences, and objects—none of which are easily linked back to a core psychological motivation, such as racism" (2001: 161). However, the Allenstown secession campaign cannot be understood without seriously engaging questions of racial entitlement and class interest operating at the level of both schooling and community politics. In this case, the secession movement clearly resonated with strategies historically employed by local White citizens to defend their neighborhoods against racial and class others.

While I am interested in how popularly conceived notions of race and racism are said to operate in the secession campaign—that is, through motivated forms of racism—I am equally interested in how racist discourses may operate without clear identification or explicit forms of racial discrimination. This means engaging in an analysis of race, and how it may function in situations where people do not necessarily see themselves as being racist.

Legal Justifications for Allenstown School Secession

To some degree, those proposing Allenstown secession had the law on their side. The shifting emphasis in federal desegregation legislation toward the desirability of "neighborhood schools" and arrangements that favored "parental choice" suggested that Allenstown's grassroots movement had a reasonable chance at success. However, its legality remained questionable in relation to state laws and other federal statutes protecting the rights of minority populations. California Education Code, Section 35753 governing the approval of school district reorganization plans, clearly states in its criteria that new proposals must neither promote racial/ethnic segregation nor result in an inequitable division of property and facilities. Approval from the state board requires that appellants show that their plan would "preserve each affected district's ability to educate students in an integrated environment and will not promote racial or ethnic discrimination or segregation." It also requires that district reorganization plans result in a reasonably "equitable division of property and facilities, including not only land and other property, but also debt and monies due but not collected."

While it was the state board of education that would ultimately rule on the legality of the school district secession proposal, the questions of whether it would hear such a proposal depended, in turn, on recommendations from lower boards: first from the PVUSD school board, then from the county board of education. The PVUSD school board, constituted by a majority of Farmingville-area trustees, maintained a 4-3 opinion against the secession proposal. In fact, in December 1995, trustees passed two measures that constituted clear setbacks to the secession campaign. The first was a decision to hire a lawyer to examine the legal and constitutional issues surrounding Allenstown secession. The second was to recommend to the county board of education that any popular vote on the secession proposal be extended to all residents in the PVUSD, rather than—as secessionists desired—only to those in the Allenstown area. The question of voting jurisdictions was crucial; extending voting rights to all PVUSD voters—particularly given the potential negative fiscal and social impact on the Farmingville area—would likely doom the proposal.

An early feasibility study on the Allenstown secession idea, commissioned by the PVUSD, found that impacts on Farmingville-area schools would include increased racial segregation, extreme overcrowding in Farmingville schools, and underenrollment in Allenstown schools. The study also anticipated the loss of a significant tax base for school support in the Farmingville area. Despite this unfavorable data, the county board of education elected to approve the Allenstown parents' "district reorganization" petition, claiming that their vote was rooted less in an assessment of the proposal's relative merit than in their belief that the state board would be best positioned to rule on such a controversial issue, particularly given the reverberating impacts it would be likely to have throughout the state.

Contesting Accusations of Racist Intent in the Secession Campaign

From the moment secession leaders went public with their petition, they were besieged with accusations that racism motivated their campaign. Opponents of the proposal were quick to call attention to the fact that serious talk about secession originated in the wake of the situation at Allenstown High, and that the parents spearheading the movement were the same who had participated in the district-sponsored parent meetings. Further fueling claims of racism was the manner in which secessionists were proposing to carve the new Allenstown school district out of the existing PVUSD. As an anti-secession school board member at the time argued: "If you look at the boundaries of the proposed Allenstown district, you'll notice they look a little weird. That's because they drew it up in order to keep all the White people together." And in truth, the district boundaries as initially proposed encompassed largely White, middle-class residential neighborhoods within incorporated areas of the Valley. Moreover, Rolling Meadows Middle School—the predominantly Latino feeder school to Allenstown High since 1987—was left out of the proposed district. Excluding the school assured that AHS would lose several hundred Latino students each year.

Allenstown secession leaders fiercely contested accusations that they were acting in a racist, exclusivist, or otherwise discriminatory manner. They grieved that opponents were unable or unwilling to empathize with their fears and their sense of frustration regarding their lack of voice in the public school system. Moreover, they claimed that the exclusion of Latino children from the new Allenstown school district was not part of their plan, pointing out that the proposed district boundaries were drawn to include a large migrant labor camp on the Allenstown/Farmingville border. They also had difficulty understanding why the plan for "secession"—which they rejected as a politically loaded term, insisting instead that it be called "district reorganization"—was so divisive, since it would do little to alter the existing racial composition in the district's schools. As one leader argued:

> The world people [students] experience doesn't change with reorganization. There is no real difference in what students see. For all practical purposes, the relations would be the same, the only difference being that Allenstown would have control over its schools.

When I asked an Allenstown resident and former school board member who favored the proposal why he believed race had become such a central issue, he explained that it resulted from a "misconception" that originally sprang from efforts to resolve tensions at Allenstown High School. "Genuine safety issues got commingled with racial issues," he said. In his view, the local media was largely responsible for this misunderstanding by "blowing the issues way out of proportion" and transforming what was a wide array of legitimate concerns among Allenstown parents into a spectacle of White racism. Racial accusations, he believed, then became "the hot button to stop reorganization and to demoralize the people involved." Although he conceded that racism existed in the Allenstown community "as it does everywhere," he assured me that racism against Mexicans was not widespread in the area, and believed it was unfair that those few marginal "bandwagon" racists were conflated with secession proponents who clearly "were not motivated by racial issues."

Despite denials that racism motivated their campaign, the *politicization* of race compelled Allenstown leaders to exercise great care in how they expressed their justifications for secession. This meant that arguments that could possibly be equated with racial anxiety—for example, concerns over student safety or the alleged lower expectations of Latino parents—gave way to more depoliticized (though perhaps no less legitimate) expressions regarding the "real problems" that motivated the secession movement. Chief among these were the district's "unruly" size and its "tyrannical" bureaucracy. These problems could be mitigated, they argued, by shifting to local control and reverting to neighborhood schools.

A desire to escape what were viewed as the stifling bureaucracy and long-existing patterns of fiscal mismanagement in the district office became the dominant justifications for secession. One Allenstown parent and secession supporter claimed that "the employee unions dominated how the PVUSD is run" at the expense of both the quality of education and parent participation. Another central frustration for Allenstown residents was the fact that they bore the largest share of the financial burden for schooling expenses in the district. While Allenstown children made up only about 20 percent of the district school population, homeowners would pay nearly half the cost of any bond measure financing school improvement or construction in the district. Perhaps the most prominent justification for secession was the claim that the district was simply "too big." The district covered over 150 square miles and included over 90,000 residents, making it bigger than the other three cities in the county combined and among the top 5 percent of California school districts in size. According to an Allenstown area school board trustee and secession supporter serving at the time, the "sprawling and unwieldy" nature of the district made it so "you can't get things done." The issue for her was how to make the Valley's schools more manageable:

> When secession talk first started, I was skeptical. I wasn't going to jump on the secession bandwagon. . . . But as I got to know more people, I thought, why try to seem small and grow large when you can be small?

This desire for "smallness" was echoed by many who supported secession, but expressions of that desire varied. One popular discourse spoke of a desire to "go back to being a small town." It was unclear, however, what this nostalgia looked back to—was it a time before Latinos were bused in or simply before district consolidation? It also begs the question of whether this narrative of returning to a better day would have been so prominent if the student population growth had been that of largely White, middle-class youth rather than of working-class youth of Mexican descent.

Articulating Race and Class in the Secession Movement

Those opposing Allenstown secession questioned the sincerity of proponent's claims that district bureaucracy and size were the primary motivating factors. They believed such claims were little more than lip service to divert attention away from deeper class interests and racist motivations. As an Allenstown High student at the time understood it, secession proponents had "all the OK-to-say reasons, but I know it is because they don't want Mexican kids in the school." Drawing attention to race, however, was not the only strategy of resistance against Allenstown secession. Opponents also condemned what they viewed as the sense of "elitism" underlying the effort. Two MPAC members offered a metaphor that linked the Allenstown secession campaign to an attempt to abandon a sinking ship:

> *Esperanza*: I will always remember the words of Mr. Ortiz [another MPAC member] who once said that we're all in the same boat, so why not work to make this boat float? And so, they [Allenstown parents] were going to throw us off the boat so that we would drown and they would make it safe to shore.
>
> *Luis*: It's like when they see that the boat is going to sink, instead of looking for a way to work together as a group, they want to get rid of us. But you can't do away with us, because they would need us to make this boat float [laughter].

These migrant parents saw Allenstown residents' interest in separating from Farmingville schools as a motivated desire to shelter their children from other working-class Latino kids whom they perceived would hold their children back. Opponents were also quick to reassert the link between Allenstown leaders' activism and local real estate concerns. There is no doubt that the secession movement was strongly supported by real estate market interests, evidenced in the fact that Allenstown real estate agents and property managers were among the most highly represented and vocal members of the secession campaign. A White AHS teacher related her feelings about how real estate values and anxiety over community "image" played an important role in the Allenstown secession movement:

> My view is that one strong group that wanted secession was the real estate group. . . . The reason some of those people wanted the secession was that when people come to buy a house, they'll say, "How are the schools?" They want to be able to say "Our schools get high test scores and they all go on to four-year schools." Well, that wasn't showing at our school because we had a lot of Latino kids

> who weren't motivated, or whatever—I mean, there was inequality—inequality in their education, the migrant students who came in here. The school didn't show well, like Berkeley High or Hillsboro High or Carmel High. It didn't show well. And that is what Realtors do, they show and tell. So that group I believe was a strong force in it. . . . And I think it was image.

A direct illustration of this anxiety about "image" was offered by one of Allenstown's more vocal and unapologetic supporters of the district split:

> I'm sure the Realtors will relax when they no longer have to lie about the schools to families moving into Allenstown. I bet they change the subject quickly when serious inquiries (beyond test scores) are made about the safety and population of our schools.

Two central arguments recurred in the narratives of those who opposed Allenstown secession. The first sees secession as grounded in a sense of class-based, elitist entitlement, where claims of deservedness to separate education are linked to the possession of economic power and high-value real estate. The other sees the justification for secession in an "out and out" racism that relies on false stereotypes that criminalize and demean Mexican-descent youth and their families. Jennifer, a White teacher at AHS who had worked closely with secession leaders on various district committees, offered an illustrative example of these critiques:

> There was a board member, and she represented this [the Allenstown] area. She said, "We are not racist, we are elitist." Publicly! It's like, for them, "We know they work hard in our fields, but they are not bringing in the test scores." That was the opinion I got after a while. But out-and-out racist remarks *were* made. You know, like "All the girls are young, they all get pregnant, they are all having babies, our county is growing." They saw them as *breeders*. Like my neighbors said "Who did you get to do your windows?" I said, "Oh, this really good company," and I said "I got a chance to speak Spanish with them." [She replied:] "Oh, I don't want Mexicans coming in." I said, "Why would that be?" [She said:] "Well, I think they look around and might take something." I mean, it's just that deep. I don't know that I can really blame these people, as I had a

> different experience when I was growing up. But the problem is that I see them as stunted . . . and you are carrying that on to your children, something that has been carried on for generations.

Jennifer portrays racism and classism as somewhat separate issues—one of "elitists" concerned primarily with their children's test scores, and the other of "those people"—real racists who are "stunted" by their ignorance and prejudice. Often, however, accusations of classism and racism overlapped, as in this commentary from migrant parent Elena Ochoa:

> They [Allenstown parents] have always known that they hold the economic power, that they have more money, and one way or another, we're just too much for them to handle. To them, we're ruining the good quality of education, and once this is reduced, in other words, it's racism. They told us in many meetings . . . that we were economically inferior and that the power was over there [in Allenstown]. Because we wanted to talk about working together, to unite and apply for education bonds to improve the schools, to finish them up, but they said no. They have more economic power and we don't have it. We wanted to use their money, they said.

The commentaries of both Elena and Jennifer highlight the connection between Allenstown residents' sense of "economic power" and their feelings of entitlement to their own district. Secession leaders did not necessarily deny this connection. Jake Simmons conceded that socioeconomic class status was a key factor in the secession movement. "Affluent, White parents have expectations for their kid's education based on their experience," he explained. "People only care about getting their kids to college." Secession, he believed, was an effective strategy to fulfill that desire. Simmons admitted that he was "stuck on this one," seeing few alternatives to creating an "elite public school" where all children are equally well prepared and college bound.

In Simmons's view, it was primarily Allenstown residents' class experience that shaped their patterns of action and reaction to the dilemmas they faced in local schooling politics. Affluent White parents were "used to running their own show and directing others." This sense of collective entitlement, he explained, promoted a sense of deservedness of "our way" that favored a rather uncompromising, class-based solidarity over a willingness to engage with the concerns of other parties:

> The community of Allenstown is highly educated. Probably over-educated. . . . We probably don't have as much respect as we should for principals and professional teachers. We are perhaps too quick to walk into school, wag our fingers at administrators, and tell them how to do their jobs. . . . The question is, are we good listeners? No. Not as good as we should be. Does it make us racist? I don't know.

Simmons believed that while charges of classism against secessionists may hold water, accusations of racism certainly did not. If race were an issue at all, he reasoned, it was as a secondary and unintended consequence of classism; that is, "to the extent it [class] correlates with race, it makes a bad situation worse." Because racist intent is not what motivated secession leaders, he considered it both misleading and unreasonable to portray race as central issue in the movement. Such accusations, he believed, served merely as a "hot button" issue that self-interested opponents used to disparage and misrepresent the merit of the proposal and the integrity of those supporting it.

Is it enough, as Simmons argues, to dismiss race as a primary factor simply because leaders offer reasonable claims that they are not motivated by racial concerns? If one accords legitimacy to arguments like Jake's, a further question remains: Should *intentions* be the primary criteria to assess the role of race in the Allenstown secession movement? Another way to appreciate the role of race—as I have developed throughout this chapter and the last—is to explore the *roots* of the popular movement, including attention to the various factors and events that provided the impetus for the movement and that helped it secure its popular support.

Race and Place

To better understand how race has operated in the Allenstown secession campaign, it is useful to look beyond a primary focus on race and class concerns to an exploration of how discourses of and about place(s) have functioned importantly in justifications for secession. Historically, battles over the content and shape of local schooling practices in Pleasanton Valley have been articulated not simply in cultural, race, and class terms, but as concerns and anxieties about places—who inhabits what places, who belongs (or doesn't belong) in particular places, and how belonging in some places connotes a sense of deservedness while in others it does not. It is precisely in talking about Farmingville and Allenstown *as places* that one hears the most honest articulations of distrust and suspicion, and of the stereotypes and notions of essential difference that condone particular arguments for (and against) secession.

Much of the early pro-secession rhetoric was framed as the need to "take back" Allenstown schools, a sentiment expressed well in the following editorial to the *Farmingville Register*:

> Thank you [secessionist leaders], whoever you are. Thanks for taking the time and the energy to restore Allenstown to the small town we thought we bought homes in and for your efforts in trying to take back our schools. We have all come to accept, even though we know it's wrong, that Allenstown citizens have no say in the way the district is run. The fact that the district meetings were moved to Farmingville permanently (rather than alternating between sites) demonstrates the total disregard given to Allenstown families. We as Allenstownians need to reiterate the statement from the movie, "I'm mad as hell and I'm not going to take it anymore." . . . Equality will be served when everyone in Allenstown can send their children to school in a neighborhood school.

This victimization narrative finds its logic in the way it represents Farmingville as simultaneously the oppressive ruler of district affairs and the root of the district's problems—in other words, it is where all the district's resources, energy, and attention go, with Allenstown getting the short end of the stick. Not only have district problems been viewed historically as originating in Farmingville, but the area has long been associated with inferiority and criminality, characteristics which were—until the conflicts surrounding Latino student empowerment at Allenstown High occurred—seen as more or less contained in the Farmingville area. In this way, it becomes possible to invest the town of Farmingville with particular agency of its own, as in the statement from an Allenstown parent who argued: "Farmingville is pro-immigration and it's killing the schools." Each claim against Farmingville, as a place, becomes a way of arguing White middle-class "victimhood," which further justifies Allenstown's bid for secession. "We're the little tail of the donkey and we have been for a long, long time," scowled one secession supporter.

In these narratives of and about places, frustration, anger, and degradation that might otherwise be projected toward Latinos in Farmingville is redirected and attributed to the place of Farmingville. This strategy of displacing the object of degradation and redirecting resentment toward the town itself provided what seemed a legitimate manner of expressing feelings of suspicion, distrust, and resentment. However, such talk can rarely separate race and place so easily. In the parent meetings, for example, Allenstown parents worried about a Farmingville "conspiracy" in which Latinos were trying to "take over" the district. In this case, Farmingville *and* its Latino residents were cast as receiving an unfair advantage to schooling resources and decision making. Yet even with these perceived "advantages," Latinos were unable to sufficiently raise test scores and achievement levels of their children, leading to blanket assumptions that located blame in Farmingville Latinos. Jake unsuspectingly offered an example of this race/place conflation when he noted that "changes will come [in Farmingville] when there is increased self-confidence of Latinos there. And self-confidence among parents, to insist that you challenge students." This sort of reasoning casts Farmingville Latinos as yet still undeserving and as largely responsible for the fact that their children are not well-served in district schools.

Allenstown parents' claims of victimization and ways of locating the problem in Farmingville served not only to justify an unwillingness to assume responsibility for the district's problems but also from feelings of responsibility for Mexican-descent children in Farmingville schools. As one Allenstown school board trustee argued:

> I don't see why we have any moral responsibility to rescue Farmingville from their problems. All of the policy (in the school district) revolves around the Latino community, and we have no say at all. Why should we have to fund their schools?

The conflation of place and race stereotypes in the narratives of secession supporters was perhaps most intriguingly expressed in Simmons's explanation of why even many influential Whites in *Farmingville* were opposing Allenstown secession. In his view, accusations of racism made by Whites in Farmingville against secessionist supporters were—at their root—an expression of their resentment that Allenstown had "escaped" the changing realities that they, as Farmingville residents, were unable to escape. He felt that Farmingville Whites despised Allenstown residents' freedom from having to deal with the consequences of the Mexicanization of the area and the conflicts engendered by this race, class, and cultural mixture. He explained that Farmingville Whites, by casting claims of racism against Allenstown secessionists, were in effect saying: "We didn't get to do it and we, by golly, aren't going to let you get out. If we can't get out, we aren't going to let you get out either . . . we can't let you go because then who is going to buy my house in a district that's so overwhelmingly Mexican?" The implicit assumption of "escape" in this argument—whether from the perspective of Whites in Farmingville or in Allenstown—is that Latinos had "ruined" Farmingville and promised to do so in Allenstown.

The State of California's Response to Allenstown School Secession

In 1996, the California State Board of Education considered the Allenstown secession proposal. After hearing testimony from concerned parties, the board's Administrative Committee decided in a 3-0 vote to recommend that the full state board deny the petition. However, on the following day, the state board split 4-4 on a vote to approve the Administrative Committee's recommendation. After further deliberation, the board eventually voted 7-1 to postpone consideration of the reorganization proposal for one year, asking that Pleasanton Valley school officials, parents, and community leaders get together, once again, to try to resolve their differences. Specifically, the state board asked the district to address concerns about the economic impact, educational performance impact, and the effect on race and segregation in the PVUSD, all of which were cited as reasons for not approving the petition.

Following the state board's advice, the PVUSD again organized meetings to bring together concerned citizens, parents, and school staff to discuss how the district could work together to better serve the diverse needs of the all the district's residents. After another six months of meetings, a compromise of sorts was reached among school board members, where the idea of three geographical "zones"—north, central, and south—was introduced. The zone concept produced the idea of a "K-12 slice," where, in each zone, principals and other school officials from the elementary, middle, and high schools levels could get together and engage in ongoing conversations about curriculum, school structure, and facilities.

A year later, the state board officially denied Allenstown's bid for its own district, but left the door open for future reconsideration, expressing a willingness to hear the proposal again after the construction of a proposed third high school in the district, scheduled for late 2003. The board wrote that if "there is still a desire by the community to break up the district [at that time], let that be a starting point so you would not have the moving of children."

Allenstown Secession, Reloaded: The Reemergence of District Reorganization in 2002

After the second state board ruling, public talk of Allenstown secession entered a period of relative remission. Frustrations still simmered below the surface, however, as when a parent coalition from Allenstown sought approval of a bond measure solely to benefit Allenstown schools, only to have it roundly rejected by school board trustees. In 2002, however, the opportunity structure for district reorganization suddenly changed. Charlie Yu, a long-time school board trustee from Farmingville and an original staunch opponent of the Allenstown secession movement, expressed his willingness to reconsider the idea. An American of Japanese descent, Yu claimed his change of heart was inspired by a "personal realization" that separate schooling arrangements might actually boost academic achievement across the district, especially among the high number of English language learners in Farmingville schools. A district split would make this possible, he contended, because it would allow each community to focus on the specific needs of its students. Yu's logic was not inconsistent with that of other minority group leaders throughout the country who have become disillusioned with the inability of desegregated school systems to provide an equitable, high-quality education for minority children.[1] "If our students were performing at high levels," Yu argued, "we wouldn't be talking about this. If [the system] is not working, then we have to look at how we can make it better."

Yu's shift in perspective thrust him into a strange-bedfellow relationship with Ellen Van Reesma, the outspoken, pro-secession trustee from Allenstown against whom he had long battled on community entitlement issues. The two agreed to begin a systematic process of gathering financial and other pertinent data to reassess the merit of dividing the district in a way that might best serve the needs of all students. The result of their partnership was the commissioning of a second district-sponsored "Reorganization Feasibility Study" in early 2003. This report, to be compiled by a team of alleged experts, would offer an "objective analysis" of the situation that would "neither draw conclusions nor present specific recommendations for action." Instead, the report would be released for public feedback, and community input would guide the trustees' decision about whether to pursue a district reorganization plan.

This second incarnation of the Allenstown secession campaign was distinctive from the first in several ways. First, the new effort was not ostensibly spearheaded by an identifiable parent or citizen group. It was school district representatives themselves who had proposed it, justifying it as a desire to fulfill the original promise made to Allenstown parents in 1996 to revisit the reorganization idea, based on the state board's counsel. Opposition to the repackaged secession idea took an expanded form as well. It thus came not just from Farmingville parents and community action groups, but from the City of Farmingville. When Farmingville's city council received a preliminary summary of the data collected for the district's feasibility study, two of its members vowed to pass a resolution opposing any new split. A month later, when the feasibility study was officially released to the public, the City of Farmingville countered with their own commissioned "Impact Report" with its own set of data that showed how, under a proposed split, the new Farmingville-only PVUSD would bulge with students and that their taxpayers would be burdened by a required $40 million investment in new school construction. To accommodate these burdens, the new Farmingville district would have to construct a new "continuation school" and at least one new elementary school, in addition to the new Pleasanton Valley High School already under construction.

The district-commissioned feasibility report, with an analysis generally more favorable to the idea of district reorganization, suggested that the split would leave a new Allenstown district with about approximately 3,000 students and Farmingville with 15,000 students. Currently serving a 75 percent Latino student body, the new PVUSD would become as much as 89 percent Latino under a proposed reorganization. Allenstown would risk losing more than 1,000 Latino students that were attending Allenstown area schools, the majority at Allenstown High.

Opponents of the split, using data from the City of Farmingville's Impact Report, claimed a split would have grave consequences, leaving Farmingville schools much poorer while providing Allenstown schools with approximately $2,500 more per student. In addition, the split would promote the loss of qualified teachers in Farmingville schools and reduce the tax base for future bond measures. They also surmised that the split would result in an unequal division of school property and facilities since a new Allenstown school district would end up with less than one-fourth of the Valley's student population but maintain 50 percent of the district's assessed valuation, on which bonding is based.

The mayor of Farmingville characterized the idea of a district split in racial terms, calling it a manifestation of "the three S's: Secession, Segregation, and Separation," and considered it a devastating move in a difficult budget time. A second council member viewed the idea as "the antithesis of what we fought for in the Supreme Court for equal education [referring to *Brown v. Board of Education*]," while another questioned the use of the term "reorganization," calling it an attempt to "hide it for what it really is [which is] unfair, outrageous, upsetting, against the law, and unconstitutional." Yet another member suggested that the reorganization would deprive Farmingville children of access to higher-performing schools in Allenstown. "We are mandated to fight this, and we will," she warned, while directing the council staff to prepare for a legal battle. While the Farmingville city council held no formal role in the decision-making process regarding district reorganization, they voted 5-2 in a nonbinding resolution to oppose a district split.

Those favoring reorganization dismissed opposition through a logic made familiar in the first incarnation of the secession proposal. They called the issue of racial segregation a "red herring," given that schools were already divided along racial lines, and they claimed that dividing the sprawling, 18,000-student district would allow for greater local control. As an Allenstown parent and business development consultant explained it:

> The reality is, if you reorganize and create smaller districts, smaller districts have always been shown to have better performance for the children. For me it's an issue of achievement and local focus, and wanting a district that's more focused on what kids need.

The seven-member PVUSD school board remained bitterly split on the issue. While trustees Yu and Van Reesma could be expected to back the reorganization idea, two school board members vehemently rejected it, another had "serious concerns" and the remaining two appeared to offer their tentative backing. Van Reesma justified her support in terms of economic efficiency, particularly given the prohibitive costs of cross-district transportation. "A lot of money is spent because of the distance between the two communities, and there is a lot of waste," she argued. She believed both communities would save money if the split occurred, and she claimed that the racial demographics would remain "essentially unchanged." Reemphasizing a strong conviction that her personal views in no way reflected an interest in racial separation, she argued: "I've always been a fan of smaller districts. Our job is to educate kids and we [supporting the split] are viewing this issue through the lens of how we can get the most 'bang for our buck.'"

Concurring with Van Reesma, Yu proclaimed: "I believed with all of my heart that a Farmingville school district focusing all of its time and money on the long-struggling Farmingville schools could perform just as well as Allenstown." His interpretation of the problem, in line with contemporary national trends, was one of academic achievement, not of race. For Yu, the "segregation problem" was primarily a housing issue, and since cross-district bussing was no longer a commonly accepted practice, it was unreasonable to view it as an acceptable solution to the problem. A Farmingville-area trustee sitting directly on the fence of the district reorganization issue was Don Golden. While he refused to believe that "kids have to be integrated with other students to be successful," he recognized the social and fiscal inequalities that would likely result from a district split. His mixed position on the issue was illustrated in his claim that he would favor a "parallel split" that assured a higher level of integration in both districts, but he admitted such a strategy would be unreasonable since it would constitute "a transportation nightmare."

Stacey Nevells, a school board trustee representing the rural, middle-lying area between the two residential centers of Allenstown and Farmingville, articulated a less heard but ultimately compelling critique of the possible separation. As a former ESL teacher, she was especially concerned about the impact of the split on English-language learners (ELLs):

> The issue of integrated schools is closely related to English language learning. One of the most effective ways to teach English is to see that English speakers and English language learners are grouped together and talk to each other. Children learn language

> from their peers! If their classmates are predominantly Spanish speaking, this deters a natural process of English language acquisition that is available in more integrated schools. . . . If you agree that more English should be spoken in the schools, we need schools that are more integrated.

Beyond the impact on ELLs, Nevells believed that, in a multicultural society, it was important for children to learn from peers with different ethnic backgrounds and for parents to have the option of enrolling their children in diverse schools. She was not opposed to a reörganization of the district per se; what concerned her most was the limited terms under which the process had been imagined from the beginning:

> I'm not dead set against the creation of smaller districts. When we started talking about this over a year ago, I wanted to see more than one alternative. That hasn't happened. The boundary lines could be drawn in a way that favors integration. Some of the wealthy beach homes are closer to (the new) Pleasanton Valley High School than Allenstown High School and closer to Rolling Meadows than Allenstown Junior High. The details of this latest attempt haven't changed since the Allenstown secessionist movement. The plan is essentially the same, with a dividing line that mirrors the Mason-Dixon. This continues to be a movement to separate the rich and the poor, Anglos and Hispanics, high-performing schools against low-performing schools. I'm very disappointed that an educational leader would not stand up for integrated schools. The idea . . . that segregated schools are better for our students is unfathomable to me. I don't see how anyone could remain neutral in this debate.

Conclusion

The Allenstown secession campaign can be located in a larger community history as well as in relation to a particular course of events inspired by Proposition 187. "Local control" was the discourse that propelled the secession campaign, and it found its strength in the way things had gotten "out of control" at AHS. Historically, resistance to school integration in Pleasanton Valley has been voiced not in terms of racial or class interest, but as a (White middle-class) fear of losing "local control" over the schooling process and the ability to rule on as a local a level as possible. Allenstown citizen groups have framed their struggles as ones meant to sustain the quality of schools, to protect community resources (particularly financial ones), and to maintain local ways of managing their affairs and finances. In this matter, community leaders and citizen activists have achieved significant success in persuading the school board to accept their positions. Yet, in Pleasanton Valley, as elsewhere in the United States, suburban White communities' felt-entitlements to their own "quality schools" has typically meant excluding minority students.

Rather than understanding Allenstown's isolationist campaign for school secession as motivated by an "out-and-out" racism that is ultimately reducible to a psychological distain for minority population, I have spoken of various manifestations of White entitlement whereby the argument could be made: I'm White, economically affluent, and live in an exclusive residential area; therefore, I deserve the discretion to organize public schooling around the needs of my children, even if that means assuring that they do not attend school with large numbers of working-class, Mexican-descent children who I fear may bring down the level of education available to my children. Such a claim of entitlement is made to appear logical, and its denial an injustice, despite incongruence with the spirit of democratic principles of fairness, equal opportunity, and equal access that have long served as the philosophical and legal foundation of public education in the United States.

PART III

Attempts to make High-Quality, Shared Schooling Work

CHAPTER 6

Cinco de Mayo, Normative Whiteness, and the Marginalization of Mexican-Descent Students at Allenstown High

Between the period of crisis at Allenstown High in the mid-1990s and when I began my school-based research several years later, a number of positive changes were made at the school. The "guidance tech" system was replaced with a counseling office that included four full-time counselors, three of whom were fully bilingual and of Mexican descent. Unfortunately, the improved representation in the counseling department was not equally achieved among the teaching faculty, where only four of over seventy classroom teachers in the school were Latino. Another positive development was the hiring of a White bilingual female principal who arrived at the school with a sincere commitment to generate a more welcoming environment for all by pursuing such strategies as extensive multicultural training for school staff, improved efforts to increase the participation of Latino parents in the school's affairs, and the active promotion of professional development training for teachers on issues of diversity and multiculturalism in the curriculum.

While incidents of interethnic and interracial fighting among students had subsided at the high school, the alienation of many Mexican-descent students endured. My own research material, along with that produced by the larger Peers Project longitudinal study of which I was a part, identified a widespread feeling of nonbelonging and discomfort among Mexican-descent students in a number of important social and academic contexts within the school. This sense of nonbelonging was often expressed as a felt lack of security to participate actively and equally with White students in various curricular, co-curricular, and extracurricular activities.

Blame for the alienating environment could not easily be pinned on the school administration since, under the new principal, they had initiated a number of strategies to increase Mexican-descent students' involvement. These included active and targeted student recruitment campaigns, improvements in the availability of transportation to and from afterschool events and activities, and increased scholarship opportunities for students who could otherwise not afford to purchase the materials for full participation in sports and clubs. Even with these institutional efforts, the school sustained only a very limited degree of success in changing patterns of Latino nonparticipation.

What constituted the largely unacknowledged limitation of AHS's strategy to counter Mexican-descent students' lack of participation was that, despite active steps to improve *access* to clubs, sports, and other activities at the school, they did little to address the social dynamics on campus that would make such opportunities seem realistically available to Mexican-descent students. Accessibility and ownership for Mexican-descent students would require an environment in which they felt able to participate on equal terms and under conditions of mutual respect in school-sanctioned activities (Fine et al. 1997), and those conditions were sorely lacking. Jorge, an academically engaged, first-generation Mexican immigrant student, expressed his experience in the following way:

> I really haven't had a chance to spend time with a lot of White people or a lot of different kinds of people. I don't play sports and I'm involved in clubs, but the ones that we're in are like AVID and MSA [Migrant Student Association]. They're Mexican. So I haven't had a chance to be there with [White students] because I would be the only Mexican. I'm more comfortable with Latinos, and I'm a little weird around White people.

This feeling of being "a little weird around White people" is given further development by Mexican migrant students Alejandra and Ana, also students involved in the school's AVID program. They explain why they prefer not to be involved in the set of activities that constitutes the school's "Spirit Week":

> *Ale*: If you go [to the spirit events], all the White people stare you down. It's embarrassing, you are taking the risk to take this step,

and they look at you like you are some kind of insect. Like you come from Mars and they are here on Earth.

Ana: And if Mexicans went, there are those [Mexican-descent students] that know more English than others. They feel they are above us. So, if you don't want them to say anything [to you], it is better to stay quiet and stay with your friends, and don't go over there.

Ana and Alejandra claimed not only to experience a sense of intimidation for feeling like nonbelonging "outsiders" among White students but also worried about "put-downs" they might receive from other, more assimilated Mexican-descent students who participate in the activities.[1]

A good deal of the insight I received from Mexican-descent students about their feelings of alienation and ambivalence on the campus drew from three years of ongoing interaction with a group of fifteen Mexican migrant students enrolled in Allenstown High's Advancement via Individual Determination (AVID) program. AVID is a nationally known, co-curricular program that identifies middle-achieving students who aspire to attend college and provides them with extra support through a curriculum designed to explicitly teach the skills, dispositions, and information students need to remain on the college track and to prosper once there (see Mehan et al. 1996 for an excellent ethnography of the AVID program and its particular success with Mexican-descent students). The AVID program at Allenstown High was originally instituted by the MEP in the late 1990s but was "mainstreamed" in the early 2000s to allow access to all students. In practice, however, it was only Mexican-descent students who tended to enroll and remain in these elective classes. The AVID courses, and the associated AVID extracurricular club, played a pivotal supportive role for Mexican-descent students at AHS, providing a unique "safe space" and community of support where they were able to develop pro-academic identities, encourage each other to enroll and remain in Advanced Placement (AP) and other more challenging courses, and monitor the extent to which they were "on-track" to fulfill the A to F course requirements necessary for admission into the California State University system. Of the fifteen students with whom I regularly interacted in the AVID program, six were born in Mexico and the rest in the United States to Mexican immigrant parents. All the students were categorized as "migrant," meaning that many returned to Mexico regularly with their families, usually during the winter months, or that they migrated with their parents for seasonal farm labor within the United States. For the most part, all of the AVID students could be considered "Mexican-oriented."[2] The narratives and experiences of AVID students illustrate the complex challenges that even academically oriented, college-aspiring Mexican-descent students faced in their attempts to negotiate pro-academic social identities in a schooling environment that often provoked feelings of discomfort and ambivalence.

Two Mexican migrant students, Rosa and Anita, enrolled in AVID classes for the first time in their sophomore year. Rosa is a relatively recent immigrant who lives with her family in one of the two high-density migrant worker camps operating in the Farmingville area. She considers herself a serious student and says she must maintain vigilance against being swayed by her friends, some of whom she feels are less interested in school. "If I want to study, I will," she says, "even if my friends say, 'C'mon, let's go!' " Despite arriving in the United States just five years earlier from a small rural rancho in Jalisco, Mexico, Rosa was earning a 3.0 GPA at AHS. Beyond her studies, she spends two days a week after school taking lessons in folkloric guitar and voice in Farmingville. Rosa excelled in her English and Spanish classes but struggled a bit in her World Cultures (social studies) and math courses. Her best friend, Anita, is also the daughter of farmworker parents with whom she had emigrated from a small Mexican *rancho* just several miles down the road from Rosa's village. Like Rosa, she was excelling academically, averaging just over a 3.0 GPA. A unique challenge facing Anita, however, was spending up to six weeks of each school year attending schools in Oxnard, California, where her parents migrated for seasonal farm work. When she accompanied them, she would take classes in Oxnard while attempting to stay current on the content of classes she would have to (belatedly) enroll in when she returned to AHS.

Anita and Rosa were among the most active and animated students in the AVID classes and tutorials, where they constantly sought academic support and information about college while playing the role of mentors to their peers. They were also actively involved in the AVID club, where they served, respectively, as club secretary and treasurer. In the first semester of their junior year, they were encouraged by their AVID teacher to enroll together in an AP English class. Now ten weeks into the course, both are struggling to remain engaged in the class and to keep up with their homework. Having shadowed the two of them in the English class, I was struck by their relative reticence and lack of active participation, particularly given the enthusiastic manner in which they contributed in the AVID context. My conversation with them about their experiences in the AP class—and their perceptions about what Mexican-descent students face more broadly in the school—merits quoting at length:

> *CH*: Why do you feel unable to speak up in class?
>
> *Anita*: We feel intimidated by them [White AP students]—we don't even know who those people are. We feel afraid that they're going to laugh at you . . . because of the way you speak or the way you respond to the question.
>
> *Rosa*: I notice that a lot, too. Just on the way you pronounce words. Like, they [Mexican immigrant students] just feel like, "I'd rather not answer than to embarrass myself so much."
>
> *Anita*: It might be someone who is speaking Spanish and barely learning English. And if it's an all-English class, they have to answer in English. They are going to answer in a different accent, to which they're going to feel inferior to how other people talk, you know? And that's what makes them feel inferior or not want to [participate] . . .
>
> *CH*: If you're in that situation where you can speak up but you don't want to—why would you *assume* that people are going to laugh at you or make fun of you?
>
> *Anita*: Because sometimes they are racist. They are going to be against you in the first place to where if you answer something, they are going to turn around and just look at you like: "That's not the right answer," even though it might be. They do laugh. No matter what.
>
> *Rosa*: I mean, everybody laughs at each other. It's just that White people tend to laugh more at us. And sometimes we laugh at them, because we're just not the same. It's a different world in a way. They think one way, we think another. They have their culture, we have ours.

Despite both students' academic potential and strong will to succeed in school, the discomfort and social separation they experienced on campus has produced a fear of negative encounters that has discouraged them from participating in schooling activities that might put them in contact with White students. They feel limited in their ability to actively participate due to what they experience as the inherent racial and social hierarchies operating within the classroom and school.

In fact, a number of AVID students could describe—some vividly and in great detail—the painful moments they have experienced in their predominantly White AP and Honors classes, including how they felt themselves to be targets of harmful stereotypes that positioned them as slow learners and how they have endured disparaging "put-downs" for their use of Spanish in class. Their narratives highlights the extent to which being "Mexican" and being "American" are viewed by students at best as distinct and somewhat parallel worlds and, at worst, as contradictory and incompatible ones. As Rosa says, "They think one way, we think another. They have their culture; we have ours." This sense of dissonance and disconnection is not simply a consequence of dissimilar class and cultural backgrounds; students are unable to get past borders of racialized difference within the school—and which are replicated in the classroom—in order to explore common interests they might have.

Vignette #1: Celebrating "Mexican Culture" at Allenstown High

Allenstown High teachers and staff acknowledged the social separation, discriminatory attitudes, and lack of mutual understanding that existed along ethnoracial lines, and they recognized it as a serious problem. One particular effort made to enhance Mexican-descent students' feeling of belonging at the school was to resume a strategy—which had fallen off in the years following the student walkouts—to actively promote celebrations of Mexican holidays like Cinco de Mayo. The school administration hoped that through intentional, thoughtful planning, such "cultural commemorations" might aid in promoting mutual respect, intercultural understanding, and equal status among students.

Reinstituted in 1999, Cinco de Mayo activities took the form of cultural celebrations held in the Quad area during lunchtime that featured entertainment-oriented activities like traditional Mexican dances and the availability of so-called Mexican food (tacos, burritos, enchiladas, etc.). This "cultural consumption" approach was considered successful and was continued without much incident until 2001. Then, under the leadership of a new principal, the administration elected to take a bolder step and sponsor a schoolwide commemoration of Dieciséis de Septiembre [September 16], the Mexican national holiday that marks the country's independence from Spain. The responsibility for planning the event was delegated to two predominantly Latino student clubs on campus, Tiburones Unidos and the Migrant Student Association (MSA). Together, they organized a schoolwide assembly during the lunch period that included a short play and a fashion show. Although the program was well executed overall, problems began soon after the assembly was dismissed. A White student from Allenstown, who had come to school with his head painted like the U.S. flag, stormed around campus holding a larger flag that he would wave, tauntingly, in the faces of Mexican-descent students who had brought Mexican flags.

When this White student was singled out by the administration and disciplined for his actions, a handful of parents in Allenstown complained, bothered that a student would be disciplined for waving a U.S. flag. Enrique Flores, an MEP teacher at the school, offered his recollection of what ensued after this incident:

> The principal came and talked to us about [the incident] and said that the parents in Allenstown were saying: "Why were we celebrating those silly holidays? We're in the States, not in Mexico." They were asking why a student would be punished for carrying the American flag when all the other boys carrying the Mexican flag weren't punished. I didn't understand. It would be the same as if there were a celebration of the Fourth of July and a boy would bring a Mexican flag to school and start provoking others who are celebrating. What they were really upset about was that we were celebrating the 16th of September here in the United States.

In response to this incident, and in a well-intentioned effort to deal more seriously with the cultural meaning of Mexican holidays, the school decided to organize a special assembly as part of its Cinco de Mayo commemoration later in the same school year. Unlike earlier Cinco de Mayo celebrations, where participation was voluntary and activities were primarily entertainment oriented, this assembly was to be mandatory and focused on the educational goal of encouraging all students to learn about La Batalla de Puebla (the Battle at Puebla) and why Cinco de Mayo is celebrated.[3]

Some parents in Allenstown expressed preemptive opposition to the event, echoing earlier resistance to having their children forfeit class time to attend an assembly that presented them with information they were not interested in learning. Again, in the words of an AHS teacher, the issue for parents was, "Why would so much time would be dedicated to the celebration of Mexico when we are in the United States?"

The 2002 Cinco de Mayo assembly renewed flag-waving competitions between students, provoking shouting matches, various expressions of ill will, and some instances of physical confrontation between groups of White and Mexican-descent students. In these flag-waving exchanges, Mexican-descent students played a more prominent role as instigators than before. "Sometimes it would be our fault," admitted Carlos, a Mexican-descent AVID student, "because they [my Mexican-descent peers] disrespected our [Mexican] flag. They'd wear it around their head or wear it as a bandana and sometimes they'd rub it in their [White students'] faces."

Although the U.S. and Mexican flags were both used as evocative symbols in these exchanges, the intent and purpose of each seemed to be distinct. The deployment of the U.S. flag seemed primarily to be for exclusive purposes, as a symbolic "call for order" and a reassertion of dominant cultural norms and status relations that required the suppression of difference, as exemplified in one student's flag-waving taunt: "It's all about the United States!" The use of the Mexican flag, however, seemed to be less about asserting the superiority of all things Mexican than about expressing a public claim of belonging, including a right to being treated as equals, with dignity, in the life of the school and the larger Allenstown community.

That does not mean, however, that all Mexican-descent students were in agreement with how the flag was used in these exchanges. Some Mexican-descent AVID students, without condoning the actions of their peers, sympathized with the feelings of anger and resentment that inspired them. Martina explained it in the following way:

> I mean, I didn't do that ["boo" the U.S. flag], but they [who did] were mad. And if they're not going to respect our flag, why should we respect theirs? Like what this girl said in my English class, she said: "Why do Mexicans flick off Americans or talk badly about the Americans if they are in this country?" I agree with that, but just because you're in a country doesn't mean you have to leave your country behind and not defend it. To me it's about justice. It means they don't understand what we've been through, and they don't

> understand what we're going through when they're talking bad about our country.

Although Martina makes no excuses for her Mexican-descent peers who took part in the "in your face" flag-waving incidents, she felt strongly that those White students who displayed U.S. flags during the assembly demonstrated a lack of respect for the Mexican national and cultural background, as well as an unwillingness to grant it equal status with an "American" background.

Martina admitted that her sense of justice developed, in large part, through conversations with her parents to whom she often turned to express her disappointment about the incidents at the high school. In a meeting over coffee in their small, two-bedroom apartment in Farmingville—which included Martina, her three younger siblings, and three caged songbirds—Martina's mother explained how she and her husband made sense of what was happening at the high school, and how they choose to counsel their daughter to best deal with the situation:

> What we have talked about is how, when Cinco de Mayo is celebrated, it's met with an indifference from the Americans toward Mexican students, an indifference that makes them feel rejection. Every single Cinco de Mayo she comes home sad. When she asks her dad, "Why do they reject us in this way?" he says to her, "Well, perhaps it isn't everyone." But they will never be able to change our origin as Mexicans, and it doesn't change the fact that we are here. Even though we are in school and we have to be in school, we must respect and know what is in our history, and we must celebrate it. If we are going to study the laws of this country, well, we will respect them. But why not know about the origins of other places in the world? It's a matter of respect. So this is what we teach her. We must remain respectful. Their dad tells them that they should take things *con calma* [calmly]. First of all, we are here and we must respect [the traditions], okay? We know how to give respect.

Although Martina's parents were clearly bothered by the indifference and hostility with which some Allenstown students and their parents regarded the commemorations of Mexican holidays, they nevertheless encouraged their daughter to take the events *con calma*. They expected her to respect the rules of the school but also to maintain a sense of pride in her own cultural heritage.

The Administration Response to the Crisis

The principal's initial response to the Cinco de Mayo incidents was that, while concerned about the xenophobic resentment harbored by some Allenstown parents and their children, she felt uneasy about taking any particular course of action:

> It seems that there's just this huge resentment. And why? I don't know, because it's really hard for me to understand it. I try to figure out. Okay, what are you afraid of? There's this huge resentment of allowing Hispanic students to celebrate; it's somehow a "slap in my face" as an American—a slap in our country's face when you do that. And I just don't get it, because I spent Fourth of July in Farmingville, watching all of these same families who all live right there, with their American flag out, waving, having a heck of a good time because it was Fourth of July and they're happy to celebrate. I don't get it.

Despite an alleged ignorance about the factors that inspired resentment from Allenstown residents, she understood that the school bore ultimate responsibility to address the situation. In her view, the primary mistake was to have *required* all students to attend the Cinco de Mayo assembly rather than leaving it as a voluntary option for those students who would most appreciate it. In adopting this interpretation of the problem, the school administration decided that the most practical way to resolve the situation was to assure that those students who resented the celebrations not be compelled to attend. Some teachers agreed with this strategy. "I agree with us having a celebration for Cinco de Mayo," expressed a White male math teacher, "but I don't agree with shoving it down their [Allenstown residents'] throats."

After further discussion, however, the AHS administration decided that the best way to avert resentment, and the heightened state of tension these events produced, was not only to make student attendance voluntary, but to move away from promoting Mexican cultural celebrations *altogether*. Instead, the administration planned to host a "more inclusive" multicultural celebration that would highlight a variety of cultural expressions. As one administrator reasoned, the new strategy was to avoid "singling out one culture to celebrate or not celebrate" and instead to promote an appreciation of a variety of cultures, showcasing folkloric and cultural "traditions" from around the world. He explained:

> We started with the idea of, well, let's get away from [Cinco de Mayo]. Why are we always singling out any one particular culture, rather than trying to show how we all have different experiences, but share similarities in those different experiences? Why don't we celebrate all of them?

This logic prompted the organization of a "World Week" celebration the following fall that would coincide with Mexican Independence Day.

The bulk of the planning for World Week was assumed by the ASB, under the direction of Allenstown High's student activities coordinator who also served as a coach of the varsity cheerleading team. The ASB decided that, during each lunch period, they would feature a cultural expression, or performance, found in one of the world's major continents. For example, Monday would highlight cultural expressions from Africa, Tuesday Europe, Wednesday Asia, and Thursday South America. On Friday, a culminating "World Day" assembly was planned. However, in the course of planning and organizing the ambitious and complex set of events, the final "World Day" commemoration was somehow translated equivocally as "USA Day" in the sense that the United States was considered the great "melting pot" of all the world's cultures. But, by building the final assembly around the idea of a USA Day—instead of the North American continent, which would have been more consistent with the week's theme—it became unclear what place, if any, Mexico would have in the activities.

Margarita Villarosa, a Mexican American counselor and former MEP staff member at the school, was among those perplexed and angered by the format. She contacted the administration to inquire about the change, and related to me the errors and follies that seemed to surround the whole World Week endeavor:

> When they celebrated Europe, Africa, and then South America, I said, "Where's Mexico?" because then on Friday it was "United States Day." And then they said, "Oh, it's [in] South America." And

> it was really embarrassing because, in their minds, they thought that Mexico was part of South America. So in the gymnasium at that time, they included the flags from all over the world—except for the flag of Mexico. The students and staff of Mexican-descent were very upset about it. For the entire week, there were dancers who performed at the school from India, Ireland, Africa—every culture except the Mexican culture. That was like a slap in the face for Mexicans.

The omission was not lost on AHS Mexican-descent students. When Friday's USA Day assembly began, the lines of ethnoracial division had clearly formed. "We were all on one side [of the gym] and they were on the other side," recalls AVID student Elena Chavez. "They were singing the [U.S. national] anthem, and then everybody started raising Mexican flags and then some White students started flicking us off." Things took a turn for the worse after the assembly when, Elena explained, an angry Mexican-descent student "took the Mexican flag and put it in a White boy's face." The White student grabbed the flag and threw it on the ground, beginning a brawl that included a handful of students and a notable ring of spectators.

According to the students I spoke with in an AVID tutorial after the event, one of the unfortunate and disturbing consequences of the conflict was that the physical separation characterizing Mexican-descent and White students in the assembly carried over into classrooms in the weeks that followed:

> *Maria*: It was just like fighting [arguing], but you could tell that half of the class was—well, I don't know how to explain it.
>
> *Elena*: Okay, let me put it this way—you could sit wherever you want, but you could tell, all the Mexicans were on one side and all the Americans were on the other.

Given the follies inherent in the school's management of cultural celebrations—even after attempting to shift to more "neutral" themes—the administration decided in 2003 to refrain from actively promoting any activities for Cinco de Mayo. This strategy proved all the more disastrous. Over 50 percent of the school population—approximately 1,000 students—were absent that day. Students from Allenstown had informally designated the occasion as a "Senior Skip Day," and a number of Allenstown parents, fearing fights that may ensue, elected to keep their students home from school. Furthermore, given that the school had failed to plan any activities to commemorate Cinco de Mayo, a good amount of Mexican-descent students skipped school, either in protest or to attend a full day of events organized in Farmingville.

Given the significant student absences and an unflattering front page article in the local newspaper, the AHS administration initially attempted to deflect blame by directing criticism toward the campus' Latino community for their failure to schedule any Cinco de Mayo activities. The administration argued that that they had not so much *opposed* having activities as that the school's Latino student organizations had not taken the initiative to organize and plan any. This explanation drew the ire of a number of teachers and staff at the high school—particularly those who worked closely with Mexican-descent students. They resented the implication that responsibility for such events should be "dumped on" Latino students and their club advisors instead of being the collective responsibility of the entire school. MEP staff member Enrique Flores expressed his frustration about an expectation that Latinos should be the ones who brainstorm, develop, and execute the various academic, organizational, and social activities designed to promote diversity and enhance a sense of belonging for Mexican-descent students on campus:

> I was more angered by the commentary of the administration because I don't feel that this should be organized by Latinos or Latino clubs, because we have the ASB who are supposed to be in charge of all school activities. The administration will turn around and say, "Oh, we'll just go talk to Migrant [Education staff], to MSA, to Tiburones Unidos, to the Spanish Department so they can get something organized." And I think that it shouldn't be that way. This kind of responsibility should not be handed over to a group because of the fact that they are Latino. If we celebrate the Chinese New Year and there's an Asian student, they aren't going to be made responsible for the whole event because they are Asian.

Although most teachers and staff had backed the administration's general World Week strategy, several were bothered by the idea that this event should be used to replace, rather than complement, the commemoration of Mexican holidays. Ronnie, a White language arts teacher, recalled an earlier faculty meeting in which the topic arose:

> I remember there was one conversation when a teacher was saying, "Oh well, on Cinco de Mayo, I bet you we won't have problems. We'll just celebrate everybody's culture. We'll just have it be like a multicultural day and everything." And I said that's not the issue. The issue is, Why is it wrong to give Mexican kids the chance and the opportunity to feel proud of who they are? Why is that so wrong?

School counselor Villarosa made the claim that the World Week concept seemed "a convenient way to tip-toe around" difficult questions of racial and cultural status and entitlement that played out in divisive ways during the commemorations of Mexican holidays. In her mind, the conflicts surrounding Cinco de Mayo and World Week were less an inevitable consequence of parent resistance and student tension than a result of a school administration that spent more time and energy preparing for the potential negatives of the events than wholeheartedly and creatively planning for the positive.

Allenstown High's principal admitted that reactionary parents from the Allenstown community were indeed those who "yelled the most" when the school presented Mexican cultural heritage as something all students should be expected to learn about, engage with, and respect:

> I have a phone message that I've saved from a parent. . . . It was Mexican Independence Day—it was our first one—just ripping me for allowing them to hang a Mexican flag. "How dare you? What are you thinking?" Those are the things that parents call about. . . . There are certain areas of this population that are really reactionary and those are the ones that have been the real pressure-cookers.

Although Mexican-descent parents may have been equally disturbed by the conflicts surrounding Mexican holidays and the administration's manner of dealing with them, they did not complain with the same frequency and vigor—nor achieve the same influence—as some of the White parents. There may be various reasons for this reticence. Some Latino parents felt a lack of entitlement to express their concerns about the social aspects of school, particularly one located in the Allenstown residential area. Another significant factor was the overall lack of Mexican-descent parents' representation on site-based management organizations like the booster club and the AHS Site Council. For example, in 2002, there was not a single Latino parent on the site council team. This situation reflects the more systematic estrangement of Farmingville's Mexican-descent parents from the high school. This estrangement may have to do, in part, with the relative distance to the school site as well as many migrant parents' long and strenuous work schedules that may preclude full participation in afterschool and evening activities. However, it is also attributable to the difficulties that these parents have in communicating with Allenstown High school staff and the sense of discomfort some have expressed in doing so.

Impact of the Conflicts on the School Participation of Mexican-Descent Students

The meaning that Mexican cultural holidays hold for many Latino students at AHS was well addressed by Sonia Mendez who, along with Enrique, served as the two-person staff of the school's MEP. Sonia explained that although many Mexican-descent students lacked precise knowledge of the historical meaning of events like Cinco de Mayo, the celebrations remained significant because they stood among the few opportunities for Mexican-descent youth to demonstrate pride in and receive public validation for their Mexican cultural heritage. She considered this particularly important given the school and larger societal context in which Latino youth often struggled to maintain a sense of belonging:

> I know that Enrique would ask these boys: "What is the 16th of September?" or "What's Cinco de Mayo?" and many couldn't even answer him. They don't know, but they simply feel a part of it because perhaps Homecoming isn't theirs, "World Week" isn't theirs, and "Spirit Week" also isn't theirs. So many of these things don't make them feel like they belong. So obviously they view this event as part of being a Mexican, and I'm going to be a part of it. I think that this holiday is just an escape for them—from an oppression of the sort where they don't identify with what's happening in the school and they use [the holiday] as a way to escape and to belong to something. . . . It's because they want acceptance and want to belong. If the community isn't embracing them or accepting them, then they are going to find a way to feel accepted.

In light of the negative ways that commemorations have played out in the school, however, many of the Mexican-descent students in the AVID program had begun to express a growing ambivalence about continuing such events. Despite the profound role that the administration seemed to have played in shaping how cultural celebrations turned into negative experiences for Mexican-descent students, a number of AVID students believed the school bore little responsibility for the tensions provoked by the events. Rosa offered the following assessment, one that a surprising number of her peers seemed to share:

> A lot of the time it's just on how kids are brought up in the first place. A lot of the White kids—most of them from my way of seeing, anyway—were brought up saying you can't like these other people, you can't interact with them a lot. So, that's just another way of bringing us down. So that makes them feel superior to where we feel inferior to them. And I've noticed that a lot with Mexican or Latino people, or whatever, who feel inferior to them. And they say, "Well, why should I do it [be involved in school events and activities]? Who cares? They're the ones that are getting all of the attention."

Several other AVID students shared similar convictions—that White and Mexican-descent students' attitudes toward one another are fairly immutable because they are determined by "people's personalities" and "the way kids are raised." It is these sorts of understandings about difference—developed in an environment of relative ethnoracial isolation and further enhanced by the way cultural celebrations have been handled at the school—that have assured the continued division and separation of White and Mexican-descent students at the school in ways that are understood to be more or less natural. In this context, interracial friendships are very difficult to establish and maintain.

The Challenges Facing Teachers

To this point, I have said little about the roles and responsibilities of teachers who are left to deal with the student and community conflicts that have become so highly politicized around celebrations of Mexican holidays. Clearly, such incidents provide fertile ground for teachers to intervene by engaging issues of racial and class entitlement with their students, and by interrogating the privileged location from which White students and parents may ask: "Why should we celebrate something pertaining to Mexico if we aren't there?"

The campus unit most active in addressing issues of this kind was the Migrant Education Program (MEP). Operating out of a classroom-sized space in the school's G-Building, MEP offers a physical space for students to work on homework or extracurricular projects, attend club meetings, or just informally "hang out" with their peers and the supportive staff (see Gibson and Bejínez 2002 for a detailed description of the MEP program at the high school). Enrique and Sonia supervise the space and serve as secondary advisors and counselors to the several hundred migrant students on campus. They communicate with students' (primarily Spanish speaking) parents, keep track of students' academic progress, and actively reach out to migrant students who appear to be "slipping," to provide formal and informal tutoring services. While MEP's mission is to serve migrant youth, the staff does not check students' statuses at the door. Nearly all students in the AVID program take advantage of MEP services on a weekly basis for homework support and social interaction with peers before and after school and during the lunch period.

Both Enrique and Sonia have used the conflicts surrounding cultural commemorations such as Cinco de Mayo to teach students that behaving well and respecting others starts with a responsibility to respect oneself and one's own cultural heritage. Enrique explains:

> Something that we try to tell our students—for example, I am against how the boys here want to use the flag. I told them about how the Mexican flag is respected, to the point at which it's almost sacred, and you all come here and you're using it for such nonsense, placing it on your head as if it were a scarf, hanging it off of your body. That's why when we see these boys who bring the American flag to school and do such silly things with them, I tell them, "We don't want you to do that with the Mexican flag, so we're going to take them away."

Enrique, in his late twenties, was once a migrant student himself. He is typically found wearing soccer warm-up pants and running shoes, given his secondary role as head coach of the varsity men's soccer and track teams. In addition to his full-time work schedule, Enrique gets up each Saturday morning to open the doors of an indoor recreation facility in Farmingville to any of his students, offering for them to come play basketball or otherwise have a place to hang out. It is through these informal weekend recreational opportunities that I came to know Enrique well.

Enrique's office is a small, short-walled cubicle tucked in the far left corner of the MEP classroom, while Sonia's is in the far right corner. The cubicles serve the dual purpose of meeting space and personal escape from the constant activity in this room. Enrique's outer cubicle walls are covered in inspirational quotes that are framed in cardboard paper and translated in both Spanish and English. Centrally placed is a miniature chalkboard that reads: *Migrant teachers make a difference*. Shelves within the office hold several *recuerdos* (souvenirs) from his hometown in Mexico, a migrant-sending community well known to students as a shared origin of many of the migrant families who live in Farmingville.

Beyond the academic and advising support services that MEP provides, Enrique also sees his role as one of advocate and mentor for Latino students on the campus. He encourages all of his students to develop self-respect and engage in self-reflection. Through his advisor-ship of the MSA, he feels it is important to prepare Latino students to defend themselves against the discrimination they may face within Allenstown High:

> I think that one of our goals in MSA is to empower students, so they feel that they can go to their classes and believe "I can defend myself, and that's what I learned [in MSA]." That's why we do the field trips. That's why we do the conferences. That's why we do these things, so that students feel that they are empowered. "I can defend myself. I don't have to take this from my teacher, or this dumb comment from the students in my class."

A female language arts teacher agreed that MEP seemed to be the only unit in the school that has prioritized engaging issues of diversity and difference with students:

> I think most of the activities that have any kind of influence for the Mexican kids on campus come from the Migrant [Education] department, and I don't really think that's their job. Their job is to help the students academically and socially, yes, but they're having to

> do all kinds of things that I don't think that they should have to do. I think there should be people in the administration that are really going to advocate for those kinds of things because all these different activities—you know, whether it's academic, social, dances, [or] activities like Cinco de Mayo, things like that—all come from Migrant [Ed].

Despite Enrique's desire to empower students to succeed socially and academically, he admits to feeling reservations about encouraging Mexican-descent students to get involved in campus activities that are dominated by White students, or to establish themselves among students in central places like the Quad area:

> I have not really encouraged students to go out and [say], "Yeah, let's put ourselves over there in the Quad," or whatever. I wouldn't want to put my students in a situation where they feel they're in danger or it's going to be worse. Because you don't know what's going to happen.

Enrique fears that by encouraging his students to "put themselves out there," he may actually be putting them at risk rather than advancing their interests or engagement. He would feel more comfortable encouraging his students to participate in mainstream activities, he said, if he felt "someone is reaching out to the Anglo kids, too." He sees this effort as lacking and believes it needs to be a higher priority among other teachers at the school.

During a slow afternoon tutorial session in the MEP office, Enrique and I got to talking about his experiences coaching the men's soccer team, which—along with the track team—are among the rare spaces on campus where White and Mexican-descent students participate in fairly equal numbers. He spoke of a recent instance in which he arranged for an intrasquad soccer scrimmage to be held on the "*football*" field—a designation he marked, cynically, with hand-gestured quotation marks, given that the field was also used for interscholastic soccer matches. He explained that the athletic administrators typically did not like the soccer team "messing up" the football field. On the day of the scheduled scrimmage, it had rained a bit and the field was somewhat soggy. While Enrique acknowledged that his choice to use the field might raise some hackles, what transpired during the scrimmage was unexpected. He recounted:

> When the football team walked by, a few were yelling: "Get off our fields, wetbacks!" Now, my team is about half Anglo and half Mexican. I told the Anglo players: "Congratulations, you've just become a wetback [too]." Some of the Latinos got really upset and wanted to respond to it. I said, "No, [and] if you respond to it, you run a mile." And they said, "Mr. Flores!"—I said, "I don't care! Don't do anything." And some of the Anglo kids [on the soccer team] got upset because of the comments that those kids made. And I said, "See? You're a team, so a lot of you are wetbacks now. You just became part of our group." And a lot of players were never before in that situation, and now they were shocked. And I think things like that got them closer and closer. But as coaches, as advisors, as teachers, if we don't do it ourselves—I mean, if we don't create that environment for our kids, it's not going to happen. They're not going to participate. We've got to do something about this. Teachers have to take responsibility to talk about this stuff with the kids.

In this incident with the football team, Enrique was particularly disappointed because "the coach was walking with them; they encourage that. These kids are being kids, and it's up to the teachers to talk to them."

Engaging Teachers

According to AHS's principal, the biggest obstacle to getting teachers to address the issues of race, status, and entitlement that contribute to tensions between students is getting them to acknowledge that a racial problem exists at the school:

> The very first time we had a discussion with the teachers about racism it was over the Cinco de Mayo issue that hit the newspaper. They looked at me like I was nuts. "We don't have a racial problem!" [they said]. . . . It had never been talked about, directly.

That issues of racial conflict had "never been talked about, directly" must be seen in relation to the school's historic reluctance to deal with the recurring racial, class, and cultural conflicts in a direct and constructive way. An assistant principal admitted that the institutional strategy—at least since the mid-1990s—has been less concerned with bringing students together than with simply getting them to behave—something that they believed was best achieved through a strong discipline policy. "We squashed all the problems; we squashed the gangs," she said. "The unspoken policy was 'We're not interested in blending. Everybody just behave.'"

Rather than focusing on the "systematic and structural elements in schooling environments within which violence is produced, perpetuated, or facilitated" (Meucci and Redmon 1997: 140), the school's leadership preferred an approach to conflict that promoted enhanced discipline and the removal of students known to be troublemakers. In practical terms, however, the school justified this preference for disciplinary action *not* in terms of a reluctance to engage with questions of diversity, difference, and status as they existed within the school, but as a claim of *institutional neutrality* toward such issues. However, assuming a position of alleged neutrality—while choosing to placate the concerns of those Allenstown parents who resist commemorations of Mexican holidays—has sent mixed messages to Allenstown High teachers. These mixed messages have impacted how teachers imagine their own responsibility to address difficult issues in their classrooms.

A former MEP staff member offered her opinion about the relationship between institutional neutrality, parent protests, and teacher reluctance to address issues of diversity and difference in the classroom:

> When there have been activities such as Cinco de Mayo—where an attempt is made to teach the history of the event and the celebration—obviously, there has always been some kind of protest. And if this protest is coming from the parents from this [Allenstown] community, and they are the ones who communicate regularly with the school about whatever they disapprove of and their complaints are heeded, then obviously the teachers aren't going to be as interested in covering these subjects as a result.

I asked the principal what she believed would be the most effective way to encourage reluctant teachers to incorporate sensitive issues of diversity and difference more centrally into their teaching practice. The challenge, she said, was that it would require "forcing a connection" with teachers, and she felt somewhat ambivalent about this approach:

> You've got to have something in the program that forces a connection (with the teachers). Because that's what's hard, how do you *force* a connection? You know, "Okay, I'm required to do this in my class, but I don't really *want* to do this." So as the teacher, I'm not really going to put my heart into it. . . . You've got to also train the teachers to be counselors, and they didn't sign up for that.

Because of this ambivalence, the school continued to rely on a strictly *voluntary* approach to curriculum innovation around the issues of politicized intergroup differences and relationships. This voluntary approach has assured that those few teachers and staff most invested and comfortable addressing these issues with students are the only ones who do so. Unfortunately, these individuals continue to be—with some notable exceptions—the relatively few Latino teachers and staff at the school, and they are becoming increasingly reluctant to do so by themselves. As Sonia put it:

> We have our jobs to do, and many people think that we're at their disposal, "Oh, well, let's go talk to Migrant Ed," or "Migrant Ed can organize this or that." What maybe they don't understand is that we can't be out there acting like revolutionaries when we have students who are failing classes that we have to reach quickly, before it's too late, and if we don't do it during this semester, they may not be able to graduate, or they'll drop out of school. And while we go around trying to put together a Cinco de Mayo celebration or a 16th of September celebration, maybe five more students will be gone.

Another important concern, which Enrique highlighted, is whether such innovative teaching practices will ever reach all students. If those teachers most open to incorporating multicultural strategies tend to be those working more closely with the Latino students, the question remains: Who is going to work with the White students?

Vignette #2: Engaging Difference with White Students

Attempting to address issues of racial, cultural, and class status and entitlement can prove a difficult endeavor in any classroom, but particularly in mixed and White-dominated classrooms like those at AHS. Rene Watson, a beginning Spanish teacher at the school, had a strong interest in having her students engage with and better understand the conditions that promoted racial segregation and the disparaged status of Latino students on the campus. A White woman in her late twenties and a first-year teacher at AHS, Watson was assigned to teach both Spanish 1 and Spanish 2 classes. She had recently returned from a teaching experience in Mexico and before that, she had taught two years at an elementary school in Farmingville.

Rene's classrooms were a fairly even split between White and Mexican-descent students. Rene describes a fair amount of the Mexican-descent students in her class as "closet Spanish speakers." By this she meant that they were capable of speaking some Spanish, but for whatever reasons—perhaps lack of fluency or lack of proficiency to read and write in Spanish—chose to enter a regular Spanish class rather than one of the "Spanish for Spanish Speakers" classes offered at the school. While she felt that a "small minority" of students in her class "were really interested and excited about learning a language, even though they won't show that much of the time," she believed many were taking the course more as a way to enhance their college application or to fulfill a requirement for graduation. "They think of learning the language as more like a [technical] skill, like in their math class," she explained. "I think they see that as everything that encompasses learning a language."

Near the end of the fall academic semester, Rene responded to students who were "begging for extra credit" by offering an optional research assignment in which they were asked to go out on campus and find five Mexican students to talk to who were either bilingual or Spanish-language dominant. She provided interested students with a questionnaire they could use to conduct interviews with Mexican-descent students, asking them how they felt about being on the AHS campus, how they felt others perceived them, whether they felt comfortable on campus, and what kind of "put-downs" they might have received. The assignment also asked students to solicit interviewees' beliefs about what might be done to create the kind of environment where Latino students might feel more comfortable on campus. The interview prompt included a list of options from which interviewees could choose—from having more music in Spanish during the lunch period to having more Latino teachers on campus. There was also a question asking interviewees what they thought White students might do "in order to make you feel more comfortable," offering again a list of possibilities that interviewees could choose from, asking them to name their top three.

Overall, Rene was impressed by the assignments she got back from her students. "I had a few papers that said, 'I don't like this assignment' and that 'I don't really think it's worthwhile,' but I also got a lot of papers that said, 'Wow, I never thought about this before,' which I thought was the importance of it." Not long after she distributed the research project prompt, Rene received an e-mail from the school principal telling her that a parent had complained about the assignment. Rene was asked to forward a copy of the assignment to the principal's office, which she did. It was not until several weeks later that she discovered the complaint had traveled all the way to the district office. At this point, the principal contacted her directly. She recalled their discussion:

> She came up to me and talked to me and said, "You know, I've had complaints about this assignment, I'm wondering what it was." So I said, "Okay, well, this is the assignment," and she said, "Well, apparently. I've just read the assignment and I think it's too biased. It's written in terms of putting more blame on the White students." And I think that's how the parents took it, [that I was saying] all these racial issues were the fault of the White students, which is not the way I intended it. But I had also slanted it that way so that they would get good responses from the students. I wasn't going to have them go interview five White students because I really felt that they already knew what their peers' responses were [going to be].

Rene disagreed with the principal's assessment of the assignment and provided reasons why:

> I said I think it's important for students to know—to have that experience of talking to [other Latino] kids, and talking to kids about this issue. And I think it's important for them to get the responses. But she [the principal] said, "That doesn't matter," basically. Those weren't her exact words but she basically said: "Well, this is what you have to comply with. You have to make it balanced."

Rene's interpretation of the principal's behavior was consistent with other staff and teachers, quoted earlier, who expressed their concern that the administration too often weighed its commitment to promote diversity and engage differences *against* its concern with the vocal White parents who were invested in seeing that these discussions about issues of difference, power, and status do not have a place in the classroom or in the school. She elaborated:

> I just thought the administration was kind of in denial . . . I think that they're very concerned about having an appearance of everything being in balance here and they're very concerned with it—no matter if it's true or not—that they try and balance everything out. Because they feel that if they support anything to do with the side of Mexicans, or Mexican culture, or anything like that, they get so much backlash from the parents that it keeps it [their commitment] down on a lower level.

Again, this notion of "being balanced" is founded on the idea that the school can somehow remain neutral on issues that are obviously not neutral for students. In the principal's handling of the case with Rene, the "problem" was not necessarily a questioning of her assignment, but that the principal failed to offer or provide the kind of support and encouragement that might assist Rene in an effort to refine her pedagogical practice to more effectively address issues of status and difference with White students. By not providing active encouragement and support, the school provided tacit support for the attitudes and ignorance that fueled the separations between students in the first place. The situation that developed over Rene's assignment also demonstrates that creating conditions for teachers to effectively engage sensitive topics of diversity and difference with their students requires work beyond the classroom level: the administration must support teachers against the loud and sometimes hostile voices of those more enfranchised parents who resist such strategies. At the same time, administrative support must go beyond irregular training opportunities and positive lip-service, and toward active encouragement and ongoing, comprehensive professional development around issues of diversity.

Rene Watson's stint as a teacher in AHS was short. She chose to return to Farmingville after only a year. She felt that as long as the school continued to maintain a position of seeming neutrality (a "neutrality" that in her case translated into a lack of active support for innovative pedagogy) on the highly politicized differences and conflicts that divide students on the campus, the school will not only fail to equally serve all of its students, it will also fail to build the kind of diverse teaching staff willing and able to successfully transform the existing social and academic patterns that students seem to fall into so "naturally" at the school.

Summary

Ethnographers of education have long noted the ways in which traditional public displays in U.S. high schools—spectacles like homecoming, football rituals, and various "school spirit" activities—can play a constitutive role in reproducing dominant norms of "American" citizenship and gender-appropriate behaviors (Foley 1996; Perry 2002). This is achieved by privileging the values, behaviors, and experiences characteristic of White middle-class populations, thereby reconstituting the superior value of European American cultural practices and their association with dominant notions of U.S. citizenship. In this specific case, however, public spectacles of "Mexican" cultural heritage are coopted, paradoxically, to perform a similar "Americanizing" function. At Allenstown High, commemorations of Mexican holidays like Cinco de Mayo and Dieciséis de Septiembre, although presenting an opportunity to promote intercultural and binational understanding and to cultivate mutual respect among students, have served instead to further intensify tensions between White and Mexican-descent students and to reinforce students' perceptions of the essential and irreconcilable differences that seem to separate them from their racial, class, and cultural "other." Although the controversies surrounding the holidays are undeniably an expression of the larger racial and cultural politics at play in the region and state, administrators and teachers at AHS—through their actions, reactions, and silences—have played an influential role in how these commemorations have been received and the conflicts they have engendered (see Gitlin et al. 2003 for similar analysis).

The experience at Allenstown High supports the conviction of researchers like Fine, Weis, and Powell (1997) who claim that "declarations of institutional neutrality actually *produce* educational hierarchy, racial and ethnic oppositions, and intergroup tensions, while peer culture more than adequately patrols these racialized, classed, and gendered hierarchies" (28). Moreover, claims of neutrality encourage reluctance among teachers to see themselves as responsible for addressing issues of intergroup respect and interaction. The unfortunate result is that there is little space or opportunity for discussions and enquiry among students that might begin to engage and ameliorate the existing racial tensions. Approaches that fail to support—or worse, that actively discourage—direct and critical engagement with the particular institutional and everyday practices that reproduce tension within the school, fail to acknowledge that race and ethnicity matter to students, as much as they might wish they did not (Jervis 1996; Pollock 2004).

At AHS, this "neutral" manner of dealing with ethnic conflict, cultural entitlement, and racial anxiety has promoted a sense of ambivalence among many Mexican-descent youth, affecting both their willingness and their ability to be actively involved in important schooling events and activities. Because engagement in such schooling contexts provides students with access to important skills, resources, experiences, and social relationships that help facilitate success in school, it can be said that Mexican-descent students' noninvolvement limits their educational opportunity. Here, equality of educational opportunity is viewed beyond the narrow focus of an "opportunity to learn" specific academic skills, to encompass a deeper understanding of the complex institutional and interpersonal politics that not only limit opportunities to learn in the classroom but impede students' access to a variety of important schooling contexts that aid in school success. In this case, Mexican-descent students have access to a school that is resource rich, but because of feelings of ambivalence and a sense of nonbelonging, they feel unable to take advantage of the benefits in the ways their Anglo peers do.

The events highlighted here, and the differential student identifications they have helped yield, may seem a reasonable reflection of the divisive racial and cultural politics at play in this region of California. However, it is important to note that public schools can play a profound role in maintaining and perpetuating either/or definitions of "Whiteness" and "Mexicanness" as well as students' perceptions of the racial and sociocultural borders that present "Mexican" and "American" as seemingly unequal and irreconcilable worlds. As Angela Valenzuela (1999) has argued, public schools in the United States have tended to promote "subtractive schooling" practices that encourage Mexican-descent students to divest in important cultural and linguistic resources, rather than empowering students to use them as tools for the further acquisition of knowledge. In this way, the formal and informal practices of public schooling have assured unequal and competing statuses for language use (English/Spanish) and cultural affiliation (Mexican/American), provoking deep conflicts over cultural and racial identity in ways consequential to success in school. At the same time, U.S.-born Mexican-descent youth may join groups of White students in disparaging more recent immigrants for their use of Spanish, their "incorrect" pronunciation of English, or the perceived "backwardness" of their national/cultural background (Hurd 2003).

What this look at Mexican cultural commemorations further suggests is that "subtractive schooling practices" are not just those that divest important cultural and linguistic resources from Mexican-descent youth; they include those that honor such expressions while imposing limits on their use and status. In other words, celebrations of "ethnic culture" are deemed acceptable insofar as they do not get in the way of—or take time away from—the "real" business of socializing students to basic literacy and other academic skills that are measurable through performances on high-stakes standardized tests. The controversies surrounding AHS *commemorations* of Mexican holidays must be understood in relation to these limits on multicultural toleration. At the same time, the analysis identifies some of the institutional practices that reinforce students' essentialized views of racial, cultural, and class differences that incline them to see each other as inherently distinct and at odds across these lines of difference. Whereas the "naturalness" of these differences is established ultimately in students' interactions (or lack thereof) with one another, the school creates and reinforces cultural, racial, and class borders between students through the way it organizes and manages contexts for student interaction. When the administration views the dilemma as one of having to "force a connection," it sidesteps its own institutional responsibility to provide contexts that promote mutually affirming interactions between students across lines of politicized and often volatile racial, gender, cultural, and class differences. To enable such contexts requires not just quick-fix tactics, but a range of strategies focused on changing the nature and quality of social relations between students, between students and teachers, and between teachers and staff.

CHAPTER 7

Waking the Sleeping Giant: The Emergence of Progressive, Latino-Led Coalitions for School Reform

Stepping up the Fight Against Educational Inequality in the PVUSD

"We are here today to declare a state of emergency for our young people and our education system," yelled Farmingville High School teacher Amanda Jenkins, via megaphone, from the interior of the gazebo in Farmingville's central plaza. "We're here today to work for equal rights for the young people in Farmingville, the Pleasanton Valley and beyond!"

Jenkins addressed over fifty high school and college students on a foggy Saturday morning, kicking off a public march to commemorate of the fiftieth anniversary of *Brown v. Board of Education* in spring 2004. The march was organized as part of a larger statewide "week of action" to draw attention to the unfulfilled promises of the historic *Brown* decision. Teachers, students, parents, lawmakers, and nonprofit community justice advocacy groups from across the state joined forces to frame the *Brown* commemoration not as a time for celebration but as an opportunity to explore and educate others about the continuing realities of school segregation and educational inequality. Through the lenses of history, politics, art, law, and social studies, activists groups from Fresno to Los Angeles staged public mock trials arraigning the state of California on charges ranging from failing to uphold *Brown*'s mandate to end racial segregation to permitting the existence of unequal and inadequate schooling conditions for the state's low-income minority students and English-language learners.

The protest activities in Farmingville were coordinated by two local citizen groups—a newly reborn chapter of the Brown Berets, and a local youth development organization called the Student Empowerment Project. Five days earlier, members of both groups had attended a PVUSD school board meeting in which trustees were expected to approve a resolution honoring the *Brown* anniversary. Over two dozen young Latino activists, many of them local high school and community college students, came to condemn the irony of the trustees' decision to honor *Brown* in light of revived plans to divide the school district. Patricia Anaya, a current Farmingville High School student and Brown Beret member, offered one of the many emotional testimonies during the public comment period:

> How dare you say you're going to celebrate *Brown v. Board* when you have done everything to increase segregation in the school district. It's like you put cake on our nose and smash a plate on our face and you think it's funny. I am so outraged!

Benito Valdez, a Farmingville public interest attorney and acting director of the Student Empowerment Project, legitimized the young peoples' presence at the school board meeting, emphasizing the need for their critical testimony:

> This is such a joke because this school board wants to commemorate *Brown*, yet they have never applied the principles of *Brown* in their policy and decision making. They continue to approve segregationist and discriminatory policies, and today they are doing nothing in terms of integration, which was at the very heart of the *Brown* decision. They make a mockery of what *Brown* stands for. We've got to call them on that. . . . What's important, and what does carry out the vision of *Brown*, is applying it to their everyday decision making as school board members. They have to live the dream of Dr. King every day and not simply pass a token resolution.

From Benito's perspective, the fight for education on equal terms, and against racial segregation and inferior schools, was not one to be passed off to supposedly good-natured school board members who could then be expected to institute the larger moral and educational project set forth in the *Brown* decision. This was especially the case, he pointed out, when it meant running up against the strong political forces invested in maintaining the local status quo of schooling. In his mind, the presence of youth from the Brown Berets served the essential function of pressuring local school board representatives to make good on their commitment to equal education.

Benito and the Brown Berets

I met Benito for the first time in 2002, although I had been familiar with him by name for the central organizing role he was known to have played in mid-1990 student protests activities surrounding Proposition 187. At that time, Benito was a nineteen-year-old graduate of Farmingville High taking classes at a local community college with the hope of transferring to a nearby four-year state university. The son of a local pastor and migrant farm-worker family, Benito's introduction to community politics came early when, from atop the shoulders of his grandparents, he had marched with Cesar Chavez and Dolores Huerta in the United Farm Workers unionizing efforts that passed through Pleasanton Valley in the early 1980s. His own foray into community organizing came in 1994, when a spike in gang violence in Farmingville had led to a drive-by shooting of a nine-year-old girl and her sixteen-year-old brother in front of a popular local bakery. Moved by the incident and motivated by his family's activist heritage, Benito helped mobilize a group of local Farmingville youth and young adults into a collective that would, a short time later, define itself as a chapter of the Brown Berets. In their first public action, the Brown Berets inaugurated a Peace and Unity March commemorating local residents whose lives had been claimed by gang violence. Benito, having just transferred to a nearby state university, extended his leadership role in the Berets to form the Student Empowerment Project, a network of local junior high, high school, and community college students who met together locally as well as participated in monthly meetings with student groups from across California's central valley. It was the Berets, and its sister organization the Student Empowerment Project, that would engage local high school students like Diego Omán in light of Proposition 187 and play a catalytic role in the youth activism that produced student walkouts across the district, including those at Allenstown High.

Thinking back a decade about his early youth organizing experiences, he recalled with fondness the groups' goal to build a cadre of educated, progressive Latino leaders in the area:

> We said to young people: "We want to see you on the school board, on the city council." If they work on these issues from an early age, then ten years down the road, with community organizing experience and a college degree, they are the kind of representatives we need. That's what we were trying to do, to develop young leaders to learn parliamentary process, push them to go to college where they get education and access to networks and organizing skills so they can return to their local community and make a real difference. Because, unfortunately, many who go off to college don't come back, and we are losing some of our best and brightest minds.

Benito's own biography provided a living example of the group's mission. After transferring to UC Berkeley and completing an undergraduate degree with honors in Political Science and Chicano Studies, Benito earned his J.D. in Public Interest Law from a prestigious California law school while also serving as a legislative aide in the California State Assembly. Following law school, Benito successfully pursued an additional Master's degree in education with a concentration in administration, planning, and social policy from a prestigious east coast university while holding a graduate research assistantship in a nationally renowned policy institute focused on issues of civil rights, racial inequality, and social justice in education. As a young, bilingual attorney with degrees from some of the country's most prestige universities, Benito returned to Farmingville in the early 2000s to fulfill the promise of dedicating himself to the cause of local community organizing and improving the lives of Latinos and the working poor in the Farmingville area. After moving back, he quickly reestablished his mentorship role with the Brown Berets and his directorship of the Student Empowerment Project.

The Farmingville Brown Berets took their namesake from the original Chicano/Mexican American rights group that appeared in Los Angeles in the mid-1960s and has since been associated with a wide range of social and political advocacy activities.[1] However, the particular inspiration young people in Farmingville found in the Berets was their political reformist ideology and their commitment to community-building strategies that combined education, cultural awareness, and direct action activism. In developing the local chapter's mission, the group consciously adopted the nonviolent teachings of Cesar Chavez and Martin Luther King, Jr., and established active connections to local cultural renaissance groups like the White Hawk Dancers whose artistry infused and valorized aspects of Aztec and Native American spirituality.

In the decade since Benito helped found the group, the Brown Berets had grown into an established youth development organization, well known for sponsoring an annual Youth Empowerment Conference and serving as a vocal watchdog group against injustices affecting the local Latino community. During the time of my research in the early to mid-2000s, it was not uncommon to find over thirty members—the majority high school and college students—gathered at weekly meetings. Their discussions touched not only on issues of local concern but a broader range of state and national social justice issues including opposition to the war in Iraq, a position against California's high school exit exam and proposed cutbacks in university and college outreach programs, and support for the rights of undocumented workers to obtain drivers' licenses.

That the Berets had endured as a vocal force in local politics for over a decade spoke to the effectiveness of their strategy to engage youth and channel their energy to be heard in local politics. "There's a lot of alienation among kids," explained seventeen-year old Francesca Rubio, a Brown Beret member who graduated from AHS in the early 2000s and was attending a nearby four-year university. "They feel isolated and angry. The Berets serve to channel that anger into positive action." The group fostered the progressive political leadership of young people by allowing a safe, cultural sphere through which they could collectively negotiate and resist the social realities of poverty, racism, and violence as well as conditions of political, educational, and economic inequality. Rather than viewing such conditions as intractable realities, the Brown Berets and Student Empowerment Project provided interpretive communities from which participants could use these same conditions as opportunities for waging struggle and gaining rights. "We're like a family," said Victor Santana who, in his mid-thirties, was among the group's elders. "There is no single group in Farmingville doing so much." Erica Suarez, a local community college student, viewed the group's development work within a larger frame of civil rights history:

> As young people we also want to honor those who came before us, who sacrificed for us, so that we can have opportunities. We have the responsibility to continue the work of the freedom fighters.

Education as a means of empowerment was a primary teaching within both groups. Youth participants were encouraged to go to college, get involved in local politics, participate in outreach, and inform themselves on local issues. Members gained important civic skills and knowledge through engagement in fundraising, event planning, and participation in statewide networking with larger educational justice coalitions, including such groups as Californians for Justice. A key political philosophy promoted in the Brown Berets was that promoting social change cannot be limited to working within narrow, insular systems of traditional government that tend to protect the status quo. Instead, effective political action may require periodic direct action strategies that interrupt business as usual in ways that compel people to listen and feel moved to act.

This direct action approach to youth civic involvement did not prove popular among all citizens in the Valley. While the group saw itself as an advocate for peace, the sight of youth heckling and "calling out" established local officials and prominent citizens in public arenas brought the ire of more enfranchised residents who considered the Berets' work counterproductive, unruly, verbally abusive, and left-leaning. Such negative characterization meant that Benito—as the group's most visible leader—would become associated with this conflictive, "anti-productive" form of citizen politics—a style some accused him of bringing to the local scene in the first place.

The "Together for a United Pleasanton Valley Unified School District" Coalition

By the time the PVUSD school board publicly announced plans for its Reorganization Feasibility Study—which it heralded as an "objective analysis" that would guide the district's decision-making process—Benito had firmly established himself as the most visible leader for the opposition. Through personal relationship-building with key members of the Farmingville City Council, he helped convince the city clerk's office to commission its own "Impact Report" exploring the long-term economic consequences of a school district split, the findings of which ultimately inspired a majority of city council members to approve a resolution against it.

Benito brought a unique set of skills to the fight against district reorganization. His status as a late twenties, highly educated public interest attorney firmly rooted in the community as a third-generation Farmingville resident and son of a migrant farm worker family provided him a unique set of skills and cultural competencies, allowing him to work as effectively with disenfranchised parents and youth as with civic leaders in positions of power.

His presence and commitment helped facilitate an alliance among diverse forces that included members of Farmingville City Council and the PVUSD school board, concerned Farmingville parents and citizens, and working-class youth through the Brown Berets and the Student Empowerment Project. Benito also brought a model of organizing and civic participation inspired by a deep understanding of the strategies that had proved successful in the civil rights and union organizing movement throughout the country's history. His approach, in line with Martin Luther King's progressive direct action agenda, was designed to dramatize key social issues in such a way that they could not easily be ignored, based on the underlying philosophy that constructive tension is necessary for community growth and transformation toward justice and social equality.[2]

Despite working nearly fifty hours a week in his role as a legal advocacy attorney, Benito became the central hub of communication for an expanding network of individuals and organizations opposing the idea of a district split, and he could constantly be found making phone calls, leading email communications, and maintaining a physical, engaged presence at a range of community events, meetings, forums, and public protests within the Farmingville community. With Benito as its catalyst, a new associational network emerged calling itself "Together for a United PVUSD" (hereafter referred to as TFAU-PVUSD), consisted of members of the Brown Berets and Student Empowerment Project, concerned Farmingville parents, Farmingville city officials (including the mayor and two additional city council members), and a handful of individual teachers and citizens from Farmingville and Allenstown—both White and Latino—united by their opposition to the district split.

The coalition's coherence was maintained largely through ongoing email exchanges, strategic ad hoc meetings, and attendance at local school district meetings and hearings. Among their central communication strategies were to make constant rhetorical appeals to the moral character of school board trustees and local citizens, emphasizing the assumed negative—and perceived racist—intents and impacts of the split. They also produced and distributed position papers to local and national media sources, calling specific attention to the "illegal" nature of the split (e.g., its incompatibility with state statutory requirements like those in Education Code 35753 that articulated specific criterion and limits for district reorganization plans), and provided summaries of academic research emphasizing the dangers of schooling conditions that promoted triple segregation and resulted in "schools of concentrated disadvantage." This communication strategy bore fruit early in the coalition's development when mainstream outlets like the *New York Times* and CNN picked up on the story.

The TFAU-PVUSD opposition to the Allenstown secession campaign was rooted in a combination of political and legal pressure, grassroots citizen mobilization, and cross-sectional relationship building with related advocacy groups. Youth from the Brown Berets played a central role in all facets, from recruiting and coordinating peers and residents for direct action activities at school board meetings and public hearings to reaching out to allies through the regional social justice networks to which they belonged. The coalition specifically targeted state and national advocacy groups with whom they shared a broad sense of purpose and whom they believed could play a role in shifting local sentiments on the issue. These included legal groups like La Raza Lawyers Association of California, California Rural Legal Assistance, League of United Latin American Citizens (LULAC), and the NAACP as well as peace and justice organizations like the Women's International League of Voters. The intent was not simply to solicit external support for their cause, but to encourage the development of "deep coalitions" (Mediratta et al. 2009: 87) based on relationships of solidarity and reciprocity that could generate trust over the long term and produce a strong and sustained consensus for mutual support. To this end, TFAU-PVUSD coalition representatives attended civic group meetings across the state, sharing details about their cause, and offering a commitment of support to their allies on future projects.

This proactive solidarity approach was tested early on when, in an unlikely development, MPAC hesitated to align itself with the TFAU-PVUSD work. Given their frustrating experience in the mid-1990s parent meetings and their deepening relationship with Farmingville area board trustee Charlie Yu, some MPAC members were expressing a growing sense that "it might be better just to get it over with." In an effort to head off the growing split within MPAC—a fracture that could endanger the legitimacy of the coalition's work and the appearance of a united front of Latino advocacy organizations against Allenstown secession—Benito and a group of fellow TFAU-PVUSD members arranged to attend a regional meeting of the Migrant Parent Association. The coalition presented their message to the larger association in Spanish and in a deliberative style that focused on the moral and social justice issues at stake in the split as well as the long-term, negative impacts that it could be expected to have on the Farmingville community. Their method of engagement with the migrant parent representatives—

highlighting and validating the committee's knowledge, work, and commitment to educational justice for Latino families in the area—played a key role in engendering trust between the migrant parents and the TFAU-PVUSD coalition members, and from that meeting on, MPAC became one of the most outspoken voices of opposition to the reorganization proposal.

Mobilizing Against Reorganization

Because the PVUSD school board trustees had assured that local citizen input would be "the deciding factor" in a decision about whether to push forward with a recommendation for a district split, they organized a series of bilingual community forums to take place in both Allenstown and Farmingville to seek residents' feedback and answer questions about the dense, 88-page feasibility study. Local citizens were also encouraged to submit written commentaries at any point during the ten-week public feedback period. Each of the four scheduled community forums was attended by a formidable contingent of coalition participants, including not only youth from the Student Empowerment Project and Brown Berets but a growing assemblage of parents, Farmingville city officials, and private citizens who spoke out against the split and posed difficult questions to school board members about the nature, legitimacy, and clarity of the data provided in their feasibility study.

A week before the final forum, Benito made an unscheduled visit to the PVUSD school district office to follow up on district superintendent Shirley Mitchell's claim, made publicly, that all written feedback submitted by citizens on the proposed division (rather than simple summaries of the data) would be included in the final version of the Community Feedback Report. Upon arrival, Benito was denied access to the full set of public feedback materials the district had collected to date. "I had to threaten a lawsuit against Dr. Mitchell who refused to let me view the documents," Benito explained. "But I sent a demand letter the following day and came back. She then allowed me to inspect all the records." Ultimately, he found that written citizen public feedback included 66 pages of signatures of local residents who opposed the reorganization (950 respondents in all), as well as letters of opposition from the Student Empowerment Project, MPAC, the county chapter of La Raza Lawyers, Pleasanton Valley's LULAC organization, and the Farmingville's city clerk's office. Notably missing were any letters from Allenstown parents, business leaders, or civic groups voicing their support for the district reorganization idea. Overall, nearly 96 percent of the submitted public feedback was in opposition to the reorganization and less than one percent of the respondents unequivocally favored the division.[3] Benito added that "even the comments in favor of a reorganization are good in the sense that they tend to show that race/segregation is indeed an issue, and that will work against reorganization when reviewed by the county and state." Benito was upbeat, but cautiously so. He remained skeptical about whether the public input would actually make a difference, despite trustees' claim that it would be "the deciding factor" in their assessment. "Even though the board doesn't want to come out and say they have made a decision," Benito explained, "I think they already have a majority decision to vote for secession."

In the days leading up to the final forum, the TFAU-PVUSD added to its list of supporters the City of Farmingville, the county office of the ACLU, and the Pleasanton Valley Federation of Teachers, the latter releasing a public statement calling the district reorganization idea "morally and ethically wrong." Benito managed to successfully negotiate a "guest column" in the *Farmingville Times*, penning an article that reemphasized how the proposed district reorganization plan would promote racial segregation and create "separate and unequal schools" in the Valley:

> In 1979, federal officials confirmed that our school district was ranked [among] the 100 most segregated school districts in the United States, and just a few years ago, the federal Office of Civil Rights found our school district in violation of federal law for unlawfully segregating students. Instead of working to integrate our schools and coming up with real solutions for the challenges facing our district, the school board has decided to waste valuable time, energy and resources on an old, failed and discriminatory idea. However, we must remind ourselves that school segregation is not inevitable. But if we are to have integrated schools, we need a new commitment by our school district officials, educators, parents, and community. We must never forget the words of Dr. Martin Luther King, Jr., who once said, "Whenever you segregate a minority, you inevitably discriminate against that minority." That's the issue.

The acting director of the Women's International League for Peace and Freedom, in a letter to the school board that was published in a regional newspaper the same day, expressed the group's opposition in a similar framing:

> We question the motives behind the idea of reorganization, especially since it has been rejected already by the State Board of Education on the grounds that it would perpetuate racial segregation. We would encourage the Board of Trustees, school administrators, parents that live in the affluent area of Allenstown and all fair, open-minded north county residents to reject secession and unite with south county parents and students to improve all our schools for all students. Through mutual cooperation we can avoid losing state funding as well as costly legal challenges (should secession happen), consolidate resources, enhance student skills both academically and socially, and finally we can show our support for and belief in cultural diversity and integrated education as a foundation for preparing students to become informed, responsible members of our society.

Defiance, Chaos, and Transformation

From the perspective of school board trustees, the final forum marked the end of a deliberative design to study the plan in a detached, objective manner. For those organizing against what they viewed as the newest incarnation of the "Allenstown secession" campaign, it was the culmination of several months of grassroots activism attempting to frame the study as a racially charged plan that would ruin Farmingville schools and harm the city's Latino children while bolstering the predominately White schools in Allenstown. The stage was set for a dramatic and impassioned fight.

As citizens gathered on the evening of the final forum, it was clear that the TFAU-PVUSD coalition had succeeded in its outreach strategies. The chambers swelled with over 120 citizens, nearly all prepared to express their opposition to a district split. A tangible sense of agitation filled the chambers as the forum got underway; it it was magnified exponentially when the first speaker of the public comment period, Frank Stone, a staunchly conservative senior citizen from Allenstown, took the microphone and—eschewing the issue of district reorganization together—began a tirade about the negative impact of illegal immigrants in Pleasanton Valley. The opposition could not have scripted a better interloper—or in this case, an overbearing caricature—to embody their claims about the racist underbelly of the

Allenstown secession movement. After a chaotic shouting match between Stone and several other attendees, the virulent speaker was rushed hurriedly out a back door. His departure was followed by a brash testimony from a member of the Farmingville Brown Berets, which further ignited the crowd:

> Well, this time it's not going to work, Yu! I'm telling you, we didn't cross no oceans; we didn't cross no rivers; we've been here forever! [*yelling and applause from the crowd*] "This country of illegal immigrants"? Give me a break! Learn your history! When our children were first bused many years ago from Farmingville to Allenstown, they needed students over there. You guys didn't even tell the Latino community "We're going to bus your children over there"—especially the migrant kids over there by the mountains [referring to a federally operated migrant farm worker camp]. That was a culture shock. A lot of them dropped out. A lot of them didn't fit in that White, Anglo school. Well, you know what? They succeeded. They lived together; they studied together; they played together. They have accomplished a great thing. And now you want to separate this? How dare you—Yu, Golden, Marshall, and Van Riesma [trustees alleged to support the plan]—we got to get you out of here!

A follow-up commentary was offered by Alicia Reyes, a young Latina resident from Farmingville who had graduated from AHS several years earlier:

> I represent my fellow students in Allenstown High School when I say [that] if you are blind and say this is not about race, it *is* about race. . . . It's just racism—plain, blind racism. You don't want to see it. Or maybe you do see it, but you just want to tell [us] that it's not. You guys are wrong. I was a product of Allenstown High School, and when I look back, you know what sticks in my mind? I had the opportunity to experience an integrated education. [*applause*]. In my experience, when I was in Farmingville, it was all Latino; when I went to Allenstown, even though it was a culture shock, I was still able to communicate with other people who were not part of my background, not part of my class, but I was still able to come together. . . . It was so fulfilling for me to experience another culture. Sometimes we have to live more than just one culture, we

> have to live with all the other cultures around us. Diversity is important, Mr. Marshall [Allenstown trustee supporting the reorganization idea]. It is. Maybe you just can't see the force as important because you don't have diversity in front of you, around you.

After more than thirty-five individual commentaries, nearly all unequivocally opposed to a district split, Benito provided the final testimony. Shifting from what had been an emotional mix of indignation, cultural pride, and personal experience, he offered a discourse rooted in well-researched legalese that brought together the full range of rhetorical strategies that had driven the coalition's work since its formation. Not to be limited by the one-minute time frame for individual testimony, Benito's oration continued for several minutes, despite the superintendent's multiple attempts to end it, with what appeared to be the full support of the crowd. Excerpts of the testimony follow:

> *Benito*: Many reasons have already been stated as to why this segregationist proposal will be a terrible thing for our students, our schools and our community. And as the community feedback shows, the community is very much opposed to this . . . The bottom line is that this reorganization will in no way conform to state law, federal law, or constitutional law, and a decision to proceed would be a clear waste of taxpayers' money that could be better spent on our students and on our schools. Thousands and thousands have already been wasted, including much time and energy, and in the end this segregationist proposal will only fail. You [school board trustees] cannot even make an informed decision, tonight or next week, because you have not even done an analysis to determine whether this proposal would conform with the 9 statutory requirements [of state law governing school district reorganizations], despite the fact that I've told you to do so numerous times. . . . But tonight I want to emphasize that this segregationist proposal will also deprive our students of an equal educational opportunity. It will deprive our students of having an integrated educational experience, and it would create separate and unequal schools for generations to come in the Pleasanton Valley. Some of you have said that this proposal is about student academic achievement and not segregation—Mr. Yu. But if you cannot even understand that racial

segregation is directly correlated with student achievement, in spite of voluminous research to prove so, then I don't know what business you have sitting on the school board. [*Loud applause and yelling from crowd; striking of gavel*]. The more segregated the schools, the worse the conditions are at those schools.

Trustee/timekeeper: His time has run out.

Woman in crowd: We have all night!

Benito: A report just came out today that showed that schools that are highly segregated have some of the worse graduation rates. A report by Harvard University today—

Trustee/timekeeper: Your time is up!

[*Jeering and yelling from the crowd*]

Man in crowd: "We listened to that guy for like five hours [referring to Stone's tirade]; we should listen to him for two minutes!

Benito: Those schools did not fail. The people who have failed are those who failed to integrate our schools. You are the ones who have failed to give our students a high-quality education. You are the ones who have failed to bring parents and our communities together. And you are the ones who have failed to come up with real solutions to increasing student academic achievement. Old, failed discriminatory ideas are simply not the solution, Mr. Yu. I just want to close by just reemphasizing that this May 17th marks the 50th anniversary of the *Brown v. Board of Education* which meant to abolish racially segregated schools throughout our country. But this board hasn't learned much since those times. We should all heed the words of the United States Supreme Court that held in its 2003 opinion upholding affirmative action and stated that integration and diversity in our educational institutions are compelling governmental interests—

Trustee/timekeeper: President Jones, if we don't [inaudible due to yelling from crowd]. We cannot be breaking rules and regulations! I'm sorry.

Man in crowd: We listened to you for two hours straight!

Benito: I'm almost done here. The justice department stated that numerous studies show that student body diversity promotes learning outcomes, better prepares students for an increasingly diverse workforce and society, and better prepares them as professionals. If you cannot understand these lessons, even coming from a conservative Supreme Court, then, again, I ask you: What business do you have on the school board? Thank you very much.

[*Yelling, applause, striking of gavel, crowd begins chants of "Charlie get out!" and "Reorganize the Board!"*]

Benito's speech, with its varied accusations and interruptions, exemplified the demeanor of "incivility" that characterized the entire meeting. It was a forum in which school board trustees received an unremitting tongue lashing from outspoken members of the opposition. Charlie Yu served as the most popular target, with boos and chants of "Get rid of Charlie!" and "Reorganize the Board!" punctuating the meeting. In the face of the heckling, Allenstown area trustee Ellen Van Reesma—an outspoken supporter of the reorganization plan—found her own attempts to respond to Benito's speech drown out by boos and shouting from the crowd, compelling her to throw down her pen in frustration and declare: "I'm done."

Given the constant barrage of yelling and personal insults, the board was forced to call an emergency adjournment. "The original intent was to study the plan in a calm, logical manner," said an exasperated superintendent soon after the meeting. "I think it's pretty clear we can't do that now." Another frustrated Farmingville area trustee considered "on the fence" about the reorganization idea, professed that "as far as I'm concerned, this is not going to come up again. Either that, or I'm going to recommend that we put the issue on the agenda for every single meeting so that people will get tired and quit coming. I don't appreciate being bullied."

The "bulliers" saw it differently, including a Farmingville High student who affirmed in his own testimony that: "During the last meeting you asked us to wave our hands in the air while you ignored our voices; tonight we are going to make noise. We are not going to be silent!" Benito provided his own assessment of the unruly behavior that characterized the meeting:

> I think the community is just tired of being polite and presenting their compelling arguments only to have the school board ignore their voices. We told them months ago that if they revived this proposal that it would create division, tension and animosity.... Despite our warnings, they proceeded and thus the energy that was present at the meeting was the expected result of their stubbornness and persistence to proceed with the reorganization.

After the forum, a handful of trustees informally expressed a desire to "postpone indefinitely" the decision on a district split. However, a week later, in a private meeting of the three-person District Reorganization Subcommittee—which included pro-district reorganization supporters Yu and Van Reesma—the decision was made to postpone the discussion for an additional twelve months to allow yet another "cooling off" period. Benito was dismayed but not surprised by the board's unwillingness to give up on the issue even in light of the compelling testimonies and obvious anger of Farmingville's Latino residents. He suggested that

> If they [the school board] were to have voted on it, it could have passed 4-2, but with such a small margin of support it would not have looked good, and it would have limited the proposal's potential success on the county and state level. They think this is going to be a cooling off period and it's not. Letting this issue simmer for another year is basically saying it does have merit. The best thing that could be done is to put it to a vote and just put this thing to an end. But I think we have made them realize that this would never have a chance at passing and that we will *strongly* oppose them every step of the way. We also made them realize that it would also subject them to unnecessary litigation. We have people from a lot of different sectors of the community. Politically, it's going to be of great concern for the school district to proceed when there is (so much) opposition.

Building for a Different Future

The coalition's success propelled it toward its next major goal: forcing a reconfiguration of the PVUSD School Board to yield a progressive majority, which it sought to accomplish by recruiting and fielding candidates for three open seats in the upcoming school board election. One was incumbent Stacey Nevells, a White former-ESL teacher, a close friend of the coalition, and a vocal opponent of the reorganization plan. The two others were Farmingville newcomers—one a female and former bilingual teacher, parent, and long-time labor organizer, the other a male who was the director of a countywide immigration assistance program and who had children in

Farmingville schools. While all three candidates were bilingual, none was of Mexican descent. The challenge facing the Latino-led coalition was that, even if all of its slated candidates won, the school board would still remain without a Latino representative. This opened the door for some criticism of the coalition leadership, particularly when another newcomer candidate, Arelio Hermosa—a former MPAC member and lettuce-picking supervisor in Farmingville—announced he would run against the incumbent Nevells. Hermosa had opposed the district split, and his campaign message was focused on improving community involvement and highlighting voices of the migrant and immigrant populations in the Farmingville area.

Responding to questions about the coalition's choice to support Nevell's candidacy over that of Hermosa, Benito expressed that while he would prefer to see a more ethnically and racially representative school board, and that it remained an essential long-term goal, he said it should not pursued at the expense of a responsive trustee:

> The issue is not just having Latinos in these positions. It's been proven time and time again, the color of your skin doesn't mean everything. There are others who have stuck their necks out for equality when it was not politically smart to do so. You don't have to be Latino but [you do] have to support the causes.

For Benito, the primary goal was to build and sustain relationships of trust among a network of citizens, teachers, supporters, and allied organizations (legal, policy, citizen groups) that could prove useful not just for the present election, but for the multiple battles that could be expected in the future, and when mutual support and a "strong showing" would again be needed. In his mind, the coalition's work should not to be framed by ethnic or racial categories per se, but by the strength of a collectivity strongly committed to the broad arena of social justice.

After three months of intense campaigning and canvassing that included the work of well over one hundred volunteers, all three coalition-sponsored candidates were elected into office. In one of the new school board's first sessions, they passed a vote to shelve the district reorganization proposal indefinitely. However, the new board made a significant accommodation for those Allenstown parents desiring more control over their "local" schools by agreeing to create three administrative "zones" within the district—a north, south, and central residential zone—which would allow principals and other school officials from the elementary, middle, and high schools in each area to engage in localized conversations about curriculum, school structure, and facilities. A board member admitted that this strategy "served to calm the waters a little bit with most of the folks pushing the re-organization" because it provided Allenstown parents with a "more direct link to the district office and the services it provides."

What Was Accomplished in the Latino-Led Mobilization Against School Resegregation

In the current era of rapidly resegregating schools, legal challenges to school desegregation plans, and waning political will for school integration, what made this particular Latino-led effort to thwart a school district secession campaign successful? There is little doubt that the increasing degree of political incorporation of the Mexican-descent population in Pleasanton Valley—made possible by the sizable growth of the Latino population and the rise in municipal electoral power that followed the late-1980s MALDEF voting rights lawsuit—played an enabling role. Incorporation was also aided by the development of—and political experience in—relatively independent, education-related civic organizations like the MPAC, Brown Berets, and TFAU-PVUSD coalition that allowed formerly marginalized youth and adults to deliberate on critical approaches to current social and educational arrangements, envision and articulate short and long-term strategies to enter the system, and and transform some of the normative assumptions on which it rests. What they were able to accomplish in this respect was not insignificant; it was a popular shift, on a regional level, in assumptions about what constitutes quality education and who is entitled to it. They managed to effectively decenter privilege by fighting against the institutional production of (White, middle class) meritocratic assumptions that some children are more deserving of access to the benefits of low-poverty, middle-class schools than are others. The groups' collective organizing activities led to a reconfiguration of the school board to reflect, for the first time in its history, a progressive majority outspoken in its commitment to the social justice tenets of equal educational opportunity and about the need to challenge long-standing norms of racial and class entitlement in the schooling process.

Benito's role as a catalyst in this organizing process should not be underestimated. His positioning as a locally raised, bilingual/bicultural, highly educated public interest lawyer provided him with a deep sense of legitimacy among both Latino working-class families and local civic leaders. Beyond his knowledge of well-tested civil rights organizing and capacity-building strategies, he possessed an obdurate commitment to the cause that made him willing, despite a litany of involvements, to act as the personal hub of communication for an expanding network of individuals and organizations—across race, cultural, and class differences—that united in opposition the idea of a district split.

From Anti-Resegregation to a Pro-Integration Agenda: Limits and Challenges

Despite the successes, many critical questions remain about the ability to sustain institutional change, and about the limits of the political organizing strategies that have been undertaken in this case. First, while the TFAU-PVUSD coalition achieved notable success in promoting the importance of shared, high-quality schooling as a fundamental right for citizens in the region, little effort has yet been made to link the campaign for equal education to a wider range of economic issues facing local, working-class Latinos including noneducational issues like fair wages and affordable housing. Second, while the newly configured PVUSD school board has assured a commitment to promoting high-quality, equity-based, and shared schooling at the district level, the difficult work remains to create relational cultures and strong partnerships between educators, parents, and school administrators, on a school-by-school basis, to assure commitment and accountability to educational models capable of successfully engaging student across racial, class, and linguistic difference (see, for example, strategies highlighted in Stone et al. 2001; Warren 2005; Warren et al. 2011). This will require that district and school-level administrators, in partnership with teacher, parent, student and civic organization collaborators, critically mine the proven school integration strategies and model programs that are currently being sustained throughout the United States (see Frankenberg and Debray 2011) and adapting methods and practices to fit local and regional contexts and concerns.

Yet if the PVUSD decides to mine and adapt existing integration strategies to meet the needs of its schools, the newly elected school board's decision to divide the district into north, central, and south "administrative zones" may end up doing more harm than good. The zone concept was established, in part, as an encouraging move toward more relational power and decentralization, features considered effective for increasing parent and community involvement and improving outcome accountability, at least in urban school contexts (Stone et al. 2001: 162). However, given the high levels of residential segregation associated with each "zone" in the PVUSD, the new system also provides a structure for defining the needs of White and Latino students separately from one another and could potentially justify zone-specific curricular and co-curricular initiatives that separate or "track" diverse learners into qualitatively different learning experiences based on their academic "potential," language proficiency, or relative scores on standardized tests.

Another challenge the TFAU-PVUSD coalition will be likely to face as it shifts at least some of its day-to-day attention to work of redesigning schools and curriculum in ways that reflect their vision, is whether it can effectively transition from its primary role as "outside agitator" to a more enfranchised, "insider" role as reformer and policymaker. Tensions and hard choices are likely to arise for some coalition members and leaders as they attempt to embody the dual role of organizer and policymaker, particularly if such positionings lead to them to being perceived "as insiders rather than representatives of the wider community" (Warren et al. 2011: 129).

Beyond these challenges, what is most likely to determine the scale of equity-based school transformation possible in this case is whether the social justice movement frame that proved so effective in motivating civic action among working-class Latinos and their justice-oriented allies in Farmingville is broad enough to capture the imagination and support of a sufficiently wide range of White middle-class parents in the Valley. The coalition's message—that integrated education is essential to human dignity and the civic health of a community, regardless of the background of its residents—played a strong and disruptive role in determining Allenstown's attempt at school district secession. In this regard, the coalition was successful in petitioning the backing of a critical mass of PVUSD teachers—the majority of whom were White and middle class—as well as in broadening its legitimacy outside the Latino community through the support it received from a host of local, regional, and national civic organizations (many not even education-based) who were willing to reiterate the important link between social and racial justice and shared, integrated schools.

It is not clear, however, that organizing efforts in this case have helped put in motion what Oakes, Welner, Yonezawa, and Allen (2005) have identified as "third order changes"—broad changes in local citizens' core beliefs about such matters as race, intelligence, and educability, as well as about the normative logics of public education that have made segregated schooling conditions seem so normal to those currently privileged. In other words, there is little evidence suggesting much has been done to co-opt or challenge the perspectives of those who have supported the school district secession effort based on an affirmation of such normative logics as resource scarcity and portrayal of public education as a "zero-sum" game in which opportunities for sought-after, high-quality education are in small supply and should be competed for by students, families, and residential communities (Oakes and Lipton 2002: 17).

Finally, the politicization of race in this case threatens to act as a double-edged sword. There is no doubt that the successful campaign against school resegregation was predicated to a significant degree on the ability to identify and rally around a tangible, emotionally laden target: the perceived "racist" and socially unjust nature of the district split. It is unclear whether the same level of political mobilization could have been mustered without such a highly charged social justice framing and clear political objective. Yet the politicization of race has other consequences as well. For example, the TFAU-PVUSD coalition's ultimate decision to back three non-Latino candidates for school board seats, even against a respected Mexican migrant leader and coalition ally, could be interpreted in divergent ways. On the one hand, it may suggest, as Benito has claimed, that the Latino-led coalition's vision of justice and inclusion necessarily trumps issues of racial representation in institutional leadership. On the other hand, it could also be taken as evidence that the politicization of race has made it difficult to generate support for Latino candidates, given a prevalent neoconservative fear among the more diverse electorate that such an action might constitute an attempt to elevate "racial interests" above those of the broader, bimodal PVUSD community. Wherever the truth may lie—probability somewhere in between—the reality is that the coalition decision has served to perpetuate the historical exclusion and underrepresentation of Latinos on the school board.

Conclusion

When the final, district-sponsored community forum to vet the District Reorganization Feasibility Study ended with an emergency adjournment and an unwillingness of school board trustees to vote on the controversial plan, it was viewed as a major accomplishment for those who had opposed the Allenstown school secession bid. However, the way in which the meeting was "shut down" was bemoaned publicly by others, including a small set of district and county school board members, who saw it as yet another example of the negative, confrontational tactics used by the Latino-led coalition to "play the race card" in a manner that obscured other important considerations surrounding the district reorganization debate. The most scathing critique came from Charlie Yu, himself target of much collective tongue lashing during the meeting, who questioned the process of "youth empowerment" pursued by adult mentors within the Brown Berets and which he saw as underwritten by the TFAU-PVUSD coalition:

> If they're teaching that you're going to empower kids by showing them how to take over a meeting and not let others speak, I'm not sure that's the empowerment we want to condone. The very thing we want to respect is civil rights, to be able to speak . . . If they're trying to convince people to change their minds based on those tactics, I don't think that is going to work.

Yu's impression that the civic mobilization of youth resembled, in his own words, a "militant association of unruly agitators undermining the democratic process," failed to appreciate that what might have appeared to him an instance of mob rule, was actually the culmination of a long-term community empowerment process that included, but went far beyond, a tactical politics of direct action and confrontation. The show of force was the result of a decade's work of civic capacity-building among Farmingville's Latino population, earned through hard-fought strategies of grassroots mobilization that included ongoing education among parents and in the community, interpersonal relationship-building across civic groups, and long-term programs of youth civic development.

What the present case of Latino-led organizing against school resegregation suggests is that, while impoverished communities of color face significant challenges in their efforts to make local schools accountable for providing high-quality education to their children, it is possible for long-marginalized citizens to successfully mobilize in ways that challenge the educational status quo arrangements that have tended to favor the affluent. In this case, success was wrought against popular and institutional efforts to exclude working-class Latino youth from the benefits of high-quality educational environments that are the trademark of low-poverty, middle-class schools. The success of Latino-led organizing groups was predicated to a large degree on the distinct forms of civic capacity-building in which they engaged. The formation of diverse, community-based spaces for working class Latino parents (MPAC, TFAU-PVUSD) and youth (Brown Berets, Student Empowerment Project) provided residents with the opportunity to see themselves—and be recognized—as change agents capable of speaking up against disadvantaging educational conditions. Asset-based civic capacity-building strategies yielded interpretive communities from which Latino citizens could collectively learn about and decode mainstream institutional settings and cultural practices and find a sense of belonging working within and sometimes against them.

Yet the successes of Latino-led organizing groups in the district secession battle does not mean that the problem of educational equity has been solved locally or that integrated education can soon be expected to flourish in district schools. In fact, conservative retrenchment has proven strong in the wake of the coalition's victories in the PVUSD school board elections. Benito has identified the emergence of a new alliance in the Valley, calling itself the "Committee for Good Governance" which, financed by a regional group of construction and real estate interests, intends to invest its own human, social, and financial capital in an effort to demonize the TFAU-PVUSD coalition's agenda and undermine the newly elected group of school board trustees by branding their leaders as agitators and noncitizens. Benito did not seem particularly surprised about these developments; in fact, he viewed them as part of the ongoing challenge of trying to beat conservative groups at their own game. "Privileged groups have always maintained power by coalition, and we must as well," he explained. "It's about practicing the science of strategies that have long proven successful for conservatives."

In the end, Benito acknowledges that accomplishments of the TFAU-PVUSD must be put in proper perspective; they should be viewed less as decisive victories than as evidence that a new process is underway. He said the coalition leadership is already considering the next level of tactics it must develop to contend with the surging efforts to undermine the recent progress that has been made. "As Dr. Martin Luther King, Jr. once said, change does not roll in on the wheels of inevitability, it comes through continuous struggle."

Conclusion: Signifying Chavez

Just months before the highly publicized denouement of the Allenstown secession campaign, the PVUSD school board met for the ceremonial and seemingly mundane task of naming the its long-awaited third high school. Controversy had been sparked weeks earlier when a district-appointed citizens' committee responsible for creating a short list of potential names from over fifty recommendations excluded the name "Cesar Chavez High School" despite a nomination package that included over 2,000 signatures. The omission angered a group of citizens favoring Chavez's namesake, including four members of Farmingville's city council and a handful of prominent local and state officials. Through their collective influence, they managed to persuade the committee to add the name to the list. In the end, four school names were offered for consideration. They were, in order of the committee's preference: Pleasanton Valley, Mar Vista, Alliance, and Cesar Chavez.

The school board meeting to decide the namesake drew a spirited, standing room only crowd of over 150 people. After two hours of public testimony from more than thirty concerned citizens—all but one speaking in favor of naming the school after the labor leader Chavez—the trustees choose to postpone their decision, saying they "needed more time" to reach a reasonable and agreeable selection. The deferment appeared unjustified given the diverse and compelling arguments offered in support of Chavez. Children, parents, and community leaders—mostly Latino but including White residents of the Valley—described Cesar Chavez as not only an inspiring Latino leader who championed the rights of farm workers, but a national and state hero who advocated for nonviolent struggle against social, economic, and political injustices. They characterized Chavez as a model citizen who tirelessly promoted freedom and equality for all, particularly for the disenfranchised and those of lower socioeconomic status. One supporter asserted that

Chavez "epitomized great human values; commitment, service to others, self-education, courage in the face of daunting odds, non-violence as a means to an end, and the notion that self-dignity is worth fighting for. He provided a united voice that insists being poor is not synonymous with being exploitable." Another community activist portrayed Chavez as an ideal role model for all the district's children, claiming that "naming our new high school after Cesar will be a stark reminder that things can be accomplished against powerful odds when people combine their strength, hope, and determination."

Not all local residents held Chavez in such high esteem, though. Among those resisting was a contingent of local agricultural growers, their families, and long-time business and political leaders in the Farmingville area. Rather than seeing Chavez as a model citizen who advanced democracy, equality, and nonviolent social justice, they saw him as primarily a "Latino leader" whose "divisive aura" and confrontational politics were largely to blame for the lost jobs and unpicked fruit during the labor union battles with Pleasanton Valley growers in the late 1970s and early 1980s. Naming the new high school after Chavez, they alleged, would not only serve to glorify his divisive legacy but would constitute a gesture of exclusivity; his selection would privilege Latinos over other ethnic groups and fail to represent the many groups that shaped the social and cultural life of the Valley. They argued for a more appropriate, neutral, and inclusive name for the high school. "We need something that would please everyone in the Valley," explained the local farm bureau president. "I don't see anything (Chavez) did in our valley that we should name a school after him." She joined a smaller but influential group of residents who favored the name Pleasanton Valley High School.

Although community and citizen support for Chavez far outweighed that for any other school name, the PVUSD school board eventually voted 6-1 in August of 2004 to name the new school Pleasanton Valley High School. To justify their decision before the more than two hundred citizens who chose to attend the meeting—the vast majority of them Chavez supporters—the school board president stunned an already exasperated crowd with these closing words of consolation: "It doesn't matter what the school name is. What matters is in your heart." The comment, which Latino activists and allies construed as facetious and insincere, inspired a chorus of shouting and chanting that compelled the board president to remove a rather substantial group of vocal citizens from the chambers.

The school board decision exhumed racial antipathies and distrust that lie forever close to the surface in the realm of education and schooling in Pleasanton Valley. Some of Chavez's supporters considered the decision a capitulation to the prevailing White power structure in a school district that had become over 70 percent Latino. Others felt the decision demonstrated a deeper, racist concern among some White leaders in Farmingville who had long feared a "Mexican takeover." On the other side were those who accused Chavez supporters of "playing the race card." By falsely establishing race as a factor in the debate, Chavez proponents were again responsible for encouraging divisiveness and disunity in the community. The farm bureau president, in a comment that seemed to conflate her view of Chavez's legacy with local Latino activists' insistent campaign to name the school after him, claimed "everybody was happy until someone started stirring the pot. The more things like this come up, the more people feel divided again." Another long-time White business leader in Farmingville—voicing sentiments that could just as well been heard thirty-five years earlier in the Valley—reasoned that "we are definitely going out of our way to name a school after [Chavez] if we look at him as a symbol of the growing power of an aggressive *Mexicanismo* at a time when many Americans sense their culture is being undermined and supplanted by a growing, aggressive, and assertive Mexican presence in California and the U.S." A disturbing aspect of this commentary was that it represents Chavez and his supporters as Mexicans who threatened Americans without recognizing that Chavez was—as were a great deal of his supporters—an American citizen.

The racial overtones and emotional fervor generated by what would appear to be the relatively incidental task of naming a new high school seem exaggerated. Yet the intensity of conflict makes sense when located within a much longer conversation and transformation taking place in Pleasanton Valley. The strong and insistent campaign of Chavez supporters, led by a largely Latino coalition in what is now an overwhelmingly majority Latino town, signified a struggle for both acceptance and recognition—that is, an acceptance of the majority Latino presence in the area, and a recognition of the ability of its leaders to make fair and informed decisions in the interest of the whole community. This was something, after all, that White political leaders had not doubted their legitimacy to do for several decades. The campaign also constituted an asserted right to representative participation in the process of defining key features (if only symbolic) of the Valley's social, economic, and institutional life. The uncompromising resolve with which Chavez supporters pursued their campaign was considered necessary to transform the political hierarchy and patronage system that had long existed in the area. It was a system that Chavez himself recognized and fought so insistently to challenge, one that had long neglected the interests of local Latinos to improve their economic lot on terms that validated their cultural and linguistic heritage. This "aggressive" manner of claiming an equal right to define and name did not—as one local, long-time business leader asserted—constitute an attack on America. Chavez was not the symbol of an "aggressive Mexicanismo," but, another White Farmingville resident insisted:

> He was an American-born leader who led a group of unrepresented and exploited laborers to organize nonviolently and protest for changes in their working conditions. He was a man who followed the teachings of Mahatma Gandhi and the example of Martin Luther King, Jr. . . . Can there be anyone more American? Chavez is not the "stereotype" of what a "Latino" should be, but the epitome of what it means to be American.

The school name controversy makes sense, and perhaps only so, in relation to the larger history of cultural politics in the PVUSD, where negotiations over racial, class, and cultural entitlement have long held a central place in the educational process. Like other conflicts I have described in this study—over desegregation mandates, Latino student activism, and Allenstown secession—the center of conflict has been less related to direct economic interests than to questions of social status; in each case, we see the anger of one group lined up against the fear of another. Yet the fears of local, middle-class Whites should not be understood primarily as anxieties about a potential reversal of the economic relationship between Latino and White residents in the area; instead it can be read as a deeper concern about losing the privilege to define the key features of social and institutional life on their own terms—that is, on their own norms and assumptions. The power to define is, in effect, the essence of privilege.

The high school naming controversy was essentially a struggle over authorship of historical memories, of the ability to define the present in terms of a particular past. The "aggressive" Chavez campaign was a strong challenge to the political and colonial relationship in which local White elites—by long-controlling the symbols and resources of the public institutions through which local social life is reproduced—have enjoyed the ability to shape local historical memory in such a way that both naturalizes their particular economic and political positioning and justifies the continuing relations of economic and political inequality that so clearly manifest themselves along lines of racial difference in the region.

Those who resisted naming the new high school after Chavez—citing its "divisive" message—did so through claims of neutrality and the need for the "unity of Americans." Such a call for "community" in the face of challenges to local status quo relations has served historically, whether intentionally or not, to pave over the contradictions posed by the particular development of social and capitalist relations in the area. At the same time, the school board, in its denial to grant the desires of the majority coalition of Chavez supports, participated (perhaps unintentionally) in a longer historical process of symbolic domination (Bourdieu 1991) whereby symbols of Latino empowerment and pride have been denied or dismissed by being characterized as threatening and divisive rather than as valid assertions of rights to equal citizenship and equal social status.

Race, Class, and Citizenship in the PVUSD

Throughout this book, I have attempted to illustrate that what underlies resistance to the demands and political agendas of Mexican-descent activists—whether over a symbolic issue such as a school name or to more substantial demands for increased economic and educational equity—is clearly not reducible to simple economic interest or to blatantly "racist" attitudes of particular individuals or groups. Instead, representing Mexican-descent residents' challenges to the educational status quo as the actions of non- or questionable citizens—a moral marking made more believable given the immigrant, socioeconomic, and educational statuses already positioning them as "undeserving"—has allowed a way of dismissing these residents' claims, often despite whatever compelling merit of their critique or dissent. This way of representing the behavior of angry Latinos—fitting them into particular, damaging stereotypes—operates as much through citizenship discourses as directly through racist and classist claims. This "blaming the victim" activism—often initiated by enfranchised Whites who themselves feel victimized by Latino anger and "aggression"—has achieved its success in great part through the way in which it capitalizes on particular and partial representations of the "immigrant situation" and the immigrant subject. These representations are then used to define the nature of educational "problems" that confront—or alternatively, are posed by—immigrant students and their families. The ability to create such convincing representations out of such partial knowledge comes from the ability to draw from extra-local opinion. As Rosaldo (1989) has noted, Whites of all class levels in California have long developed the peculiar ability to "see" Mexican-descent people as essentially "foreign" and not an integral part or as substantial contributors to American society. Moreover, the social and economic separation produced by residential and labor market segregation, along with the social polarization enhanced by White backlash to the direct action strategies of Mexican-descent activists and their allies, has led to a very one-sided popular understanding of the immigration situation.

The harmful stigmas endured by Mexican-descent youth and their families in the educational arena are not just those perpetuated by "racist" individuals or groups of individuals who might express a particular distain for people of color; nor are they limited to cases in which school staff maintain lowered academic expectations for Latino students based on cultural deficit assumptions (see Foley 1997). Equally stigmatizing are the recurring campaigns of backlash to Latino empowerment in which Latino claims of inequality and calls for equal citizenship status are dismissed and subverted. These cases are made all the more damaging when those dismissing such assertions further pathologize the intensity of Latino anger by reducing it to unwarranted concerns over a "trivial" issue—portraying it as "only" about a school name, or "only" a mural, or "only" a Chicano Studies course. Clearly, these dismissals are productive; recurrent resistance to supposed "trivial" rights to cultural affirmation, pride, and equal status for language and culture sends a strong message about what is acceptable, sayable, doable—and indeed thinkable—not just for those "dissenters" but citizens of all backgrounds. This is achieved by invoking limited notions of national character and expectations of citizenship behavior that reaffirm particular (Anglo-centric, middle-class) norms and practices, justifying a larger hierarchical order of distinctions, relationships, and symbols that define both social life and social history. Not only do these recurrent campaigns of resistance against Latino empowerment significantly shape the culture, structure, and practices of local schooling, they also severely impact how local Whites and Mexican-descent youth and families differentially respond to schooling and the level of entitlement that members of each group feel to participate in school functions and decision making.

Clearly, the exclusionary processes operating against Mexican-descent residents in Pleasanton Valley are not to be understood in a simple, unidirectional way—that is, as a one-way exercise of power by one privileged group unilaterally against another (less privileged) one. In the PVUSD, it is important to note that the enhanced exclusion of Latinos has served, in many cases, only to enhance their desire to belong. This desire to belong has not always facilitated a more efficient process of "assimilating" Latino immigrants to particular middle-class, Anglo-centric norms; in cases of exclusion, it has also increased the intransigence of dissent and the reaffirmation of cultural practices within the working-class Latino community (Portes and Zhou 1993). These formal and informal practices of dissent and affirmation—and the evolving political and economic institutions within which such dissent manifests itself—constitutes a productive process of redefining terms of national citizenship through the assertion of rights to maintain cultural distinctions within a single institutional framework in order to enable shared control, equal respect, and equal status—in other words, to assure equal citizenship.

My interest has been to frame the struggles of working-class Mexican-descent residents for equal opportunity in the educational realm as manifestations of Latino cultural citizenship, that is, as assertions of entitlement to respect and full participation in the public, institutional life of the communities they share with race and class "others" (Flores and Benmayor 1997; Rosaldo, Flores, and Silvestrini 1994). The recurrent conflicts described in this book have tended to pit equal citizenship norms rejecting stigma and domination against particular cultural norms based on expectations of Anglo-conformity (i.e., expectations of conformity to White middle-class norms in public institutional contexts and a divestment in other cultural practices or symbols) and unacknowledged expressions of White entitlement and privilege—that is, when groups with superior material resources use their political capital to effectively define institutional contexts in ways that favor specific understandings of "merit" and "equal opportunity."

Since the unification of the Pleasanton Valley school district in the mid-1960s, it has yet to function in a way that equally serves the Latino and White populations that make up the bulk of the district's school children. Yet the failure of the district to achieve conditions of equal opportunity for all students—a failure now being touted by Allenstown secessionists and other district reorganization proponents as a justification for splitting the district in ways that reinstitute segregated, "locally controlled" schools—is the result of a set of particular historical processes. It should not be reduced, therefore, to a dilemma definable by a set of empirical factors among which standardized test scores seem to be the most significant. Those who will claim with confidence that "desegregation hasn't worked" in the PVUSD and that "it's time for a change," must be willing to acknowledge the political and educational processes that have contributed to this failure and identify the dimensions of shared responsibility for the district's deficiencies. In this sense, the current debate on "district reorganization" is entirely lacking in historical perspective.

School Resegregation and Educational Inequity: What Can Be Done?

Given the historic difficulty of establishing conditions of equal status and opportunity in desegregated schools, shifting federal laws that continue to deprioritize integration as an equity-based reform measure, and an increasing desire among more affluent residential communities for schooling arrangements on their own terms—is there anything that might be done in places like Pleasanton Valley to promote, create, and maintain desegregated environments where middle-class White and working-class Latino students might be provided with relatively equal opportunities and access to participation in the schooling activities that promote engagement and academic success? Ultimately, the primary challenges are neither technical nor pedagogical, but normative. Until we address the normative issues that challenge equity-based school reform, and imagine paths and strategies for altering them, our technical reform endeavors will continue to fall flat (Oakes et al. 2005; Rogers and Oakes 2005). This includes the enduring assumptions that opportunities for high-quality education are in small supply and therefore should be "competed for" by students, families, and residential communities, which sustains a normalized context in which social wealth trumps social priority, and superior funds are expected to flow to those who have "earned" it by virtue of their relative socioeconomic standing and privileged residential location. In this normative environment, equity-based reform strategies—including some of the technical reform accountability measures prescribed by NCLB—appear threatening to middle-class residents who feel caught in a "zero-sum" struggle to assure the intergenerational transfer of opportunities and socioeconomic standing to their children, even if it requires exercising class and racial privileges that may have the effect of disadvantaging others.

The ubiquity of these normative cultural logics, and their embeddedness in schooling politics and practice, strains the ability to imagine how to generate broad-based political will to fight for inclusive, equitable, high-quality education that might be shared across socioeconomic and racial differences, particularly in the current political climate that has seemed largely to yield to an acceptance of school segregation. To the extent that such a comprehensive shift in favor of integrated schooling is possible, it would demand first and foremost—as Jeannie Oakes and her colleagues have argued—an alternative framing and broad public rearticulation of what is meant by "educational rights." The normative idea that educational quality is a scarce resource that should be differentially distributed to those who most "deserve" it would need to be reframed popularly as a *fundamental right* for which all citizens have equal entitlement and a *social priority* that engenders assumptions of public resource abundance rather than scarcity (Oakes et al. 2008). As well, the notion of "quality education" would need to be expanded sufficiently in breadth to encompass both concerns about student safety and commitments to fairness and inclusion, and in equal measure. Finally, such a reframing of educational rights would have to attend, in equal measure, to concerns about equal access to and support for challenging curriculum *in full cognizance* of the inherent costs and challenges posed by student and family characteristics such as race, income, parent's educational attainment, disability, and so forth (353).

This kind of reframing of the public education reform agenda was, in fact, a central part of the TFAU-PVUSD strategy to fight district separation, and their relative success illustrates the importance of education reform strategies that move beyond a focus on technical innovations to challenge and disrupt the dominant norms of schooling that sustain status quo conditions. The provisional success of the coalition, through its specific strategies of organizing and action, suggests that there are things that can be done locally to challenge active school resegregation efforts. Here, the formation of diverse, community-based spaces for working class Latino parents (MPAC, TFAU-PVUSD) and youth (Brown Berets, Student Empowerment Project) provided residents the opportunity to see themselves—and be recognized—as change agents capable of speaking up against disadvantaging educational conditions. The coalition accomplished its short-term goals of disrupting and then "reorganizing" the local school board through a social justice framing that successfully linked a public mandate for inclusive, high-quality education with broader issues of community well-being and respect for human dignity. This ability to connect the campaign for fair, high-quality schooling to other "noneducational" values and quality of life issues permitted broader-based social alliances and facilitated connections to progressive government, nonprofit, legal, and labor groups, from local to international levels. In essence, the demand for equitable, high-quality education was effectively transformed from a "Latino issue" to one essential to the social interests and values of the broader community, appealing on some level to a larger, multiracial and cross-class constituency of individuals and civic groups. Armed with "disruptive knowledge" (Oakes et al. 2008: 361) and supported by legal allies, this coalition successfully established a new school board majority willing to act as an advocate for new educational norms and political arrangements that were more responsive to the district's low-income Latino residents and more sensitive to the marginalizing norms and conditions that put their children at an inherent disadvantage in the schooling realm.

While the TFAU-PVUSD offers a strong moral framing, its human resources and cross-class support remain delicate, as do its financial resources for future struggles. Even with substantial mobilization from within the working-class Latino community, the coalition's support among middle-class Whites, particularly those residing in Allenstown, remains fragile and largely underdeveloped. To maintain its momentum, the coalition will need to dedicate substantial energy to nourishing convictions among White parents regarding the usefulness and viability of high-quality integrated education, including a clear understanding of the academic and social benefits associated with it, in order to overcome any perception that parents are being asked to choose between "diversity" and "excellence" in the schooling of their children.

A second question is whether the coalition and its new majority in the school board can maintain "sufficient allies and resources to sustain concerted action over time and in the face of significant resistance" (Oakes et al. 2008: 364). This remains to be seen, and there is some cause for doubt. A significant challenge will be in the coalition's ability to sustain collective leadership over time. When Benito moves out of the coalition's leadership position—or if he is subject to sufficient and sustained character assassination—the motivated but fragile fellowship could easily lose its momentum. At the same time, the coalition's "disruptive knowledge" approach and social justice framing is already under attack and being put on the defensive by more conservative forces in the Valley who are gathering their own data to frame educational arguments to their advantage. The Latino-led coalition, without more conventional means for developing or buying power, will likely need to rely even more on grassroots efforts than in the past.

Personal Thoughts on the Future of Integrated Education

Despite the myriad challenges associated with creating and sustaining effective integrated schooling environments in places like Pleasanton Valley, I would agree with Gary Orfield and Susan Eaton (1996) in their assessment that if equal educational opportunity remains a true value and concern for public schools in the United States, the current dilemma cannot be reduced to a question of whether increased segregation is more or less desirable; any move toward resegregation and "separate but equal" schooling is likely only to create new barriers to equal opportunity for working-class Mexican-descent communities. This is because "separate but equal" schooling conditions—which in some circumstances would seem to promise working-class communities of color more direct control over their schools—typically produce promises of "control" that are inherently fleeting. First, White middle-class norms—and for the most part, White middle-class people—will continue to control the public and private distribution of educational resources at the state and federal levels. Second, as Orfield and Eaton maintain, "once racial and class separation are accepted as legitimate, and leaders (of color) affirm the possibility of 'separate but equal,' they will be blamed for the school system's failure" (1996: 48). Finally, returning to "separate but equal schools" will be anything but equal for communities of color, particularly in urban and other high-poverty contexts where students will continue to suffer in inferior "schools of concentrated disadvantage."

Alternatively, there are a number of well-tested school integration options still available, with model programs operating more or less sustainably throughout the United States. Such efforts are being maintained through a diverse, and often shifting, array of models and strategies including magnet programs and dual immersion schools; the use of intradistrict zoning (rather than the creation of new school districts); the development of school reassignment, open enrollment, and interdistrict transfer policies that encourage and facilitate both socioeconomic and racial diversity in schools; housing policy that encourages development of racially and socioeconomically integrated neighborhoods; and through attention to race implications in the construction of new schools and redrawing of school and school district boundaries (see Frankenberg and Debray 2011; Frankenberg and Orfield 2007; and Tefera et al. 2011 for case studies, discussion, and profiles of these existing programs). There is some concern that the Supreme Court 2007 decision in *Parents Involved in Community Schools v. Seattle School District No. 1 (PICS)* has effectively sounded a death knell for integration mandates of the kind proffered in *Brown v. Board of Education*. And, indeed, the *PICS* decision is significant for the ways in which it has limited how race can be used by school districts in decisions about student assignments—specifically, through the mandate that individual students cannot be classified solely by their race in the school assignment process. However, the *PICS* decision also reaffirmed the idea that school districts have a "compelling interest" in promoting racial diversity and in avoiding racial isolation in schools (Frankenberg and Debray 2011). Contrary to popular interpretations of the decision, race-conscious measures for assigning students to schools are still permitted; among the measures *explicitly endorsed* in *PICS* are (a) the strategic selection of new school sites, (b) the drawing of attendance zones with general recognition of the racial demographics of neighborhoods, (c) allocation of resources for special programs, (d) recruitment of students and faculty in a targeted manner, and (e) the tracking of enrollment, performance, and other statistics by race (Tefera et al. 2011: 42).

Ultimately, the ability to sustain support for integrated schooling programs, and the public will to fight for them, will require a fundamental shift in the ways most educators, parents, citizens, and students think about the meaning of equal citizenship and about the role of deliberative democracy in the schooling process. As sociologist Pamela Perry has noted, there is a strong need in multiracial, socioeconomically diverse societies to "go beyond the current, almost pathological, obsession with schools as training grounds for the workforce and re-introduce the value of schooling for teaching youth personal and interpersonal respect, cooperation, tolerance, and reflection, skills necessary for effective, democratic participation" (2002: 194). Ensuring conditions of equal status and equal opportunity for all students is possible only when low achievement is taken to be a schoolwide problem and when the central concern of schooling practice and organization is to foster learning communities in which all children can be smart

(Oakes 1995). This requires moving beyond an exclusive focus on test scores as the sole criterion of school "success," particularly if the ultimate goal of schooling is to prepare students for responsible participation in the larger society.

To effectively infuse public schools with democratic values of support, diversity, and community requires a political climate of shared responsibility and trust that is achievable only by establishing new political relations among teachers, administrators, parents, students, and community members (Oakes 1995: 8). In the school context, sustaining such communities of difference requires not just *equal access* of school resources for all students, but *institutional conditions for inclusive participation* that assure all students and parents have the ability to share in the choices that define and redefine the school's community of collective interests. For example, to promote what might be considered "safe spaces" for Mexican-descent youth in traditionally White-dominated schools would require accepting that there is no essential contradiction between a claim of equal citizenship and room for separate cultural expression and development (Gibson and Bejínez 2002). It would also necessitate believing that equal status and a widespread sense of belonging in the school could be best achieved not through (Anglo) conformity to a "common culture" that stresses sameness without differences, but through envisioning and cultivating a community of difference in which citizens are bonded together through a politics of solidarity rather than sameness, based on the "mutual respect for reasonable intellectual, political, and cultural differences" (Ovando and McLaren 2000: xvii). Here, solidarity "begins when people have the confidence to disagree over issues of fundamental importance precisely because they 'care' about pluralized and diversified forms of contemporary democracy" (212).

Clearly, such visions of deliberative democracy in the schooling context have the potential to generate conflict. That would be the case, however, with any attempt to create conditions for a more inclusive community in a context of widespread economic, educational, racial, and gender inequalities. For example, students will inevitably experience a sense of unease should they be invited to engage across lines of difference with "others" whom they may have long considered alien, inferior, threatening, or altogether different. Under conditions of cultural pluralism, there is no guarantee that racial and class coexistence over time will remain peaceful, or that it necessarily must. Yet this sense of conflict or unease can and should be taken as a productive, educable opportunity in multiracial, socioeconomically mixed school settings for the way it allows youth to "sharpen [their own] perspectives through the friction of dialogue" (Boostrom 1998, 20) inviting them to discuss, critique, or refashion the very notions of race, class, and gender that can be so limiting and that remain so widely accepted in the larger community (Fine et al. 1997). Here, conflict should be envisioned as an opportunity to address a need or meet a challenge, not as something to stomp away or sweep under the carpet. The damaging consequences of the later approach are well documented in this book.

Highlighting the need for inclusive forms of deliberative democracy in schools does not deny the importance of school-based achievement and learning; there is no question that schools should be centrally concerned with the personal, social, and intellectual development of all students to their highest potential. Yet educators must acknowledge the need within our society for intercultural competent citizens who are endowed with tools to comprehend existing dimensions of social differences and social inequality, and who have the ability to combat prejudice and discrimination in ways that empower them to make informed, responsible judgments about their lives and about the larger social policies that will shape the increasingly interdependent world in which they live. As well, it should be clear that a pluralist model of deliberative democracy serves White middle-class students as well. Our nation's future is one that will be increasingly characterized by multilingual and multicultural environments and will require that all citizens be well-prepared to function comfortably, adequately, and fairly beyond the communities in which they grew up.

In the experience at Allenstown High, it is clear that the challenges to equal status and equal opportunity for Mexican-descent students do not derive from the widespread existence of racist or uncaring teachers. It is also apparent, however, that many teachers have failed to develop an enhanced sense of what Bartolomé and Trueba (2000) have called "political clarity," which they define as a professional acknowledgment that the "clarity of [one's] political beliefs, practices, and commitments is as important as the actual pedagogical strategies used in instruction" (278). Political clarity requires a heightened awareness of the important political and ideological dimensions of teaching that often go unacknowledged. For teachers, this means an ongoing willingness to reflect critically on how one's teaching practices and perhaps one's own belief system—to the extent that it may be rooted in an assimilationist orientation or function on a romanticized view of White middle-class (mainstream) culture—may inadvertently support unfair and inequitable schooling conditions and practices. Unfortunately, this sort of reflection is not something most educators have been specifically trained to consider or do, largely because teaching has long been considered a political neutral undertaking in which professional development training focuses almost exclusively on the acquisition of particular methods of instruction and the transmission of specific technical skills in management and curriculum. Rarely do teacher preparation programs adequately encourage or provide teachers with the tools to reflect upon "the greater political and ideological challenges that [will] face them in their attempt to work with immigrant and U.S. born low-status minority populations" (Bartolomé and Trueba 2000: 279). In this sense, the responsibility to take seriously the political dimensions of education lies not just with teachers, but with those educators, administrators, and public officials who develop or make available preservice and ongoing professional development training programs. It is important that such programs move beyond an exclusive focus on instructional methods and technical skills to assure that "concepts such as 'equality,' 'democracy,' 'fairness,' and 'justice' . . . serve as ever present anchors across the teacher education curriculum so as to remind prospective teachers that teaching is ultimately a moral and ethical undertaking" (2000: 289).

Ideally, an emphasis on political clarity would encourage all educators—White or not—to engage in a democratic politics of solidarity with immigrant and other low-status minority students as well as the communities from which they come, challenging themselves—as Paulo Freire would have it—to "become courageous in [their] commitments to defend subordinated populations even when it is easier not to take a stand" (Bartolomé and Trueba 2000: 289).

NOTES

Introduction

1. The U.S. Census rightly represents "Latino" as an ethnic rather than a racial category. However, attention to White/Latino school segregation as a *racial* issue recognizes the extent to which Latinos are positioned as a highly racialized group in the U.S. context, one that has been subject to a long history of interpersonal and structural racism across social, economic, political, and cultural spheres. This history of racialization, and its impact on the schooling experiences of Latino youth, are elaborated in detail throughout this book.

2. Here I follow Orfield and Lee's 2006 designation of the U.S. Western states as Arizona, California, Colorado, Montana, Nevada, New Mexico, Oregon, Utah, Washington, and Wyoming. A full accounting of the authors' regional distinctions can be found in (2006: 7n13).

3. This argument is well articulated in Chemerinsky 2003. Other comprehensive analyses of the history of Supreme Court decisions related to school desegregation can be found in the work of Orfield and Eaton 1996 and Weiler 1998.

4. A more extensive discussion of the social, health, and educational challenges posed by high-poverty, racially isolated schools will be presented at the beginning of Chapter 1.

5. This includes the expansive research associated with the Civil Rights Project/Proyecto Derechos Civiles at UCLA, http://civilrightsproject.ucla.edu/research.

6. This claim draws from analysis of extensive survey data by Gary Orfield and Susan Eaton 1996.

7. I use the terms "Latino" and "Mexican-descent" interchangeably throughout the text, largely because nearly all my Latino informants (and the majority of Latino residents) in the Pleasanton Valley region are of Mexican descent. I note all exceptions. When relevant, I draw particular attention to intra-ethnic differences such as those related to gender, immigrant generation, assimilation, socioeconomic status, and language preferences.

8. All names of people and places in this study are pseudonyms. I have done this to protect the identities of those who provided their candid commentaries.

9. For exceptions, see the excellent work of Alvarez (1986); Donato (1998); Donato and Hanson (2012); San Miguel and Valencia (1998); and Valencia (1998).

10. For example, while the segregation of African American children was predicated on exclusions related to their non-White racial status, Mexican Americans generally maintained a *legal* status as "White," even as they endured a distinct *social* status and treatment as a stigmatized and racialized group across the U.S. Southwest (Donato and Hanson 2012). Therefore, their widespread school segregation was justified on a pedagogical rationale: their "need" for assimilation (via an Americanization curriculum) and targeted English-language training. While the idea that Mexican American children could be legally segregated for educational purposes was rejected as early as 1946 in the Supreme Court *Mendez v. Westminister* decision, the desegregation process put in motion by *Brown v. Board of Education* remained applicable primarily to African Americans in the South through the 1960s. It was not until the Supreme Court decision in *Cisernos v. Corpus Christi* (1970) that Mexican Americans were granted the status of an "identifiable ethnic-minority group" and the right to a desegregated education under *Brown*.

11. From the perspective of critical race theory, the significance of race is viewed and analyzed not primarily in terms of skin color or some notion of a static "content" of racial or cultural identity (e.g., "White person" or "Mexican culture") but in terms of processes and practices of inclusion and exclusion through which categorical boundaries of "race" are maintained in specific historical moments and in particular institutional contexts.

12. Yasso and Solórzano (2007) define "cultural wealth" as the accumulated assets and resources (which they refer to as various forms of capital defined by characteristics such as aspirational, navigational, social, linguistic, familial, and resistance) that exist in working-class Latino communities (129). This focus on community-based cultural wealth (similar to what Moll et al. 1992 have called "funds of knowledge") is understood as an important corrective to deficit-based and "race neutral" research and policy-making that has long served to silence and distort the living experiences of people of color.

13. This can lead in some cases to what Virginia Dominguez 1993 has called the "culturalization of sociopolitical difference," referring to the multiple manners in which society's structural inequalities can become culturally constituted in ways that divide racial minority groups internally.

14. Population and income figures are based on data from the 2010 U.S. Census.

15. Asian and Filipino-descent students each make up about 1 percent of the district's student population; African Americans, Native Americans, and Pacific Islanders collectively constitute less than 1 percent.

16. The Peers Project, directed by Principal Investigator and UC Santa Cruz educational anthropologist Margaret Gibson, received generous grant support from the Spencer Foundation, the National Science Foundation, the U.S. Department of

Education Office of Educational Research and Improvement (OERI), and the University of California Linguistic Minority Research Institute (UCLMRI). Published studies associated with this research include (as a nonexhaustive listing): Gibson and Hidalgo (2009); Gibson et al. (2004); Gibson and Bejínez (2002); and Hurd (2008, 2004).

17. Acknowledging one's own "positionality" means being self-reflective about the role one plays, as a subject and actor, in the very experiences of "others" one intends to describe. This means acknowledging political and positional biases in ways that treat one's own experiences—not just the experiences of "others"—as primary data. Ethnography is not a transparent rendering of some independent order of reality. It is always a mediated story fraught, unavoidably, with ethical and political concerns including, but not limited, to the conditions of possibility that allow researchers to work in specific areas with particular populations; the institutional factors that shape how a research agenda is developed and the framing questions that guide it; the management of one's political inclinations; the exploitation of one's positional privileges; and the "write up" of field data in ways that meet the divergent goals, expectations, and conflicting interests of a dynamic literary/academic market (de Genova 2005).

18. Ultimately, the story of the "lost" manuscript constituted a mild controversy in the district, with a small faction of school board members threatening to call out their colleague's actions as violations of various California freedom of information acts (the California Brown Act and Public Records Act) and other copyright infringements. In the end, the situation was resolved without great incident, but it speaks volumes to the divisions and animosity that existed among factions on the school board, which mirrored those in the community, and how my presence was transposed onto those conflicts.

Chapter 1. White/Latino School Resegregation, the Deprioritization of School Integration, and Prospects for a Future of Shared, High-Quality Education

1. Orfield and Lee (2006: 29). The *Bunche Report* (2004) also highlights how social stratification in access to higher education is associated with racial segregation as well as inequalities in educational resources.

2. Frankenberg, Lee, and Orfield (2003: 152); Orfield and Eaton (1996: 22, 42).

3. I realize that by choosing to selectively synthesize a broad and diverse body of scholarly work into two dominant frameworks, I run the risk of being overly reductive. However, I present the scholarship in broad strokes here primarily for the purpose of suggesting a more integrated approach to the study of resegregation processes as it pertains to suburban school contexts.

4. See, specifically, landmark decisions in *Green v. County School Board* (1968), *Swann v. Charlotte-Mecklenburg Board of Education* (1971), *Ciserno v. Corpus Christi* (1970), and *Keyes v. School District No. 1, Boulder, CO* (1973).

5. As Omi and Winant (1994) have claimed, much of the anger directed at civil rights advocates at the time might be considered largely displaced. They argue that economic dislocations felt by working-class Whites had less to do with civic rights activism and more to do with the (1) deindustrialization of the U.S. Northeast (felt through increased factory shutdowns, worker layoffs due to redundancy with more efficient technologies, and a labor market shift to more limited employment opportunities in the high tech sector); (2) U.S. manufacturers' loss of market share to foreign competitors; (3) a growing trade deficit; (4) surging inflation (which eroded purchasing power and curtailed investment); and (5) humiliating military losses in Vietnam, Nicaragua, and Iran in the 1970s.

6. See landmark cases *Board of Education of Oklahoma City v. Dowell* (1990), *Freeman v. Pitts* (1992), *Missouri v. Jenkins* (1995), and *McFarland v. Jefferson County Public Schools and Parents Involved in Community Schools v. Seattle School District No. 1* (2007), aka, the *PICS* decision).

7. The Court's 2007 *PICS* decision constitutes the most recent blow to school desegregation policy-making in further restricting how race-based criteria (alone) can be used by school districts in student assignment decisions, even in cases of voluntary integration.

8. As Cashin (2001) has argued, residents of CIDs have come to "view themselves as taxpayers rather than citizens, and they often perceive local property taxes as a fee for services they should receive rather than their contribution to services local government must provide to the community as a whole" (1677).

9. This liberal interpretation of territory as the "voluntary aggregation of members' real estate holdings" (Lehning 1998) offers a strong and well-tested rationale; it is the same logic that propelled the passage of California's Proposition 13 (1978), a voter referendum measure prohibiting government from taxing property to provide "inessential" redistributional services against the wishes of the property-owning majority.

10. While claims of this kind remain largely conjectural at this point, historical analyses focusing on the increasingly privatized nature of social and political life in United States would seem to support the possibility of such developments.

11. Here, Barlowe views such destabilizing developments to be a consequence of a broader politico-economic shift in the United States, away from what resembled a basic social welfare state in the post-World War II period, and toward an "ideal" type of private accumulation state in which redistributional social welfare programs (e.g., retirement, health care, education) are portrayed as being in need of replacement by personal capital investments and individuals are expected to be increasingly responsible for their own personal welfare. In this ideal private accumulation state, people

should expect to "get what they pay for" and social entitlements formerly understood as publically granted are now increasingly seen as individual's responsibility to attain through the private marketplace.

12. These early interventions of Black Nationalist leaders have been sustained in the continued writings in the Critical Race Theory (CRT) tradition, where inquiry has moved away from thinking about race solely in terms of discrimination and prejudice toward a wider consideration of the role of power, subordination, and colonialism in the establishment and maintenance of structures of racial domination.

13. In other words, as Gary Peller has aptly pointed out, in failing to "recognize the cultural specificity of White schools, and instead only see them as 'superior' education," such a perspective assumed only positive characteristics in White, middle-class environments and primarily negatives attributes in minority, working-class ones (1996: 141)

14. See Ruben Donato (1998) for an excellent historical case study, done in the same region that is the focus of this case study, that covers political organizing and activism on the part of the Mexican American community to sustain equal schooling conditions from the 1960s to early 1980s.

15. Broadly speaking, "social capital" is a term used to describe a matrix of social relationships, built over time, that connects individuals and social groups together in ways that facilitate their access to resources and forms of support and promote the achievement of shared goals and a sense of collective identity that is based on reciprocity, resiliency, trust, and belonging (Portes 1998; Stanton-Salazar 1997; Stanton-Salazar and Dornbusch 1995).

16. Warren et al.'s 2011 volume on community organizing and school reform, while not structured specifically around the concept of social capital, offers several case studies that highlight the effectiveness and limitations of leadership development and cross-sector coalition-building activities for school improvement among U.S. Latino populations.

17. Contentious politics play an essential rather than an incidental role in such "pro-poor" social capital-building, given that power-sharing with the poor necessarily involves redistributional stances that threaten entrenched interests and will likely generate resistance from those who typically benefit from socializing institutions (like public schools) that tend to operate though norms of meritocracy that favor the affluent (Fox and Gershman 2000; McAdam et al. 2001).

18. Trueba et al. (1993) coined the term "castification" to refer to the ongoing processes of marginalization and disenfranchisement U.S. Latinos have historically endured. This marginalization has been perpetuated not necessarily by means of legal exclusions, but by recurring attempts to reduce the social status of the group so that it cannot enjoy the same rights and obligations possessed by other groups.

19. Raley (2004) provides a useful discussion of the importance of educational spaces for Latinos that are relatively *safe from* societal and educational stigmas of discrimination, low expectations, and devaluing of culture and language, as well as

safe for such things as taking risks and establishing personal relationships with others focused on self-efficacy, mutuality, and collective action.

20. Such attributed—and often felt—"deficiencies" include those related to language proficiency, parent support, intelligence, cultural background and educational experiences.

Chapter 2. Historicizing Educational Politics in Pleasanton Valley

1. The Peers Project engaged both White and Latino students in an extensive social mapping project as a means of gaining insight into how they experienced and understood social relationships on the campus. There was a remarkable level of congruence in how they placed and named students groups. Their personal assessments of the groups, as could be expected, varied more significantly.

2. "Migrant" status is given to school-age children whose families regularly relocate to seek temporary or seasonal work in agriculture, fishing, or related industries, including food processing. Some move seasonally to follow cultivation, picking, and processing opportunities in Mexico and Southern California; others return to Mexico during the winter months when they have neither employment nor income. Having the status of a migrant qualifies students for supplemental educational services provided by the federal Migrant Education Program. On verification of eligibility, students typically qualify for three years.

3. As Ruben Donato (1987) contends in his own historical research in the region, consolidation was made to seem financially and organizationally attractive by promising to provide a coordinated and consistent K-12 program and curriculum, a fixed tax rate to support all schools, more efficient spending of funds, and an equalization of educational opportunity to children of various socioeconomic backgrounds. However, federal and state directives were deemed to be crucial in compelling the local schooling officials to pursue consolidation and in shaping public opinion about the relative virtues of consolidation.

4. Donato (1987: 31). Their treatment must also be seen in relation to the increasingly contentious relations between the U.S. and Japanese governments in the interwar period. This would help explain the perception of their "dangerousness" and the assumption they would only support "their own kind."

5. This quote is from the transcript of a 1985 oral history interview with a longtime Farmingville activist, accessed from the McHenry Library Special Collections at the University of California, Santa Cruz.

6. The non-Hispanic population in Farmingville is largely White, although it includes those of Filipino, Chinese, African American, and Japanese descent who make up less than 10 percent of the non-Hispanic group.

7. Miriam Wells's 1996 excellent ethnography of the historical development of the strawberry industry along the California central coast provides a deft analysis

of the political construction of labor in this area from the 1940s through the late 1980s .

8. One of these predominantly White communities is a hillside neighborhood of Victorian homes just east of downtown that has historically housed the more wealthy farm-owning families in the region. The second is a middle-income but increasingly mixed neighborhood of single family homes near the center of town, and the third is a newer subdivision of condominiums and single family homes adjacent to a recently constructed outdoor shopping mall that promises to provide residents with "a taste of suburban living."

9. "River-by-the-Sea directors bothered by 'rooming house' Situations," *Santa Cristo Sentinel*, January 9, 1979.

10. Details of this campaign were released by multiple local media sources, including in the following articles: "River-by-the-Sea Improvement Association Wants to Improve Student Test Scores," *Santa Cristo Sentinel*, July 3, 1984; "RDM Directors Quarrel over Education Report," *Green Sheet*, October 9, 1985; "Rio Director Resigns in Protest," *Farmingville Register*, January 20, 1986.

11. It included representatives from the Pleasanton Valley PTA and Student Council, the Allenstown and Farmingville chambers of commerce, the Pleasanton Valley Federation of Teachers, La Coalición (a Mexican American educational support organization), Chicano Leadership Council, and Japanese-American Citizenship League (Donato 1987: 217).

Chapter 3. Latino Empowerment and Institutional Amnesia at Allenstown High

1. Another important factor at play, as regional historian Paule Cruz Takash (1990) has pointed out, was the local, longstanding practice of political *patron-clientelism* in which aspiring Latino public servants were hand-picked by enfranchised White civic leaders to serve on city commissions. This initiated a "political grooming" process in which Latinos were expected to prove themselves sufficiently acculturated to merit the support of the local White establishment (controlled by an elite group of local farm-owners and their interests) and to represent the interest of the entire community, not the Latino one. Takash considered this an example of institutional racism because it was a process required of all Latinos, but not necessarily of all White candidates. In other words, the ability of Whites to represent the entire community was not doubted, while that of Latinos was.

2. The Brown Berets are a citizen-led Chicano/Mexican American civil rights group that appeared in Los Angeles in the mid-1960s. The group promoted social justice work such as initiating social programs to serve and empower the poor, combat police brutality, and improve schooling conditions for immigrant and nonimmigrant Latino students. A deeper inquiry into the development and activities of the Farmingville chapter of the Brown Berets is pursued in Chapter 7.

3. MEChA, an acronym for El Movimiento Estudiantil Chican@ de Aztlán, is a national student leadership organization first established as a college student coalition in California in the late 1960s. MEChA seeks to promote the unity and political empowerment of young Mexican Americans through educational and social activities as well as political action and mobilization.

4. For example, the headline from a widely circulated regional newspaper read: "Leader or Loser? Former Allenstown High President Now Watching His Back."

5. These accusations of "acting White" are similar to what Fordham (1996), Morgan (1996), and Ogbu and Fordham (1987) have found with some working-class African American youth.

6. Clearly, issues of gender are central here, as they have been in "Chicano" political activism since the 1960s (see Garcia 1997 for a collection of a historical writings by feminist scholars critical of Chicano nationalist rhetoric and political practice). The centrality of gender is well illustrated in the way Rebecca was expected to "stand by her man" when Diego was impeached from ASB office.

Chapter 4. The Road from Dissent to Secession

1. At the same time, gang violence must be understood in terms of battles over notions of "proper" and "valued" citizenship at play in the larger regional context that impacted, in detrimental ways, relationships between Mexican-descent youth themselves. Battles over citizenship have traditionally shaped Norteño/Sureño gang affiliations and confrontation. Mendoza-Denton's (1999: 42–45) analysis of Norteño/Sureño gang divisions is instructive for a general understanding of the dynamics of gang affiliation in Farmingville.

2. See AB1382, 1982, and California Educational Code 54441, 54443, and 54444.

3. Making the exclusionary gesture all the more insulting was that it came from the superintendent who was himself an American of Mexican descent, one many of the migrant parents saw as capitulating to the wishes of the Allenstown community.

Chapter 5. Race and School District Secession: Allenstown's District Reorganization Campaign, 1995–2004

1. See Derrick Bell (1995) for a thoughtful critique of the desegregation approach mandated in *Brown v. Board of Education*. Bell finds in *Brown* the antisegregation mandate to be "educationally destructive" to minority students in many instances, particularly given the widespread reluctance of middle-class White communities to give up their superior societal status. He argues that resource allocations and concerns regarding educational reform should be perhaps less focused on desegregation than on

"the improvement of presently desegregated schools as well as the creation or preservation of model black [or, as he might suggest, other racial minority] schools" (1995: 26).

Chapter 6. Cinco de Mayo, Normative Whiteness, and the Marginalization of Mexican-Descent Students at Allenstown High

1. In another publication (see Hurd 2004), I offer a more detailed analysis about how fears of "put-downs" by more assimilated Mexican-descent peers limit other students' participation (especially that of more recent immigrants and ELLs) in school activities as well as their ability to practice and learn English.

2. Here I refer to Matute-Bianchi's definition of "Mexican-oriented" students as those "with strong ties to both Mexico and the United States, but claim an identity as Mexicano. . . . They see themselves as different from Mexican *recien llegados* [but] they exhibit pride in their Mexican heritage, which they feel distinguishes them from other, more Americanized students of Mexican descent in the school" (1986: 238).

3. Cinco de Mayo commemorates La Batalla de Puebla, an 1862 battle in which the Mexican army successfully beat back advancing French forces, considered at the time the premier army in the world. Although somewhat militarily insignificant given France's eventual advance, it remains culturally significant as a national victory against tremendous odds. Its commemoration is celebrated with a sense of patriotism and cultural pride for being "Mexican."

Chapter 7. Waking the Sleeping Giant: The Emergence of Progressive, Latino-Led Coalitions for School Reform

1. The activities associated with the Brown Berets include positive social justice work such as initiating social programs to serve and empower the poor, combat police brutality, and improve schooling conditions for immigrant and nonimmigrant Latino students. They have also included more radical forms of political protest that have included seizures of private property and alleged paramilitary operations. For a deft, first-person account of the foundational activities of Brown Berets in California during the 1960s and 1970s, see Carlos Muñoz (1989).

2. King's direct action agenda included a clear path of tactics: first to collect facts to document the injustice exists and then to negotiate with enfranchised citizen and government groups to address that injustice. If or when such negotiation should fail or break down, it was necessary to organize and mobilize people and resources to bring to the surface hidden tensions in the community, forcing citizens and public officials to confront issues they might have wished or fought to avoid (King 1997 [1963]).

3. One percent provided "mixed" feedback, meaning feedback that included arguments both in favor and against reorganization but not appearing to favor one particular view. About 3 percent did not provide feedback for or against the reorganization, but commented on the difficulty of understanding the data as presented in the report.

BIBLIOGRAPHY

Acuña, Rodolfo. 1972. *Occupied America: The Chicano's Struggle Toward Liberation.* San Francisco: Canfield Press.

Allport, Gordon. 1954. *The Nature of Prejudice.* Cambridge, Mass.: Addison-Wesley.

Almaguer, Tomás. 1994. *Racial Fault Lines: The Historical Origins of White Supremacy in California.* Berkeley: University of California Press.

Alvarez, Robert R., Jr. 1986. "The Lemon Grove Incident: The Nation's First Successful Desegregation Court Case." *Journal of San Diego History/San Diego Historical Society Quarterly* 32, 2.

Andersen, Margaret. 2003. "Whitewashing Race: A Critical Perspective on Whiteness." In *White Out: The Continuing Significance of Racism,* ed. Ashley Doane and Eduardo Bonilla-Silva, 23–34. New York: Routledge.

Apple, Michael. 1993. "Constructing the 'Other': Rightest Reconstructions of Common Sense." In *Race, Identity, and Representation in Education,* ed. Cameron McCarthy and Warren Crichlow, 24–39. New York: Routledge.

Balfanz, Robert, and Nettie Legters. 2004. "Locating the Dropout Crisis." In *Dropouts in America,* ed. Gary Orfield, 85–106. Boston: Harvard Education Press.

Baquedano-López, Patricia. 2000. "Narrating Community in Doctrina Classes." *Narrative Inquiry* 10, 2: 1–24.

Bardacke, Frank. 1994. *Good Liberals and Great Blue Herons: Land, Labor and Politics in the Pleasant Valley.* Santa Cruz, Calif.: Center for Political Ecology.

Barlowe, Andrew. 2003. *Between Hope and Fear: Globalization and Race in the United States.* Lanham, Md.: Rowman and Littlefield.

Barrera, Mario. 1979. *Race and Class in the Southwest: A Theory of Racial Inequality.* South Bend, Ind.: University of Notre Dame Press.

Bartolomé, Lilia I., and Enrique (Henry) Trueba. 2000. "Beyond the Politics of Schools and the Rhetoric of Fashionable Pedagogies: The Significance of Teacher Ideology." In *Immigrant Voices: In Search of Education Equity,* ed. Enríque. T. Trueba and Lilia I. Bartolomé, 277–92. New York: Rowman and Littlefield.

Bell, Derrick, Jr. 1995. "*Brown v. Board of Education* and the Interest Convergence Dilemma." In *Critical Race Theory: The Key Writings That Formed the Movement,* ed. Kimberlé Crenshaw, Neil Gotanda, Gary Peller, and Kendall Thomas, 20–29. New York: New Press.

———. 2004. "Brown Reconsidered: Was Education Equity Rather Than Integration Idealism the Appropriate Goal?" *The Crisis* 111, 3 (May/June).

Bettie, Julie. 2003. *Women Without Class: Girls, Race, and Identity.* Berkeley: University of California Press.

Betts, Julian, Kim Rueben, and Anne Danenberg. 2000. *Equal Resources, Equal Outcomes? The Distribution of School Resources and Student Achievement in California.* San Francisco: Public Policy Institute of California.

Boostrom, Robert. 1998. "Safe Spaces: Reflections on an Educational Metaphor." *Journal of Curriculum Studies* 30, 4: 397–408.

Boudreau, Julie-Anne, and Roger Keil. 2001. "Seceding from Responsibility? Secession Movements in Los Angeles." *Urban Studies* 38, 10: 1701–31.

Bourdieu, Pierre. 1991. *Language and Symbolic Power.* Cambridge: Polity Press.

Brodkin, Karen. 1998. *How Jews Became White Folks and What That Says About Race in America.* New Brunswick, N.J.: Rutgers University Press.

Bunche Research Report. 2004. *Separate But Certainly Not Equal: 2003 CAPAA Findings*, Vol. 1(2). Los Angeles: Ralph J. Bunche Center for African American Studies, University of California, Los Angeles.

Burris, Carol, and Kevin Welner. 2007. "Classroom Integration and Accelerated Learning Through Detracking." In *Lessons in Integration*, ed. Erica Frankenberg and Gary Orfield, 207–27. Charlottesville: University of Virginia Press.

Caldeira, Teresa P. R. 2000. *City of Walls: Crime, Segregation and Citizenship in São Paulo.* Berkeley: University of California Press.

Cammarota, Julio. 2007. "A Social Justice Approach to Achievement: Guiding Latina/o Students Toward Educational Attainment with a Challenging, Socially Relevant Curriculum." *Equity & Excellence in Education* 40, 1: 87–96.

Cashin, Sheryl. 2001. "Privatized Communities and the 'Secession of the Successful': Democracy and Fairness Beyond the Gate." Georgetown Law Faculty Publications and Other Works, Paper 518. http://scholarship.law.georgetown.edu/facpub/518/.

Chemerinsky, Erwin. 2003. "The Segregation and Resegregation of American Public Education: The Court's Role." *North Carolina Law Review* 81: 1597–1622.

Chesler, Mark, Melissa Peet, and Todd Sevig. 2003. "Blinded by Whiteness: The Development of White College Students' Racial Awareness." In *White Out: The Continuing Significance of Racism*, ed. Ashley W. Doane and Eduardo Bonilla-Silva, 215–30. New York: Routledge.

Clifford, James. 1994. "Diasporas." *Cultural Anthropology* 9, 3: 302–38.

Clotfelter, Charles, Helen Ladd, and Jacob Vigdor. 2005. "Who Teaches Whom?" *Economics of Education Review* 24, 4: 377–92.

Coleman, James. 1968. "The Concept of Equality of Educational Opportunity." *Harvard Educational Review* 38, 1: 7–22.

Collins, Jim. 1988. "Language and Class in Minority Education." *Anthropology and Education Quarterly* 19: 299–321.

Comaroff, Jean, John Comaroff, and Richard Weller, eds. 2001. *Millennial Capitalism and the Culture of Neoliberalism.* Durham, N.C.: Duke University Press.

Conchas, Gil. 2001. "Structuring Failure and Success: Understanding the Variability in Latino School Engagement." *Harvard Educational Review* 70, 3: 475–504.

Crain, Robert L. 1981. "Making Desegregation Work: Extracurricular Activities." *Urban Review* 13, 2: 121–27.

Davidson, Anne Locke. 1996. *Making and Molding Identities in Schools: Student Narratives on Race, Gender, and Academic Engagement.* Albany, N.Y.: SUNY Press.

De Genova. 2005. *Working the Boundaries: Race, Space, and "Illegality" in Mexican Chicago.* Durham, N.C.: Duke University Press.

Delpit, Lisa. 1995. *Other People's Children: Cultural Conflict in the Classroom.* New York: New Press.

Delgado-Gaitan, Concha. 1996. *Protean Literacy: Extending the Discourse on Empowerment.* Washington, D.C.: Falmer Press.

Dominguez. Virginia. 1993. *White by Definition: Social Classification in Creole Louisiana.* New Brunswick, N.J.: Rutgers University Press.

Donato, Ruben. 1987. "In Struggle: Mexican Americans in the Pleasanton Valley Schools, 1900–1979." Ph.D. dissertation, Stanford University.

———. 1998. *The Other Struggle for Equal Schools: Mexican Americans During the Civil Rights Era.* Albany, N.Y.: SUNY Press. Donato, Ruben, and Jarrod Hanson. 2012. "Legally White, Socially 'Mexican': The Politics of *de jure* and *de facto* School Segregation in the American Southwest." *Harvard Educational Review* 82, 2: 202–25.

Du Bois, W. E. B. 1992 [1935]. *Black Reconstruction in America.* New York: Atheneum.

Dyrness, Andrea. 2008. "Research for Change Versus Research as Change: Lessons from a *Mujerista* Participatory Research Team." *Anthropology and Education Quarterly* 39, 1: 23–44.

———. 2011. *Mothers United: An Immigrant Struggle for Socially Just Education.* Minneapolis: University of Minnesota Press.

Eaton, Susan. 2001. *The Other Boston Busing Story: What's Won and Lost Across the Boundary Line.* New Haven, Conn.: Yale University Press.

Eckert, Penelope. 1989. *Jocks and Burnouts: Social Categories in the U.S. High School.* New York: Teachers College Press.

Erickson, Frederick. 1987. "Transformation and School Success: The Politics and Culture of Educational Achievement." *Anthropology and Education Quarterly* 18, 4: 335–56.

Espinoza-Herold, Mariella. 2003. *Issues in Latino Education: Race, School Culture, and the Politics of Academic Success.* Boston: Pearson.

Fennimore, Beatrice. 2004. "Brown and the Failure of Civic Responsibility." *Teachers College Record* 107, 9: 1905–32.

Fine, Michelle. 1991. *Framing Dropouts: Notes on the Politics of an Urban Public High School.* Albany, N.Y.: SUNY Press.

Fine, Michelle, and Lois Weis. 2003. *Silenced Voices and Extraordinary Conversations: Re-Imagining Schools*. New York: Teachers College Press.

Fine, Michelle, Lois Weis, and Linda C. Powell. 1997. "Communities of Difference: A Critical Look at Desegregated Spaces Created by and for Youth." *Harvard Educational Review* 67, 2: 247–83.

Fitzpatrick, Laura. 2009. "Continuing Segregation Is Hurting U.S. Competitiveness." *Time*, December 8.

Flores, William V., and Rina Benmayor, eds. 1997. *Latino Cultural Citizenship: Claiming Identity, Space, and Rights*. Boston: Beacon Press.

Foley, Douglas. 1996. *Learning Capitalist Culture: Deep in the Heart of Tejas*. Philadelphia: University of Pennsylvania Press.

———. 1997. "Cultural Deficit Theories: The Anthropological Protest." In *A Critical Appraisal of Deficit Theory in Education*, ed. Richard Valencia, 113–31. London: Falmer Press.

Fordham, Signithia. 1996. *Blacked Out: Dilemmas of Race, Identity, and Success at Capital High*. Chicago: University of Chicago Press.

Fordham, Signithia, and John Ogbu. 1987. "Black Students' School Success: Coping with the Burden of 'Acting White.'" *Urban Review* 18, 3: 176–206.

Fox, Jonathan. 1996. "How Does Civil Society Thicken? The Political Construction of Social Capital in Rural Mexico." *World Development* 24, 6: 1189–1203.

Fox, Jonathan, and John Gershman. 2000. "The World Bank and Social Capital: Lessons from Ten Rural Development Projects in the Philippines and Mexico." *Policy Sciences* 33: 399–419.

Frankenberg, Erica, and Elizabeth Debray. 2011. *Integrating Schools in a Changing Society: New Policies and Legal Options for a Multiracial Generation*. Chapel Hill: University of North Carolina Press.

Frankenberg, Erica, and Chungmei Lee. 2002. *Race in American Public Schools: Rapidly Resegregating School Districts*. Cambridge, Mass.: Civil Rights Project at Harvard University.

Frankenberg, Erica, Chungmei Lee, and Gary Orfield, eds. 2003. *A Multiracial Society with Segregated Schools: Are We Losing the Dream?* Cambridge, Mass.: Civil Rights Project at Harvard University.

Frankenberg, Erica, and Gary Orfield. 2007. *Lessons in Integration: Realizing the Promise of Racial Diversity in Our Nation's Public Schools*. Charlottesville: University of Virginia Press.

———. 2012. *The Resegregation of Suburban Schools: A Hidden Crisis in American Education*. Boston: Harvard Education Press.

Gándara, Patricia. 2002. "A Study of High School Puente: What We Have Learned About Preparing Latino Youth for Postsecondary Education." *Educational Policy* 16, 4: 474–95.

Gándara, Patricia, and Megan Hopkins. 2009. *Forbidden Language: English Learners and Restrictive Language Policies*. New York: Teachers College Press.

Garcia, Alma, ed. 1997. *Chicana Feminist Thought: The Basic Historical Writings*. New York: Routledge.

Gibson, Margaret A., and Livier F. Bejínez. 2002. "Dropout Prevention: How Migrant Education Supports Mexican Youth." *Journal of Latinos and Education* 1, 3: 155–75.

Gibson, Margaret, Livier Bejínez, Nicole Hidalgo, and Cony Rolón. 2004. "Belonging and School Participation: Lessons from a Migrant Student Club." In *School Connections: U.S. Mexican Youth, Peers, and School Achievement*, ed. Margaret Gibson, Patricia Gándara, and Jill Koyama, 129–49. New York: Teachers College Press.

Gibson, Margaret, Patricia Gándara, and Jill Koyama, eds. 2004. *School Connections: U.S. Mexican Youth, Peers, and School Achievement*. New York: Teachers College Press.

Gibson, Margaret, and Nicole Hidalgo. 2009. "Bridges to Success in High School for Migrant Youth." *Teachers College Record* 111, 3: 683–711.

Gifford, Bernard, and Guadalupe Valdes. 2006. "The Linguistic Isolation of Hispanic Students in California's Public Schools: The Challenge of Reintegration." *Annual Yearbook of the National Society for the Study of Education* 105, 2: 125–54.

Gilroy, Paul. 1987. *Ain't No Black in the Union Jack*. Chicago: University of Chicago Press.

Gitlin, Andrew, Edward Buendia, Kristin Crosland, and Fode Doumbia. 2003. "The Production of Margin and Center: Welcoming and Unwelcoming of Immigrant Students." *American Educational Research Journal* 40, 1: 91–122.

Gomez, Santos, and Arlene Wong. 1998. A *Glimpse of Farmingville's Past: How It Got to Where It Is: The Case of Farmingville Today*. Oakland, Calif.: Pacific Institute for Studies in Development, Environment and Security.

González, Norma, and Luis Moll. 2002. "Cruzando el Puente: Building Bridges to Funds of Knowledge." *Journal of Educational Policy* 16, 4: 623–41.

González, Norma, Luis Moll, and Christina Amanti, eds. 2005. *Funds of Knowledge: Theorizing Practices in Households and Classrooms*. Mahwah, N.J.: Lawrence Erlbaum.

Grady, Karen. 2002. "Lowrider Art and Latino Students in the Rural Midwest." In *Education in the New Latino Diaspora: Policy and the Politics of Identity*, ed. Stanton Wordham, Enrique Murillo, Jr., and Edmud Hamann, 169–91. Westport, Conn.: Greenwood.

Gregory, Stephen. 1998. *Black Corona*. Princeton, N.J.: Princeton University Press.

Gupta, Akhil, and James Ferguson. 1992. "Beyond Culture: Space, Identity and the Politics of Difference." *Cultural Anthropology* 7, 1: 6–23.

Gutiérrez, Kris, Patricia Baquedano-López, and Héctor H. Álvarez. 2000. "The Crisis in Latino Education: The Norming of America." In *Charting New Terrains of Chicana(o)/Latina(o) Education*, ed. Christina Tejada, Corinne Martínez, and Zeus Leonardo, 213–32. Cresskill, N.J.: Hampton.

Hartigan, John, Jr. 1999. *Racial Situations: Class Predicaments of Whiteness in Detroit*. Princeton, N.J.: Princeton University Press.

———. 2001. "'White Devils' Talk Back: What Anti-Racists Can Learn from Whites in Detroit." In *The Making and Unmaking of Whiteness*, ed. Birgit Brander Rasmussen, Eric Klinenberg, Irene Nexica, and Matt Wray, 138–66. Durham, N.C.: Duke University Press.

Harvey, David. 1991. *The Condition of Postmodernity: An Enquiry into the Origins of Cultural Change*. Boston: Wiley-Blackwell.

———. 2007. *A Brief History of Neoliberalism*. Oxford: Oxford University Press.

Hawley, Willis. 1981. "Equity and Quality in Education: Characteristics of Effectively Desegregated Schools." In *Effective School Desegregation: Equity, Equality, and Feasibility*, ed. Willis D. Hawley, 297–307. Beverly Hills, Calif.: Sage.

———. 2007. "Designing Schools That Use Student Diversity to Enhance the Learning of all Students." In *Lessons in Integration*, ed. Erica Frankenberg and Gary Orfield, 31–56. Charlottesville: University of Virginia Press.

Haycock, Kati. 1998. *Good Teaching Matters*. Washington, D.C.: Education Trust.

Heath, Shirley Brice. 1996. "What No Bedtime Story Means: Narrative Skills at Home and School." In *The Matrix of Language: Contemporary Linguistic Anthropology*, ed. Don Brenneis and Ron Macaulay, 12–38. Boulder, Colo.: Westview Press.

Hill, Jane. 1999. "Language, Race, and White Public Space." *American Anthropologist* 100, 3: 680–89.

hooks, bell. 2000. *Where We Stand: Class Matters*. New York: Routledge.

Hurd, Clayton. 2004. "Acting Out and Being a 'Schoolboy': Performance in an ELD classroom." In *School Connections: U.S. Mexican Youth, Peers, and School Achievement*, ed. Margaret Gibson, Patricia Gándara, and Jill Koyama, 63–86. New York: Teachers College Press.

———. 2008. "Cinco de Mayo, Normative Whiteness, and the Marginalization of Mexican-Descent Students." *Anthropology and Education Quarterly* 39, 3: 293–313.

Jackson, Kenneth.1985. *Crabgrass Frontier: The Suburbanization of the United States*. Oxford: Oxford University Press.

Jervis, Kathe. 1996. "'How Come There Are No Brothers on That List?': Hearing the Hard Questions Students Ask." *Harvard Educational Review* 66, 3: 546–76.

Kailin, Julie. 1999. "How White Teachers Perceive the Problem of Racism in Their Schools: A Case Study in 'Liberal' Lakeview." *Teachers College Record* 100, 4: 724–50.

Karst, Kenneth L. 1989. *Belonging to America: Equal Citizenship and the Constitution*. New Haven, Conn.: Yale University Press.

Kelley, Robin. 1997. *Yo' Mama's Disfunktional! Fighting the Culture Wars in Urban America*. Boston: Beacon Press.

King, Martin Luther, Jr. 1997 [1963]. "Letter from Birmingham Jail." In *Norton Anthology of African American Literature*, ed. Henry Louis Gates, Jr., and Nellie Y. McKay, 1854–66. New York: Norton.

Kohl, Herbert. 1994. *"I Won't Learn from You" and Other Thoughts on Creative Maladjustment*. New York: New Press.

Kruse, Kevin M. 2005. *White Flight: Atlanta and the Making of Modern Conservatism*. Princeton, N.J.: Princeton University Press.

Labaree, David F. 1997. *How to Succeed in School Without Really Learning: The Credentials Race in American Education*. New Haven, Conn.: Yale University Press.

Labov, William. 1972. *Language in the Inner City: Studies in the Black English Vernacular*. Philadelphia: University of Pennsylvania Press.

Landsman, Julie, and Chance W. Lewis. 2006. *White Teachers/Diverse Classrooms: A Guide to Building Inclusive Schools, Promoting High Expectations, and Eliminating Racism*. Sterling, Va.: Stylus.

Laureau, Annette. 2000. *Home Advantage: Social Class and Parental Intervention in Elementary Education*. 2nd ed. Lanham, Md.: Rowman and Littlefield.

Lehning, Percy, ed. 1998. *Theories of Secession*. London: Routledge.

Levinson, Bradley, and Dorothy Holland. 1996. "Introduction: The Cultural Production of the Educated Person." In *The Cultural Production of the Educated Person*, ed. Bradley Levinson, Douglas Foley, and Dorothy Holland, 1–53. Albany, N.Y.: SUNY Press.

Lewis, Amanda. 2003. *Race in the Schoolyard: Negotiating the Color Line in Classrooms and Communities*. New Brunswick, N.J.: Rutgers University Press.

Lipsitz, George. 1998. *The Possessive Investment in Whiteness: How White People Profit from Identity Politics*. Philadelphia: Temple University Press.

Lipsitz, George, and Melvin Oliver. 2010. "Integration, Segregation, and the Racial Wealth Gap." In *The Integration Debate: Competing Futures for American Cities*, ed. Chester Hartman and Gregory Squires, 153–167. New York: Routledge.

Lowe, Setha. 2003. *Behind the Gates: Life, Security, and the Pursuit of Happiness in Fortress America*. New York: Routledge.

Lydon, Sandy. 1996. "Lingering Legacies of Segregated Housing." *Santa Cristo Sentinel*, June 24.

———. 1998. "All That Glitters: An Argument in Support of Commemorating (and Lamenting) the California Gold Rush." *Santa Cruz County History Journal* 4: 6–11.

Mahoney, Martha. 1997. "Residential Segregation and White Privilege." In *Critical White Studies: Looking Behind the Mirror*, ed. Richard Delgado and Jean Stefanic, 273–76. Philadelphia: Temple University Press.

Marcuse, Peter. 1997. "The Ghetto of Exclusion and the Fortified Enclave: New Patterns in the United States." In "The New Spatial Order of Cities," special issue, *American Behavioral Scientist* 41, 3: 311–26.

Martínez, Elizabeth. 1998. *De Colores Means All of Us*. Cambridge, Mass.: South End Press.

Massey, Doreen. 1994a. "Double Articulation: A Place in the World." In *Displacements: Cultural Identity in Question*, ed. Angelika Bammer. Bloomington: University of Indiana Press.

———. 1994b. *Space, Place, and Gender.* Minneapolis: University of Minnesota Press.

Massey, Douglas, and Nancy Denton. 1998. *American Apartheid: Segregation and the Making of the Underclass.* Cambridge, Mass.: Harvard University Press.

Matute-Bianchi, Maria Eugenia. 1986. "Ethnic Identities and Patterns of School Success and Failure Among Mexican-Descent and Japanese American Students in a California High School: An Ethnographic Analysis." *American Journal of Education* 95, 1: 233–55.

McAdam, Doug, Sidney Tarrow, and Charles Tilly. 2001. *Dynamics of Contention.* Cambridge: Cambridge University Press.

McDermott, Ray. 1997. "Achieving School Failure, 1972–1997." In *Education and Cultural Process: Anthropological Approaches*, 3rd ed., ed. George Spindler, 110–31. Prospect Heights, Ill.: Waveland Press.

McKenzie, Ewan. 1996. *Privatopia: Homeowner Associations and the Rise of Residential Private Government.* New Haven, Conn.: Yale University Press.

McLaren, Peter, and Juan Munoz. 2000. "Contesting Whiteness: Critical Perspectives on the Struggle for Social Justice." In *The Politics of Multiculturalism and Bilingual Education: Students and Teachers Caught in the Cross Fire*, ed. Carlos J. Ovando and Peter McLaren. Boston: McGraw-Hill.

Mediratta, Kavitha, Seema Shah, and Sara McAlister. 2009. *Community Organizing for Stronger Schools: Strategies and Successes.* Cambridge, Mass.: Harvard University Press.

Mehan, Hugh, Irene Villanueva, Lea Hubbard, and Angela Lintz. 1996. *Constructing School Success: The Consequences of Untracking Low-Achieving Students.* New York: Cambridge University Press.

Mendoza-Denton, Norma. 1999. "Fighting Words: Latina Girls, Gangs, and Language Attitudes." In *Speaking Chicana: Voice, Power, and Identity*, ed. D. Letticia Galindo and Maria Dolores Gonzales, 39–56. Tucson: University of Arizona Press.

Meucci, Sandra, and Jim Redmon. 1997. "Safe Spaces: California Children Enter a Policy Debate." *Social Justice* 24, 3: 139–51.

Mickelson, R. A. 2008. Twenty-First Century Social Science on School Racial Diversity and Educational Outcomes. *Ohio State Law Journal*, 69, 9: 1173–1228.

Moll, Luis, Cathy Amanti, Deborah Neff, and Norma Gonzalez. 1992. "Funds of Knowledge for Teaching: Using a Qualitative Approach to Connect Homes and Classrooms." *Theory into Practice* 31: 132–41.

Morgan, Marcelyna. 1996. "Conversational Signifying." In *Grammar and Interaction*, ed. Elinor Ochs, Emanuel Schegloff, and Sandra A. Thompson. New York: Cambridge University Press.

Morrison, Toni. 1992. *Playing in the Dark: Whiteness and the Literary Imagination.* Cambridge, Mass.: Harvard University Press.

Muñoz, Carlos, Jr. 1989. *Youth, Identity and Power.* New York: Verso.

Murray, Dale. 2009. "Presumptions Against School District Secession." *Theory and Research in Education* 7, 1: 47–63.

Nieto, Sonia. 2010. *Affirming Diversity: The Sociopolitical Context of Multicultural Education*. Boston: Pearson Education.

Noguera, Pedro. 2004. "Racial Isolation, Poverty and the Limits of Local Control in Oakland." *Teachers College Record* 106, 11: 2146–70.

Nygreen, Kysa. 2006. "Reproducing or challenging power in the questions we ask and the methods we use: A framework for activist research in urban education." *The Urban Review* 38, 1: 1–26.

Oakes, Jeannie. 1995. "Normative, Technical, and Political Dimensions of Creating New Educational Communities." In *Creating New Educational Communities*, ed. Jeannie Oakes and K. Hunter Quartz, 1–15. Chicago: University of Chicago Press.

———. 2000. *Keeping Track*. New Haven, Conn.: Yale University Press.

Oakes, Jeannie, and Martin Lipton. 2002. "Struggling for Educational Equity in Diverse Communities: School Reform as Social Movement." *Journal of Educational Change* 3: 383–406.

Oakes, Jeannie, John Rogers, Gary Blasi, and Martin Lipton. 2008. "Grassroots Organizing, Social Movements and the Right to High-Quality Education." *Stanford Journal of Civil Rights and Civil Liberties* 4, 2: 339–71.

Oakes, Jeannie, Kevin Welner, Susan Yonezawa, and Ricky Lee Allen. 2005. "Norms and Politics of Equity-Minded Change: Researching the 'Zone of Mediation.'" In *Fundamental Change: International Handbook of Educational Change*, ed. Michael Fullan, 282–305. Dordrecht: Springer.

Olsen, Laurie. 1997. *Made in America: Immigrant Students in Our Public Schools*. New York: New Press.

Omi, Michael, and Howard Winant. 1994. *Racial Formation in the United States*. Philadelphia: Temple University Press.

Orfield, Gary. 1978. *Must We Bus? Segregated Schools and National Policy*. Washington, D.C.: Brookings Institution.

———. 2000. "Latin@s in School: The Most Segregated . . . Soon the Largest Minority." *Revista: Harvard Review of Latin America* (Spring).

———. 2001. *Schools More Separate: Consequences of a Decade of Resegregation*. Civil Rights Project at Harvard University. Cambridge, Mass.: Harvard University.

Orfield, Gary, and Susan Eaton. 1996. *Dismantling Desegregation: The Quiet Reversal of Brown v. Board of Education*. New York: New Press.

Orfield, Gary, Erica Frankenberg, and Genevieve Siegel-Hawley. 2010. "Integrated Schools: Finding a New Path." *Educational Leadership* 68, 3: 22–27.

Orfield, Gary, and Chungmei Lee. 2005. *Why Segregation Matters: Poverty and Educational Inequality*. Cambridge, Mass.: Civil Rights Project at Harvard University.

———. 2006. *Racial Transformation and the Changing Nature of Segregation*. Cambridge, Mass.: Civil Rights Project at Harvard University.

———. 2007. *Historic Reversals, Accelerating Resegregation, and the Need for New Integration Strategies*. Los Angeles: Civil Rights Project at UCLA.

Orfield, Myron, and Thomas F. Luce. 2012. *America's Racially Diverse Suburbs: Opportunities and Challenges.* Minneapolis: Institute on Metropolitan Opportunity, University of Minnesota Law School, July 20.

Ovando, Carlos, and Peter McLaren, eds. 2000. *The Politics of Multiculturalism and Bilingual Education: Students and Teachers Caught in the Cross Fire.* New York: McGraw-Hill.

Peller, Gary. 1996, "Race Consciousness." In *Critical Race Theory: The Key Writings That Formed the Movement*, ed. Kimberlé Crenshaw, Neil Gotanda, Gary Peller, and Kenneth Thomas, 127–58. New York: New Press.

Perry, Pamela. 2001. "White Means Never Having to Say You're Ethnic: White Youth and the Construction of 'Cultureless' Identities." *Journal of Contemporary Ethnography* 30, 1: 56–91.

———. 2002. *Shades of White: White Kids and Racial Identities in High School.* Durham, N.C.: Duke University Press.

Pettigrew, Thomas, and Linda Tropp. 2006. "A Meta-Analytic Test of Intergroup Contact Theory." *Journal of Personality and Social Psychology* 90: 751–83.

Phelan, Patricia, Anne Locke Davidson, and Hahn Yu. 1993. "Students' Multiple Worlds: Navigating the Boundaries of Family, Peer, and School Cultures." In *Renegotiating Cultural Diversity in American Schools*, ed. Patricia Phelan and Anne Locke Davidson, 52–88. New York: Teachers College Press.

Philips, Susan Urmston. 1983. *The Invisible Culture: Communication in Classroom and Community on the Warm Springs Indian Reservation.* New York: Longman.

Pollock, Mica, ed. 2004. *Colormute: Race Talk Dilemmas in an American School.* Princeton, N.J.: Princeton University Press.

———. 2008. *Everyday Antiracism: Getting Real About Race in School.* New York: New Press.

Portes, Alejandro. 1998. "Social Capital: Its Origins and Applications in Modern Sociology." *Annual Review of Sociology* 24: 1–24.

Portes, Alejandro, and Min Zhou. 1993. "The New Second Generation: Segmented Assimilation and Its Variants." *Annals of the American Academy of Political and Social Science* 530: 74–96.

Raley, Jason. 2004. "Like Family, You Know? School and the Achievement of Peer Relations." In *School Connections: U.S. Mexican Youth, Peers, and School Achievement*, ed. Margaret A. Gibson, Patricia C. Gándara, and Jill Peterson Koyama, 150–72. New York: Teachers College Press.

Reich, Robert. 1991. "The Secession of the Successful." *New York Times*, January 20.

Reyes, Maria de la Luz, and Eloise Laliberty. 1992. "A Teacher's 'Pied Piper' Effect on Young Authors." *Education and Urban Society* 24, 2: 263–78.

Rivera-Bonilla, Ivelisse. 1999. "Building Community Through Gating: The Case of Gated Communities in San Juan, Puerto Rico." Paper presented at the Annual Meeting of the American Anthropological Association, Chicago.

Rogers, John, and Jeannie Oakes. 2005. "John Dewey Speaks to *Brown*: Research, Democratic Social Movement Strategies, and the Struggle for Education on Equal Terms." *Teachers College Record* 107, 9: 2178–2203.

Roithmayr, Daria. 2007. "Racial Cartels." Law and Economics Working Paper Series-Paper 66. University of Southern California Law School.

Rosaldo, Renato. 1994. "Cultural Citizenship and Educational Democracy." *Cultural Anthropology* 9, 3: 402–11.

———. 1989. *Culture and Truth: The Re-Making of Social Analysis*. Boston: Beacon Press.

Rosaldo, Renato, William V. Flores, and Blanca Silvestrini. 1994. *Identity, Conflict, and Evolving Latino Communities*. Stanford, Calif.: Stanford Center for Chicano Research.

Rouse, Roger. 1991. "Mexican Migration and the Social Space of Postmodernism." *Diaspora* 1, 1: 9–23.

———. 1992. "Making Sense of Settlement: Class Transformation, Cultural Struggle, and Transnationalism Among Mexican American Migrants in the U.S." In *Towards a Transnational Perspective on Migration: Race, Class, Ethnicity and Nationalism Reconsidered*, ed. Nina Glick-Schiller, Linda Basch, and Cristina Blanc-Szanton. *Annals of the New York Academy of Sciences* 645. New York: New York Academy of Science.

Rury, John L. 2002. "Democracy's High School? Social Change and American Secondary Education in the Post-Conant Era." *American Education Research Journal* 39, 2: 307–36.

Said, Edward. 1979. *Orientalism*. New York: Pantheon.

San Miguel, Guadalupe, Jr. 2005. "The Impact of Brown on the Mexican-American Desegregation, 1950s-1980s." *Journal of Latinos and Education* 4, 4: 221–36.

San Miguel, Guadalupe, and Richard Valencia. 1998. "From the Treaty of Guadalupe Hidalgo to Hopwood: The Education Plight of Mexican-Americans in the Southwest." *Harvard Educational Review* 68, 3: 353–96.

Scheper-Hughes, Nancy. 1995. "The Primacy of the Ethical: Propositions for a Militant Anthropology." *Current Anthropology* 36, 3: 409–40.

Schmidt, Ronald. 2000. *Language Policy and Identity Politics in the United States*. Philadelphia: Temple University Press.

Sergiovanni, Thomas. 1994. *Building Communities in Schools*. San Francisco: Jossey-Bass.

Shirley, Dennis. 2002. *Valley Interfaith and School Reform: Organizing for School Power in South Texas*. Austin: University of Texas Press.

Slavin, Robert. 1985. Cooperative Learning: Applying Contact Theory in Desegregated Schools. *Journal of Social Issues* 41, 3: 45–62.

———. 1995. "Enhancing Intergroup Relations in Schools." In *Toward a Common Destiny*, ed. Willis Hawley and A. W. Jackson, 291–314. San Francisco: Jossey-Bass.

Slavin, Robert, Nancy Madden, Lawrence Dolan, and Barbara Wasik. 1996. *Every Child, Every School: Success for All*. Thousand Oaks, Calif.: Corwin.

Solóranzo, Daniel, and Dolores Delgado-Bernal. 2001. "Examining Transformational Resistance through a Critical Race and LatCrit Theory Framework." *Urban Education* 36, 3: 308–42.

Staiger, Annegret. 2004. "Whiteness as Giftedness: Racial Formation at an Urban High School." *Social Problems* 51, 2: 161–81.

Stanton-Salazar, Ricardo. 1997. "A Social Capital Framework for Understanding the Socialization of Racial Minority Children and Youth." *Harvard Educational Review* 67, 1: 1–40.

———. 2004. "Social Capital Among Working-Class Minority Students." In *School Connections: U.S. Mexican Youth, Peers, and School Achievement*, ed. Margaret A. Gibson, Patricia Gándara, and Jill P. Koyama. New York: Teachers College Press.

Stanton-Salazar, Ricardo, Olga Vásquez, and Hugh Mehan. 2000. "Engineering Academic Success Through Institutional Support." In *The Academic Achievement of Minority Students: Perspectives, Practices and Prescriptions*, ed. Sheila T. Gregory, 213–47. Lanham, Md.: University Press of America.

Stanton-Salazar, Ricardo, and Sanford Dornbusch. 1995. "Social Capital and the Reproduction of Inequality: Information Networks Among Mexican-Origin High School Students." *Sociology of Education* 68 (April): 116–35.

Stewart, Kathleen. 1996. *A Place on the Side of the Road: Cultural Politics in the "Other America."* Princeton, N.J.: Princeton University Press.

Stone, Clarence, Jeff Henig, Bryan Jones, and Carol Pierannunzi. 2001. *Building Civic Capacity: The Politics of Reforming Urban Schools*. Lawrence: University of Kansas Press.

Sunderman, Gail, James Kim, and Gary Orfield. 2005. *NCLB Meets School Realities, Lessons from the Field*. Thousand Oaks, Calif.: Sage/Corwin.

Takaki, Ronald T. 1993. *A Different Mirror: A History of Multicultural America*. Boston: Little, Brown.

Takash, Paule Cruz. 1990. "A Crisis of Democracy: Community Responses to the Latinization of a California Town Dependent on Immigrant Labor." Ph.D. dissertation, University of California, Berkeley.

Taussig, Michael. 1987. *Shamanism, Colonialsim, and the Wild Man: A Study in Terror and Healing*. Chicago: University of Chicago Press.

Tefera, Adai, Erica Frankenberg, Genevieve Siegel-Hawley, and Gina Chirichigno. 2011. *Integrating Suburban Schools: How to Benefit from Growing Diversity and Avoid Segregation*. Los Angeles: Civil Rights Project/Proyecto Derechos Civiles at UCLA.

Troop, Linda, and Mary Prenovost. 2008. "The Role of Intergroup Contact in Predicting Children's Inter-Ethnic Attitudes: Evidence from Meta-Analytic and Field Studies." In *Intergroup Attitudes and Relations in Childhood Through Adulthood*, ed. Shari Levy and Melanie Killen, 236–48. London: Oxford University Press.

Trueba, Henry, Cirenio Rodriguez, Yali Zou, and Jose Cintrón. 1993. *Healing Multicultural America: Mexican Immigrants Rise to Power in Rural California*. Washington, D.C.: Falmer.

Urciuoli, Bonnie. 1995. "Language and Borders." *Annual Review of Anthropology* 24: 525–46.

Valdes, Guadalupe. 1996. Con Respeto: *Bridging the Distances Between Culturally Diverse Families and Schools: An Ethnographic Portrait*. New York: Teachers College Press.

Valencia, Richard. 2008. *Chicano Students and the Courts: The Mexican American Legal Struggle for Educational Equality*. New York: New York University Press.

Valenzuela, Angela. 1999. *Subtractive Schooling: U.S. Mexican Youth and the Politics of Caring*. Albany, N.Y.: SUNY Press.

Villenas, Sofia. 2001. "Latina Mothers and Small-Town Racisms: Creating Narratives of Dignity and Moral Education in North Carolina." *Anthropology and Education Quarterly* 32, 1: 3–28.

Villenas, Sona, and Donna Deyhle. 1999. "Critical Race Theory and Ethnographies Challenging the Stereotype: Latino Families, Schooling, Resilience and Resistance." *Curriculum Inquiry* 29, 4: 413–45.

Warren, Mark R. 2005. "Communities and Schools: A New View of Urban Educational Reform." *Harvard Educational Review* 75, 2: 133–68.

Warren, Mark R., Karen Mapp, and the Community Organizing School Reform Project. 2011. *A Match on Dry Grass: Community Organizing as a Catalyst for School Reform*. New York: Oxford University Press.

Waters, Mary C., and Tomás R. Jiménez. 2005. "Assessing Immigrant Assimilation: New Empirical and Theoretical Challenges." *Annual Review of Sociology* 31: 105–25.

Weiler, Jeanne. 1998. *Recent Changes in School Desegregation*. New York: ERIC Clearinghouse on Urban Education.

Wells, Amy Stuart. 1995. "Re-examining Social Science Research on School Desegregation: Long-Versus Short-term Effects." *Teachers College Record* 96: 691–706.

Wells, Amy Stuart, Awo K. Atanda, Jennifer J. Holme, Amina Humphrey, and Anita Revilla. 2009. *In Search of* Brown*: The Unfulfilled Promise of School Desegregation in Six Racially Mixed High Schools*. Berkeley: University of California Press.

Wells, Gordon. 2001. *Action, Talk and Text: Learning and Teaching Through Inquiry*. New York: Teachers College Press.

Wells, Miriam. 1996. *Strawberry Fields: Politics, Class and Work in California Agriculture*. Ithaca, N.Y.: Cornell University Press.

Willis, Paul. 1981 [1977]. *Learning to Labor: How Working Class Kids Get Working Class Jobs*. New York: Columbia University Press.

Winant, Howard. 1998. "Racism Today: Continuity and Change in the Post-Civil Rights Era." *Ethnic and Racial Studies* 21, 4: 755–66.

Woolard, Kathryn. 1999. "Voting Rights, Liberal Voters, and the Official English Movement: An Analysis of Campaign Rhetoric in SF's Proposition 'O'." In

Perspectives on Official English: The Campaign for English as the Official Language of the USA, ed. Karen L. Adams and Daniel T. Brink. Berlin: de Gruyter.

Yasso, Tara. 2005. "Whose Culture Has Capital? A Critical Race Theory Discussion of Community Cultural Wealth." *Race, Ethnicity and Education* 8, 1: 69–91.

Yasso, Tara, and Daniel Solórzano. 2007. "Conceptualizing a Critical Race Theory in Sociology." In *The Blackwell Companion to Social Inequalities*, ed. Mary Romero and Eric Margolis, 117–46. Malden, Mass.: Blackwell.

Yun, John, and Michael Kurlaender. 2004. "School Racial Composition and Student Educational Aspirations." *Journal of Education for Students Placed at Risk* 9, 2: 143–68.

Zavella, Patricia, and John Borrego. 1999. *Policy Implications of the Restructuring of Frozen Food Production in North America and Its Impact on Farmingville, California*. Working Paper 28. Santa Cruz: Chicano Latino Research Center, University of California, Santa Cruz.

Zentella, Ana Celia. 1997. *Growing Up Bilingual: Puerto Rican Children in New York*. Malden, Mass.: Blackwell.

INDEX

ACKNOWLEDGMENTS

Since beginning work on this book nearly a decade ago, I have experienced a number of circumstances—personal and professional—that have interrupted my capacity to see this project through to publication. It is only now, in the conclusive act of writing these acknowledgments, that my fear about missing the opportunity to share this important story with a broader audience has begun to seriously subside. That I have persevered in the writing process is a credit to family, friends, colleagues, and community collaborators who have offered me, throughout the years, their constant and profound support, encouragement, and—when necessary—prodding.

I wish to thank first of all my parents, John and Mary, for providing me with their unconditional love despite some unconventional career choices. They have never asked me—as others would—what sort of job skills I might be acquiring in my movements between anthropological fieldwork and community development projects. That being said, I will not miss my father's habitual inquiry: "So, how's the writing going?"

I also owe a great debt of gratitude to colleagues at UC Santa Cruz who read and commented on early drafts of the manuscript; to Professor Triloki Pandey for his wisdom, inspiration, and guidance throughout the years; to Professor Don Brenneis for his insights, off-beat humor, and willingness to let me stray from my particular training to write about what seemed most important; to Professor Dan Linger for our engaging conversations and for his close and critical reading of my original manuscript; and to Professor Margaret Gibson for her mentorship, support, and the opportunities she made available for me to develop as a scholar, researcher, and teacher. Finally, I thank all the young people and adults who shared pieces of their lives with me throughout my field research. It is my hope that this study does justice to their words, ideas, frustrations, and passions.

This research was made possible, in part, by generous grants from the Spencer Foundation, University of California Linguistic Minority Research Institute (UCLMRI), and U.S. Department of Education Office of Educational Research and Improvement, as well as from a number of small grants from the Department of Anthropology at UC Santa Cruz.